Bittersweet Sounds of Passage

Bittersweet Sounds of Passage

Balinese *Gamelan Angklung* Cremation Music

ELLEN KOSKOFF

UNIVERSITY OF ILLINOIS PRESS
Urbana, Chicago, and Springfield

This book will be made open access within three years of publication thanks to Path to Open, a program developed in partnership between JSTOR, the American Council of Learned Societies (ACLS), University of Michigan Press, and The University of North Carolina Press to bring about equitable access and impact for the entire scholarly community, including authors, researchers, libraries, and university presses around the world. Learn more at https://about.jstor.org/path-to-open/

Publication of this book is supported by a grant from the Bruno Nettl Endowment for Ethnomusicology.

Library of Congress Cataloging-in-Publication Data
Names: Koskoff, Ellen, 1943– author.
Title: Bittersweet sounds of passage: Balinese gamelan angklung cremation music / Ellen Koskoff.
Description: Urbana: University of Illinois Press, 2025. | Includes bibliographical references and index.
Identifiers: LCCN 2024059692 | ISBN 9780252046629 (hardcover) | ISBN 9780252088735 (paperback) | ISBN 9780252047930 (ebook)
Subjects: LCSH: Gamelan angklung music—Indonesia—Bali Island--History and criticism. | Gamelan angklung music—Indonesia—Bali Island—Analysis, appreciation. | Funeral music—Indonesia—Bali Island—History and criticism. | Gamelan angklung—Indonesia—Bali Island—History. | Music—Social aspects—Indonesia—Bali Island. | Hindu funeral rites and ceremonies—Indonesia—Bali Island. | Cremation—Indonesia—Bali Island. Bali Island (Indonesia)—Social life and customs.
Classification: LCC ML3758.I537 B355 2025 | DDC 781.5/880959862—dc23/eng/20241212
LC record available at https://lccn.loc.gov/2024059692

To the men of *Sekehe Gamelan Angklung* Taman Sari,
for their patience and good humor,
and for their beautiful music;

and,

To I Nyoman Suadin, Latifah Alsegaf, and their Balinese family,
who lovingly watched over me, and gave me
the support and encouragement I needed
to write this book.

Contents

Companion Website

Readers of *Bittersweet Sounds of Passage: Balinese* Gamelan Angklung *Cremation Music* are invited to visit the supplemental materials found at the University of Illinois Press website and accessed through the web page for the book. The site contains selected audio clips relevant to each chapter and complete recordings of all pieces in the cremation repertoire. The symbol ◉ in the text indicates a reference to these materials.

List of Recordings

List of Complete *Gending*

1. "Santun" (Politeness), *pemungkah, pemungkah, pengiba*
2. "Tambun" (Belonging Together), *pemungkah, pengiba*
3. "Katak Ngongkek" (Croaking Frog), *pemungkah, pengawak, pengiba*
4. "Tungtung Tangis" (Forever Weeping), *pemungkah, pengawak, pengawak/pengiba* hybrid
5. "Capung Gantung" (Hovering Dragonfly), *pemungkah, pengawak, pengiba*
6. "Sekar Jcpun" (Japanese Flower), *pemungkah, pengawak, pengiba*
7. "Bapang" (a metric pattern), *pemungkah* (same as 4 *pemungkah*), *pemungkah, pengiba* (same as 6 *pengiba*)
8. "Lutung Loncat" (Jumping Monkey), *pengawak, pengawak, pengawak, pengiba* (same as 2 *pengiba*)
9. "Prebangsa," *pemungkah* (same as 6 *pemungkah*), *pengawak* (same as 6 *pengawak*), *pengawak*
10. "Capung Manjus" (Bathing Dragonfly), *pengawak/pemungkah* hybrid, *pengawak* (same as 4 *pengawak*), *pengawak/pengiba* hybrid
11. "Sekar Gadung" (Gadung Flower), *pemungkah* (same as 6 *pemungkah*), *pengawak* (same as 6 *pengawak*), *pengiba* (same as 2 *pengiba*)
12. "Cerukcuk Punyah" (Drunken Bird), *pengawak/pemungkah* hybrid (same as 10 *pengawak/pemungkah* hybrid), *pemungkah, pengiba*
13. "Alis-Alis Ijo" (Green Eyebrow), *pemungkah, pemungkah, pemungkah/pengawak* hybrid, *pengawak*

14. "Jangkrik Ngibing" (Dancing Cricket), *pemungkah/pengawak* hybrid, *pengawak* (same as 10 *pengawak/pengiba* hybrid)
15. "Jaran Nginjek" (Runaway Horse), *pengiba*

List of Illustrations

Photographs

(all photographs by the author)

Diagrams

Acknowledgments

I am profoundly grateful to the many people who have contributed to the writing of this book. First and foremost, I thank my teacher, I Nyoman Suadin. I could not have accomplished this without his help and support and our countless discussions in the backyard. I also wish to thank the members of the *Sekehe Gamelan Angklung* Taman Sari, with whom I worked, played, and laughed over the year I lived in Bali (2007–08): I Wayan Ladera (cohead); I Nyoman Rideng (cohead and treasurer); Anak Agung Rai Winaja (*pemangku*); Pak Marwi (*ugal*); Pak Madia (*ceng-ceng*); I Madé Landra; I Nyoman Budiarta; I Wayan Minadi; I Gung Ratig; I Nengah Ruih; I Wayan Debet (my *jegogan* partner); Pak Badrie; I Nyoman Nadra (*suling*); I Madé Bagiarsa; I Wayan Renjing; I Wayan Kesek; I Nyoman Rapug; I Nyoman Kamiana; I Nyoman Radra; I Madé Puger; Pak Dina; Pak Ari; Pak Pra; Jero Mangku Ratna; and I Nyoman Wira (translator). I loved every minute I was with you—even when I was making mistakes. Thank you so much.

Much love and many thanks to my longtime friend and colleague, Michael Tenzer, who has been there from the beginning. Always supportive and graciously helpful, Michael has followed the progress of this book from its start, checking in now and then with support, encouragement, and helpful suggestions. His wonderful work on Balinese music has long been an inspiration to me. Thanks also to Michael Bakan and Lisa Gold, who graciously provided answers to my many (often strange) questions and encouraged me in countless ways. And, although no longer with us, I owe a debt of thanks to the Canadian composer and scholar Colin McPhee (1900–1964), with whom I share a love for *gamelan angklung* and its enchanting music. His work was of tremendous value to me as I contemplated and struggled with my own.

I am also grateful for the help and support of Dr. I Wayan Rai, who took me under his wing during my first weeks in Bali while I studied Indonesian, providing not only a place to sleep, but also chauffeured rides through the Denpasar traffic; and thanks also to his son, Dr. I Made Indra Sadguna, who talked with me about the many varieties of *gamelan angklung* ensembles and their music. I thank I Putu Tangkas Adi Hiranmayena and his wife, Ni Dewa Ayu Eka Putri, for their support and enthusiasm, but most importantly, for helping me to better understand the fluid nature of emotions experienced at a cremation.

To Mary McArthur, Ken Luk, and Evan Henry—all former students, now friends—thank you for your gracious help in making sure that what I was writing made sense, as well as for your generous time and support. Thanks also to Laurie Matheson of the University of Illinois Press for not giving up on me, and to the two anonymous peer reviewers who read the book's first draft and offered helpful suggestions. Finally, heartfelt love and hugs to Rebecca Morris, Margaret Leenhouts, and Gretchen Wheelock for being the perfect guinea pigs for my text and listening guides, and again to Gretchen and Margaret for pep talks and riotous luncheon laughter.

Bittersweet Sounds of Passage

Introduction

This is a book about cremation music performed by the Balinese *gamelan angklung*. The history and meaning of *gamelan angklung* and its importance to contemporary Balinese cremations is hazy; written sources, recordings, and other forms of scholarship—as defined by the West—are almost nonexistent, nor are most contemporary Balinese musicians, scholars, or community members familiar with, or interested in, its general history or specific repertoire. Yet, this music, most often performed by everyday villagers, most with no special musical interest or training, is considered by all Balinese to be a necessary component of village life and death.

There are many stories surrounding *gamelan angklung* and its presence at Balinese cremations that have little to do with music, as we generally understand this term. Some stories are bolstered by written documentation; others remain in the realm of oral history or conjecture. Thus, throughout this book, we will occasionally encounter seemingly ambiguous, often contradictory, accounts of *gamelan angklung* that have been, and continue to be perceived, articulated, and given meaning by different groups of people.

How did my interest in *gamelan angklung* cremation music begin? In 1991 the University of Rochester's Eastman School of Music, where I taught, bought a four-tone, bronze-keyed *gamelan angklung*, Lila Muni (Heavenly Sound), from Bowling Green State University. When the *gamelan* first arrived, I had no idea what to do with it, so I contacted José Evangelista, a composer who had set up a Balinese *gamelan* program at the University of Montréal a few years earlier. For the first few years of our program, we shared teachers brought in from the Institut Seni Indonesia

(Institute of Indonesian Arts, or ISI; see figure 2.2 on page 35). Our first year of sharing, 1993, brought Pak Wayan Suweca (d. 2023), one of Bali's most renowned musicians, to Eastman.

One day, after having spent a few months learning some contemporary pieces composed for other ensembles that had been arranged for *gamelan angklung*, Pak Suweca introduced a piece that he described as "really old," one played by the *gamelan angklung* for cremation ceremonies. He started with the second section, the slow one, and introduced it laughingly, saying that many in Bali thought it long and boring, and that nobody really enjoyed playing it because it was so sad and hard to remember. Although this section used the same four-note set of pitches as the other pieces we had learned, it sounded completely different.

First, there were no *gong* strikes to mark the cycle! There was no cycle! All the timings seemed to be off; some of the phrases contained an odd number of beats—seven, ten, eleven—and one seemed to be nine-and-a-half beats long! Was Pak Suweca making mistakes? Was my hearing off? I am purposely using exclamation marks here, because from the start I was shocked into relearning, re-feeling, and reorienting myself to new musical sounds and structures that did not fit comfortably within my previous understandings of music. I was riveted—where was this music going? Why was it so quirky, so uneven? Why were there so many unexpected (at least to me) shifts in texture and meter? How did Pak Suweca remember what came next? I loved it! And I immediately wanted to know more.

I began to visit Bali in the summer of 1997, but it was not until 2003 that I first heard the men of *sekehe gamelan angklung* Taman Sari (*gamelan angklung* club, Sweet Nectar) play. By this time, the Eastman School had permanently hired I Nyoman Suadin, a Balinese musician and graduate of the Sekolah Menengah Karawitan Indonesia (SMKI, High School for Music, formerly known as KOKAR) in Denpasar, who now lived in Maryland. Nyoman traveled home to Bali every other summer to see his family and to reconnect with his *banjar* (neighborhood association). I went with him in the summer of 2003 and stayed in his home in *banjar* Wani, Kerambitan, Tabanan, in the southwest of the island (see map, page 14).

Nyoman's father, I Wayan Dapet (Nang Suadin),[1] was also a musician and frequently played in the local *gamelan luang*, a sacred and rare ensemble that still exists in *banjar* Wani (see figure 1.6, page 16). Nyoman had told his father that I liked *gamelan angklung* music, so one midafternoon the men of *sekehe gamelan angklung* Taman Sari suddenly appeared at our compound carrying instruments. They had come from *banjar* Baturiti, a neighborhood about a half-mile away. They set up their instruments—about fifteen in all—and began to play. They played seven pieces, as though at a concert, but none was like the one I had learned from Pak Suweca. I asked if they played these pieces at cremations. No, they said; there was another set of pieces they used for cremations. Aha!

For the next four years, I worked on a plan to return to Bali to work with this group, hoping to learn and play their cremation repertoire. During that time, I also read as much as I could about Hinduism in Bali, death rituals, and Balinese music history. There was almost nothing written about the bronze, four-keyed *gamelan angklung* (apart from a helpful chapter in Colin McPhee's book *Music in Bali: A Study in Form and Instrumental Organization in Balinese Orchestral Music* (1966)) and some passages in Michael Tenzer's *Balinese Music* (1991) and his *Gamelan Gong Kebyar: The Art of Twentieth-Century Balinese Music* (2000).[2] Even recordings of cremation music were difficult to find. Although there were many recordings of *gamelan angklung* out there, they invariably featured arrangements of pieces taken from other ensembles, much like those I had learned in Rochester and that Taman Sari had played at its concert, or newly created ones with added instruments, such as large drums and cymbals.

During this time, I also talked constantly with Nyoman when he was in Rochester. I would read about a certain ensemble or music and then do a "reality check" with Nyoman. Things first began to falter over the concept of mode (what else?), and whether *saih angklung* (the four-tone set of pitches used in *gamelan angklung* music) was part of the *pélog-slendro* tuning and modal system. Mode was, and still is, a contentious issue among some scholars, and much of the older literature is filled with graphs showing interval sizes, tunings, and names assigned to pitch sets (e.g., McPhee 1966; Rahn 1996; Rai 2004). I said no, *saih angklung* was its own scale; Nyoman said yes, it was *slendro* (a five-tone scale with more or less equidistant intervals) missing its first pitch. "How do you know that?" I asked. "I learned it in school," he said.

I returned to Bali in 2007 to spend a year with *gamelan* Taman Sari, gathering information for a case study on this group and its performing activities at cremations. I had a reasonable plan, somewhat different from most other Western music scholars who work in Bali, most of whom study with a master musician or teacher from ISI, or KOKAR. I would be on my own here. I knew that the men of the Baturiti *sekehe gamelan angklung* had never worked with a Western researcher (or a woman) and that my language skills were not up to deep music or theoretic conversations, especially in Balinese, the language they used among themselves. I expected misunderstandings, anticipated misinterpretations, and looked forward to blank moments that would (and did) eventually dissolve into wild gestures and laughter.

I never worked directly with one teacher or with any Balinese master musicians while I was there, but I occasionally met with them on my excursions to Denpasar and Ubud. I would frequently be invited to see a *gamelan angklung* concert performance or attend a competition that fed into the annual Bali Arts Festival (Pesta Kesenian Bali, or PKB). My Balinese friends often wondered why I was so interested in working with village musicians and in playing with them at cremations when I could hear "really great performances at concerts in Denpasar—even music played by women" (telephone conversation, Gusti Ayu Srinatih, October 6, 2007).

And, as I quickly discovered, the players with whom I worked did not see themselves as musicians, or what they played at cremations as music, and they were largely unfamiliar with the more formal literature, concert performance practices, or the contemporary terminology commonly used by scholars and expert Balinese musicians to describe the music analytically. Some had performed in other, local, more contemporary *gamelan*, such as the now-ubiquitous *gamelan gong kebyar*; some had inherited their positions in the *gamelan angklung* from their fathers or grandfathers; others had been dancers in their youth, performing for Balinese royalty, Dutch administrators or, after Independence (1945), for government ambassadors visiting their villages.

Most were rice farmers, *warung* (small eatery) owners, or local government workers who understood the primary spiritual significance of cremations and who chose to play in the ensemble more from a sense of ritual obligation than from the promise of an artful musical performance. Thus, during fieldwork, the men often seemed perplexed by my interest in what they were doing as "performers" or "musicians," rather than in what they saw themselves doing—simply carrying out their normal, everyday spiritual responsibilities to their families and communities.

Gamelan Angklung Stories

Soon, I began to separate what I saw and learned into three different *gamelan* stories that overlapped here and there, as in a Venn diagram, each informing the other, but ultimately generated from different pools of situated knowledge. The term *situated knowledge*, in its most basic sense, describes knowledge that is created, embodied, and performed by people within specific contexts, and which reflects an implicit, underlying worldview or perspective (Davidson 1992). It proposes that knowledge is constructed and contextualized by the knower's subject position within specific social contexts and, because these positions are generally part of larger structures of power and influence, certain knowledges, over time, become privileged and others ignored or forgotten.

The first story I refer to here is the conventional one, told through existing scholarship conducted largely by Western scholars, composers, and Balinese cultural experts—those Balinese musicians, singers, and dancers with whom Westerners worked during their time in Bali. Balinese cultural experts often provided access to other musicians and performances and supplied needed insider information to these early scholars. Many of these Balinese experts, or their descendants, are now the teachers and administrators of state-run arts schools, such as those mentioned above, or have become visiting artists in the West and elsewhere, like Nyoman and Pak Suweca. This close, reciprocal connection between Balinese cultural experts and European/American scholars and composers, over roughly 125 years, has resulted in both a wider exposure of Balinese music outside Bali and the adoption of many Western ideas about music, its training, and professionalism in Bali.

The conventional story left a scholarly legacy based on contemporaneous Western historical and ethnomusicological issues, such as the importance of tuning and mode, and the distribution of ensembles throughout the island that has continued to inform newer generations of scholars and composers, including me. Thus, much of the information on Balinese music we have today, although written primarily by outside scholars, driven by shared Western and Balinese interests, and primarily using Western-based analytical tools and methods, has been overseen, directed, and (largely) approved by Balinese experts interested in sharing their culture with a wider world.[3]

However, Balinese cultural experts were, and still are, also intimately connected to the players in groups such as the *sekehe angklung* Taman Sari in that they remain close to their families, their local *banjar*, and their spiritual communities. They frequently return home from the city or from overseas to their villages and participate in local ritual and musical practices, often recruiting young performers. Many today see their roles as leaders in simultaneous efforts to both preserve Balinese culture and enable it to flourish outside Bali.

The second story, largely unknown, belongs to the players. *Gamelan angklung* cremation music, such as that discussed in this book, has been under-researched and generally ignored by scholars and inside cultural experts alike, who see it as not relevant to their interests and who tend to regard its ubiquitous presence simply as humble, ambient sound. The player's story, unlike that of scholars or cultural experts, is more a *dharma*-infused one, communicated to me by the men of Taman Sari through their embodied

musical and spiritual practice at cremations. Their story is mainly one of
obligation and offering to the community.

They regard performing at a cremation as a religious duty, an individual's contribution to maintaining the law of cosmic balance between
dharma (order) and *adharma* (disorder/chaos), seen as a fundamental
principle of Hinduism and Buddhism, as practiced in contemporary Bali.
They are governed more by a sense of place, of groupness, and of the resulting *rasa* (feeling, or flavor) of cremations than by a shared abstraction of
the music's structure or a desire to perform concerts for new audiences.
They are connected to the cultural experts through their families, their
shared spiritual practice, and by their overall sense of Balinese identity,
but they are only minimally connected to the now professional Balinese
performance and scholarly communities.

The third story is mine, derived from the privileged perspective of a
female, white, Western-trained musician and academic who, in later life,
unexpectedly fell in love with a music unlike any she had ever known. It
was the first time in my academic career that the music itself captivated
me. I admit that early on I was also taken with the romanticism of con-
ducting fieldwork in Bali, a fantasy that had been fueled for decades by
countless stories told by previous scholars, such as Margaret Mead (1935),
Jaap Kunst (1934), Colin McPhee (1966), Clifford Geertz (1966), and many
others. I could at last join the mythological heroes of my imagination, a
notion I now recognize as a form of academic exoticism.[4] Over the years,
I have read and absorbed the conventional story of scholars and experts,
and, through ethnographic fieldwork, have come to better understand
the players' story. But my story is not entirely theirs; although I hope that
I have given as accurate an account as possible of what I experienced, I
also acknowledge that my writing may obscure the obvious unequal social
relations, resources, and consequences that are inherent in a project of
this kind.

When I first heard this music in Rochester, my main interest was to
understand the music's structure, how it worked, what made its wonderful,
wandering melodies and quirky metric shifts so enchanting. I wanted to
analyze it, to master it, to suss out its structure and underlying grammar.
But, as an ethnomusicologist, I also understood that this was a form of
musical colonialization that could only more firmly reify those unequal
power relations I knew existed. So, during the years I visited and lived
in Bali, I began to think more about what the men and I had in common
that could help us come closer together and bridge this gap. Although they
never spoke to me directly about "musical" things, I sensed that we not
only shared a love for this music, we had also developed similar methods

of learning it aurally and recalling it through various sound maps, with well-developed pathways and guideposts.

Eventually, I began to develop my own analytic method based on this assumption. I had always learned *gamelan* pieces aurally; I had never used notation, or any notes at all—so why start now? The men of *gamelan* Taman Sari had not learned these pieces from notation; why should I, just because I could? The men had never taught anyone how to play this music (why would they—everyone knew it), so I would just have to listen carefully, record what I heard, and learn the repertoire as fast as I could.[5] About halfway through the year, one of the men (I Nyoman Budiarti) took pity on me and made a bamboo *gangsa*, giving it to me so I could "practice at home."

Much later, when I returned to Rochester and began transcribing the music, I realized, as many have, that how and what I had learned aurally did not fit comfortably within the constraints of Western notation. I had always known that notating music, especially from an oral/aural tradition, was problematic, but was not prepared for the many difficulties and confusions I encountered trying to be truthful to the flow of the music

FIGURE 0.1 Bamboo *gangsa* and two *panggul* made by I Nyoman Budiarta, *banjar* Baturiti, Kerambitan, Tabanan.

while committing its sounds to the written page. Many ethnomusicologists face this challenge at some point, and often find creative solutions. Indeed, Balinese scholars themselves, such as I Ketut Gedé Asnawa (1991), I Wayan Surdirama (2013), and more recently, I Gdé Made Indra Sadguna (2021), have developed creative ways to illustrate the musics they discuss. So, I decided to avoid standard Western notation and, instead, provide recorded examples, listening guides, and diagrams to illustrate my points.

All the stories presented here (as well as countless others, no doubt) are equally valuable and important to an understanding of *gamelan angklung* cremation music in Bali. They exist simultaneously but more or less independently, like parallel universes—perhaps overlapping on occasion—having originated in different knowledge-worlds, and having been constructed, refined, retold, and re-musicked for different purposes. But I do not want to choose or privilege one over another here. I take the position that no one story is complete or completely accurate—all are true in some sense; they all exist together, each contributing a different color, shape, and connection to the kaleidoscopic universe of *gamelan angklung* and its music.

The organization of this book reflects these perspectives: chapters 1 and 2 are introductory, giving a sense of the physical and musical contexts of *gamelan angklung* and its cremation music, as experienced in contemporary Bali, as well as a summary of relevant history pertaining to *gamelan angklung*. Chapters 3 and 4 present the conventional story, what is already known about *gamelan angklung*, through the writings and recordings of previous scholars and musicians. Chapters 5 and 6 tell the players' story—one of obligation and connectedness—that characterizes the worldview of most Balinese today as they negotiate a rapidly changing socioeconomic world. And, in chapters 7 and 8 I grapple with the ephemeral features of this music that continue to enchant me in unexpected ways. In the final chapter, chapter 9, I try to come to terms with the intersecting worlds these stories reveal and how they are told in the context of performance at a cremation.

The book is based on research, fieldwork, and active performance carried out over many years, but mainly between May 2007 and June 2008. During that time, I lived in *banjar* Wani, at the family home of my teacher, I Nyoman Suadin, and worked with the *gamelan angklung* group Taman Sari, from *banjar* Baturiti, a bit down the road. I played with this group of men for over twenty-five cremations, as well as for many other temple and private ceremonies.

CHAPTER 1

Balinese Village Life

This chapter briefly explores the historical and cultural foundations of Balinese village life and ritual practice that are relevant to an understanding of contemporary *gamelan angklung* cremation music. It traces certain social and ritual practices surrounding wet-rice agriculture and early Hindu/Buddhist practices that fostered a sense of family, place, and order. It then moves to more recent political and cultural negotiations that affected *gamelan angklung* and its music in modern times. It begins in the recent past (2007) with a description of a typical day as I experienced it during my fieldwork, and some of the "oddities" I encountered as I began to live there.

A Day in Kerambitan

I wake up to the raucous sounds of the next-door neighbor's rooster, whose cries seem to form the English phrase, "Come and help me!" It is still dark, but I'm up and that's that.

My Balinese family, Men Iluh, Pak Iluh, Ayu, and Kadek are arising and will soon be getting ready for the day. Today, I am going with Men Iluh to the market at the center of the village. She is taking me to a seamstress who will make two kebaya *(blouses) for me to wear when I play for an* odalan *(temple ceremony) or enter a temple. I already have a Lacoste-like, bright orange jersey to wear for cremations—the Taman Sari uniform—but a* kebaya *will be necessary for other performances. I see the sign, Desa Kerambitan (Kerambitan Village), marking the entrance to the market and slowly weave my way in and out of the hundreds of people streaming in from neighboring* banjar *to buy today's wares.*

FIGURE 1.1 Rice field outside Suadin family compound.

The smells of raw meat, vegetables, and fruit, combined with the hot, sizzling odor of frying coconut oil remind me that I am hungry. We return to the family compound by the main road, turning right to pass the small warung *(food kiosk) where many of the men sit snacking, talking together, and wistfully engaging in* cuci mata *(getting some air while eyeing the women); we move onward to the* balé banjar *(neighborhood meeting place) where the* gamelan gong kebyar *is stored, and past the pigsty at the turn of the road where Nyoman's family lives.*

Back at home, Men Iluh cooks a glorious breakfast for me of egg-filled pancakes and fruit. Kadek, her son, who is six, has taken a liking to me (and I to him), often climbing into my room through the back window, wanting some chocolate or simply to say hi. He is adorable and funny, and every morning before he leaves for school, we snuggle up to watch "SpongeBob SquarePants" together (English, voiced-over in Indonesian) on the floor of the big family pavilion. Before setting off for school, Kadek stands with his beloved blown-up balloon statue of Spiderman in front of my door, hoping this will serve to protect me while he is away.

FIGURE 1.2 Kadek and Spiderman outside my living quarters.

After Kadek and Ayu leave, I'm pretty much on my own for a few hours. Sometimes, I take early morning walks through the neighborhood, visiting Kadek's school or laughing at the youngsters who follow me on their bikes, shouting "Mr. Money, Mr. Money!" I know I am an oddity here and am watched over by the villagers who protect me from seen and unseen forces. Unlike in the larger tourist areas, such as Ubud or Sanur, white people are rarely seen here.

As I pass their houses, neighbors and strangers come out to say hello, asking if I have bathed yet—a common greeting, like "What's up?" I pick up some food from the market or eat what is left in the pantry for lunch. When Kadek comes home, he likes to take me for a walk, holding my hand and leading me around like a pet; he practices his English and I practice my Indonesian. We are at about the same level of language acquisition, so these attempts usually end by dissolving into laughter or stopping to have an ice cream cone.

Around 6:30 p.m. I head up the main road to banjar Baturiti, the neighborhood next to banjar Wani where the men of sekehe gamelan Taman Sari live, about half a mile away, and wave to the men and boys resting on wooden benches and walls along the way. I arrive on time, at 7:00, but no one's there, not even Pak Rideng (head of the group), who thinks my ideas about being on time are amusing. He frequently reminds me that the Balinese are never on time—they work on the principle of jam karet (rubber time). Arriving about twenty minutes later, he enters the balé and climbs the ladder to the kulkul (large, suspended bamboo slit drums; see the photo below) where he plays the percussive pattern for calling the men of Taman Sari to the balé banjar. (🔊 Recording 1.1, Kulkul) In the background are the sounds of everyday life: a motorcycle, a passing car, and some people chatting.

Over the next half-hour or so, the men slowly drift in, smoking and chatting, anticipating an easy evening of playing, where Ibu Ellen will ask strange questions about what they are doing, and then they will have some tea and cigarettes. Tonight, we are recording the three sections of "Sekar Jepun" (Japanese Flower). The second section sounds like the second section of another piece—is it the same? Probably

FIGURE 1.3 *Kulkul* at *banjar* Baturiti *balé banjar.*

not, but only transcribing will tell. There are about fifteen men here tonight—pretty much the whole group. They are mostly my age or older (sixties or seventies). They are invariably friendly and seem glad I'm there, some even anticipating that I will take them to the United States on a tour. We laugh a lot, and the group sometimes breaks down when one kotekan *(interlocking passage) veers off into another, but a quick signal from Pak Rideng gets us back on track. My* jegogan *(lowest metallophone) partner, Pak Debet, smokes continuously, his cigarette permanently hanging from the right corner of his lower lip. The music still enchants me—how do they remember it all? Only four notes and a universe of music!*

Bali is about ninety-five miles east to west and about seventy miles north to south (see the map below). The island is bisected by a large east-west mountain range that divides it into two distinct areas. Tabanan is part of the southcentral plains, for centuries known as the heartland of wet-rice agriculture. To the west of Tabanan lie the dense forests of Jembrana, home to the large bamboo used to make *gamelan jegog* (see figure 4.1 on page 67); and beyond the mountains to the north, sloping foothills stretch down to the coast of the Bali Sea, home of the centuries-old trading centers and beautiful beaches of Singaraja and Lovina.

Tabanan and its surrounding areas are well known for their wet-rice production.[1] High rainfall, radiant sunshine, and multiple *subak* (local irrigation groups) ensure an abundance of food. Individual houses and compounds lie almost on top of one another, while flourishing, flat, and terraced rice fields fan out from the village center. The daily market (*pasar*), soccer field, temples, *warung*, and family compounds are connected by a series of footpaths and alleys that meet at narrowly paved roads and often lead to springs of pure mountain water (*pancoran*).

Most Balinese still live in or have family homes in villages, such as Kerambitan, some commuting to businesses or government offices in Denpasar or to work in the southern tourist centers, but returning frequently to their villages, *banjar*, and families. And, although they may live elsewhere, they are still expected to attend, celebrate, and support the three main *pura* (temples) in their villages (Interview, Wayan Arshana, October 4, 2007).

Family compounds (*pakarangan*), like temples, adhere to basic directional and spiritual principles.[2] For example, kitchens and bathrooms—places where human bodily functions and activities occur—lie in the compound's south, closer to the sea, which is considered a dangerous place. The family temple and ancestral shrine are placed in the north—closer to the gods who reside in the mountains. An individual family

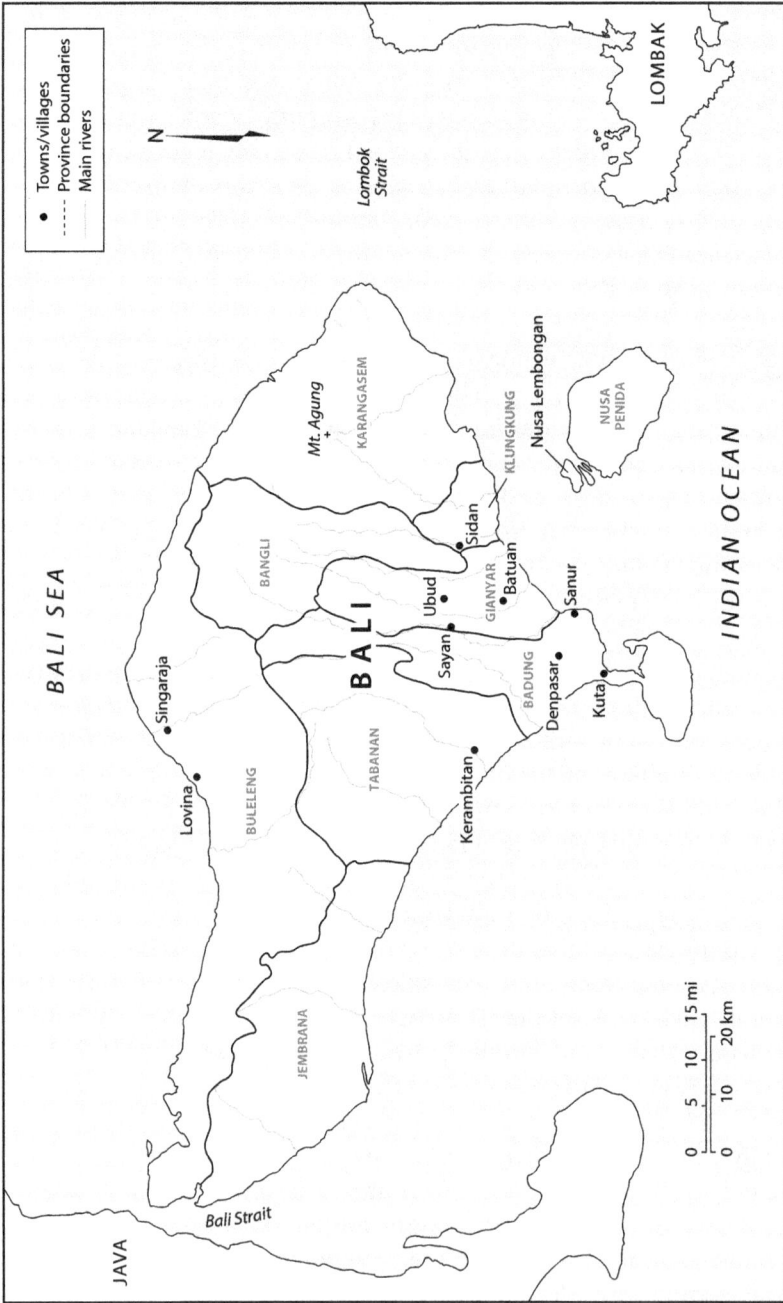

FIGURE 1.4 Map of Bali. William Nelson, cartographer.

compound has three areas that are considered less to more sacred: a large gate, approached from the outside walkway, opens into the main area, housing the largest communal space. This is where most of the family activity takes place and where visitors socialize and eat snacks. In the northwest of the compound, the family temple sits elevated and enclosed by a small stone gate and steps; in the northernmost area of the compound is the ancestral shrine, where effigies of deceased family members reside within small, highly decorated containers.

Walking through the village at almost any time of the day or evening, one is likely to hear Balinese music. Frequent celebrations at local temples, stores, or family compounds; local rehearsals for upcoming competitions; afterschool *gamelan* programs (see the picture below); cremations; welcoming dances; or simply the practicing of a homemade instrument all enliven the *balé banjar*, the streets, and compounds as the community goes about its day. *Banjar* Wani, where I live, maintains an active *gamelan luang*, an ancient seven-tone ensemble (see figure 1.6 on p. 16), one of only four or five on the island, in which Nyoman's father participated for decades.

FIGURE 1.5 Girl's after-school *gamelan angklung* rehearsal.

FIGURE 1.6 *Gamelan luang, banjar* Wani.

The *banjar* also supports a large *gamelan gong kebyar*, which is frequently used as a sort of default *gamelan* for many occasions, including *odalan* (temple ceremonies) and largescale weddings at the *puri* (local palace). For cremation ceremonies, the *gamelan angklung* group, Taman Sari, comes down the road from *banjar* Baturiti, and other ensembles, such as *gender wayang* (accompanying *wayang kulit* stories), *gambang* (an ensemble of wooden xylophones also used for cremations), and others, are hired from neighboring *banjar*.

The Roots of Village Life

Living in a village such as Kerambitan, one sees and experiences daily a complex collage of the old and new: beliefs and practices, centuries old, adapted to contemporary times; social and political structures changed and rechanged over centuries; an economy based on traditional practices, somewhat modernized to enter a global economy; and a sense of community and competition that has always existed yet is performed anew in the present. To understand how *gamelan angklung*, the subject of this book, fits into this intricate picture today, we must examine some of the recent and not so recent histories of the island to consider why and how this ensemble and its music continues, as it has for centuries, to be a necessary component of today's village life and death.

What is central to the study of *gamelan angklung* and its cremation music today is its underlying connections to a much older Bali. Social structures based on specific place, family and ancestor veneration, the importance of cooperative groups, the necessity for elaborate cremation rituals, deep concerns with seen and unseen forces, as well as the displaying of appropriate social behavior in public all provide centuries-old beliefs and practices that predate the commonly understood beginnings of contemporary Balinese history, yet are still present today. Although much of this older story has long been forgotten (and little documentation exists), it is daily reconstructed and made present in the beliefs and practices of everyday villagers whose voices are seldom heard in the standard retellings of their history. What follows is a brief look at some of the roots of contemporary Balinese culture and *gamelan angklung* performance that continue to be reconstructed and performed today as Bali attempts to integrate into a larger Indonesia and into a more global economy.

Prehistorical Beginnings

The conventional story of modern Bali begins in 1343 when remnants of the great Hindu kingdom of Majapahit are believed to have left their homeland in eastern Java and migrated across the Bali Strait to the island. When the Majapahit arrived, they encountered people with whom they had long been in contact through trade, exploration, and cultural exchanges. Although much of the archipelago's early history remains hazy, archeologists surmise that the Bali Strait separating Bali from Java, now only a mile and a half wide, was once a single landmass, and travel, especially between east Java and Bali, was common. Originally descended from successive waves of immigrants from what today are known as the Philippines, China, and Austronesia, scholars believe that humans have been present on the island for over 30,000 years (Pringle 2004).

Very little is known for certain about the pre- and early history of this area, but various artifacts and documents show that in the first millennium CE, inhabitants of the island had coalesced into stratified, extended family groups, or clans, with a forged-metal technology that sustained both a dry- and wet-rice agriculture, especially in the south (Wessing 1998:47–55; Pringle 2004:31); in the north, a thriving economy, based on trade with neighboring islands, especially Java to the west and Lombok to the east, also existed at the end of the first millennium. Austronesian social structure, based on clan lineage (descent from a common ancestor), and spiritual practices, focusing on local deities, ancestor veneration, and extensive cremation practices, were also present (Hutterer 1998:32–47).

The importance of family and place in Bali's early history and in contemporary life cannot be underestimated. One's identity, spiritual practice, and community responsibilities have long been linked to place of birth (where the placenta of newborn babies is buried), to local and extended family, and most importantly, to one's deceased and deified ancestors who still live on, in effigy. Proper death ceremonies ensuring the safe passage of the deceased from *sekala* (the seen world) to *niskala* (the unseen world) remain crucial for the protection and wellbeing of still-living family members (Eiseman vol. 2, 1990:115–26; Connor 1995:537–59).

Indianization

Historians of Bali often refer to the time from c. 400–1400 CE as the period of Indianization, during which traders, missionaries, soldiers, and artist/performers, primarily from India, traveled extensively throughout Southeast Asia, often marrying into local families. This is the period before the entrance of the Majapahit Kingdom in Bali, and is felt, as Michael Tenzer writes, "to be not so much the actual past as [one that] is suspended in a mythic prehistory that is discontinuous with the origins of the Bali they know" (2000:150). Bringing an early form of Vedic practice that focused on Shiva as the primary deity (Saivism or Shaivism), as well as a different form of social order (*varna*, color) based primarily on occupation, these travelers provided a sort of social and ritual scaffolding for the more classic Hinduism and Buddhism, said to have arrived with the Majapahit Empire and later.

Many theories of how early Indic culture evolved throughout the area have long existed within religious and anthropological studies. The spread of early Vedic beliefs, along with Buddhist, and later, Muslim and Christian practices have been examined extensively elsewhere; what is important here is the relationship of these beliefs to contemporary Bali and to its expressive culture. A form of this social and ritual system has persisted over centuries and today, known by many names, it provides not only a solid structure for daily and ceremonial life, but also a unique site for a specifically Hindu Balinese culture within Indonesia, a country that has the largest Muslim population in the world.

One of the most important beliefs that linked early Hinduism and Buddhism, and resonated with pre-Majapahit Balinese, was the basic concept of preserving cosmic balance between *dharma* and *adharma*. *Dharma* was conceptualized by early Indian texts and missionaries as the underlying structure that preserved cosmic balance, and by early Buddhists as a name for the Buddha's teachings that provided a form of practice to obtain this balance (Eiseman vol. 1, 1990:12). *Dharma* encompasses all traditional duties and responsibilities that humans perform for themselves, for their families and communities, and for the spirits that protect them against *adharma*; *dharma* is also a description of the ordered world itself: as Michel Picard writes, "Dharma is both an account of the world and a norm on which to base social life, at once describing how things are and prescribing the way they should be" (2012:121).

One performs thoughtful and appropriate actions (*karma*) in accordance with one's own *dharma*, constrained by one's place and time. As everyone and everything is connected, the universe will remain ordered when each entity is in its own place in an established relation to everything else. It is precisely this ordered relationship that is *dharma*. Fred Eiseman states, "The Balinese conceive that all things in the universe, living or not, have some connection with each other. There is no clear distinction made between oneself and some other self or between oneself and some other object. There is no clear distinction made between what will happen, what has happened, and what is happening right now" (vol. 1, 1990:12).

J. Stephen Lansing, in his article "The 'Indianization' of Bali" (1983), suggests that the basic Indic belief of balance between *dharma* and *adharma* through sacrificial ritual was spread in the first millennium throughout the Indonesian archipelago, mainly through what would today be called the performing arts—music, dance, drama, and puppetry (seen as offerings by early Indigenous peoples)—rather than through conquest or colonialization. He surmises that the performances of musicians and other artists traveling between villages carried the essence of the Indian worldview more successfully than missionaries or holy texts. Further, Lansing argues that the central ideas of early Hinduism's social order and ritual practices in Bali were accepted voluntarily by Indigenous Balinese (often encouraged by local rulers and Brahmin priests) and were easily embedded within already-existing familial social structures. Hence, it appears that the Indianization of Bali "was a voluntary—indeed enthusiastic—project of the Balinese themselves; that it consisted in the selective adoption of a broadly Indic worldview that involved a redefinition of the relationship of the social sphere to the cosmos; ... therefore, Bali was 'Indianized' by the power of Indian ideas—ideas given expression, for the most part, in works of art" (1983:19).

The Importance of Collectives: *Subak, Banjar,* and *Sekehe*

Balinese today attribute their centuries-old sustainable economy to their ability to work together communally, a principle that derives, in part, from the spiritual practice of Tri Hita Karana, roughly translated as the "three causes of wellbeing" or "three reasons for prosperity" (Fox 2010:370). These include harmony between people, between people and the natural environment, and between people and various local deities, achieved through the many offerings, rituals, and celebrations that go on daily. Most scholars of Balinese history and culture have commented on the significance of collaborative groups present on the island as far back as the beginning of the common era.[3] What follows here is a brief, general discussion of the *subak, banjar,* and *sekehe*—three important traditional group structures still found on the island today, and central to the study of *gamelan angklung.*

Early practices shared with other Austronesian migrating peoples, such as burial rites, ancestor worship, and interactions between the living and the dead, have marked Balinese culture, over centuries, as particularly cooperative. Indeed, one of the primary organizational principles of contemporary village life today is cooperative reciprocity, provided by groups of all kinds that have existed there for centuries. Collectives such as the *subak* (a group of neighboring rice growers who regulate irrigation),[4] the *banjar* (a more or less permanent group of extended families largely responsible for celebrations, festivals, and cremations), and the *sekehe* (also *sekaha*) (a specific group or club, formed for a special purpose, such as *sekehe gamelan angklung*, Taman Sari—a group that performs *gamelan angklung* music) continue today to provide help and support for their communities. Analyses of Balinese collaborative groups have frequently been used in the scholarly literature to illustrate both hierarchic (caste-based) and democratic social structures (see especially Geertz and Geertz 1975).

The *Subak*

The philosophy of Tri Hita Karana, mentioned above, is perhaps best manifested in the *subak*, a communally based water-management system tended and watched over by neighboring families and local deities who inhabit small water temples within the fields, as well as other temples along the navigation stream, and the head water source. About twelve hundred *subak* exist in Bali today, but the traditional *subak* system is many centuries old—some scholars say it developed around 800–900 CE, and its communal nature is deeply rooted in all aspects of Balinese culture.

Today, members of each *subak* decide propitious dates for planting and harvesting, as well as for offerings and ceremonies to Dewi Sri (Goddess of Rice), materialized in small figures made from dried rice stalks. So important is rice to Balinese culture that some scholars suggest the 210-day Balinese calendar, consisting of six, thirty-five-day months, was originally constructed to mark the ends of the two annual crop cycles (*padi tahun*) (Lansing 1987:330).

The wet-rice growing, harvesting, drying, and cooking processes have evolved over centuries into a multi-staged, multi-crop-a-year industry. Eaten at every meal and part of every offering, rice is so central to daily living that, in the absence of money, it was and continues to be used as a form of payment for work, or as part of trade between neighbors. Fred Eiseman, a longtime observer and scholar of Balinese culture, has observed that "rice and rice ritual occupy a major portion of the time, energy, and money of the people of Bali" (vol. 1, 1990:284).

How Rice Is Grown in Kerambitan

While living with Nyoman's family, I became fascinated by the rice growing and harvesting process and with the many words used to name the results of each stage: padi *refers to the growing plant (not the field itself, as I always thought);* jijih *is the unhusked, brown rice taken from the mature* padi; *the newly husked, but uncooked, white rice is* baas; *and* nasi *is the cooked, white rice that is eventually eaten, as in* nasi goreng *(fried rice).*

But what was even more fascinating to me was the rice field itself— a complete sound, spiritual, and ecological system, constantly busy, noisy, and thriving. By day, it was often filled with workers, knee-deep in water, or with the neighbor's chickens pecking for grain. At night, it teemed with the loud chirping of frogs, crickets, and other night creatures, or hosted teams of eel-catchers, with their miner-light hats and spears, laughing and lunging in the murky wetness.

The planting and harvesting require many steps: first, the seeds are taken from the jijih *and planted in small nurseries next to the rice fields, where they are covered with burlap and allowed to sprout until they turn into* padi. *The* padi *grows to about two to three feet high and produces a slim, green stock packed with rice grain (*jijih*). When the grain turns yellow, it's time to harvest. Lots of people show up to harvest the rice. They bring their own machetes and walk through the fields, whacking away at the top half of the* padi. *They then combine the grain stocks into large bales (somewhat like wheat or hay in the United States), which are then covered with plastic tarps to dry out for a few days.*

Other workers then show up with a rice-husking machine. They feed the partially dried stalks through the machine and the grains fall out onto a tarp. Sometimes, they take a handful of stalks and whack them against a wooden board, which loosens the grains. They put the grains into large white sacks and cart them home, where over the next week or so they spread them out on plastic tarps all over the alleys and compound yards to dry out. Every day they rake them and toss them up and down in small woven baskets to loosen mud, plant debris, dust, or any other foreign matter from the grains.

At the end of each day, the workers repackage the grain in sacks and take them home, and after many days, they take their bags to a processor, a machine that takes off the outer, brown husk and turns the grains into baas. In earlier times, and still occasionally today, the unhusked grains would be poured into large wooden troughs and teams of men and women would beat the grains with bamboo poles, creating interlocking patterns, a practice discussed more fully in a later chapter. The rice is then packaged in large, white bags and sold to stores or given to the workers and owners as payment (personal conversation, Nyoman Suadin, November 15, 2005). People buy the rice and cook it to become fluffy, white nasi.

FIGURE 1.7 Drying rice.

The *Banjar*

The *banjar* is the smallest unit of local, traditional government (*desa adat*) in Bali and has existed as a primary social group for centuries. Its membership consists of a neighborhood's married men (about sixty to a hundred men) who represent their families at meetings (about four hundred to eight hundred people). Independent from, but now working in tandem with, the centralized Indonesian government (*desa dinas*), members of the *banjar* attend the same village temples, and they are responsible for ritual and ceremonial events, such as finding appropriate dates for celebrations, as well as the financial arrangements and traffic control involved in such events. In addition, they must provide ritual offerings and maintain the temples and cremation site, musical instruments, costumes, and much more.

During colonial times (c. the nineteenth century, as described below), the *banjar* took on more importance, in part to distinguish it from the more centralized Dutch administrative government, but also to help the Dutch consolidate the village population in their efforts to standardize certain community undertakings, such as the building of roads, and later, collecting taxes. The *banjar* is also responsible for local protection against both seen and unseen forces.[5] Members are summoned by the *kulkul*, introduced earlier, and various rhythmic patterns (*tabuh*) known to the community are tapped out with a large stick, just as Pak Rideng did to call the men of *gamelan* Taman Sari. Meetings are conducted in Balinese, not Indonesian (Eiseman vol. 2, 1990:72–80). Today, the *banjar* remains the heart of the local community and much time and effort are spent here making sure all runs smoothly.

Perhaps the most important service of the *banjar* to the community is its role in a *ngabén* (cremation). The *banjar* is "fundamental in the cyclical passage between the worlds of the seen and unseen (*sekala* and *niskala*), and in the maintenance of relations between the living and deceased ancestors" (Warren 1996:5). When a member of a *banjar* dies, it is the responsibility of all the other members to make offerings, to ensure that the body is properly washed and dressed, to purchase adequate amounts of burial cloth for wrapping the body, as well as to carry the body to the cemetery, and to dig a shallow grave if the body is not cremated immediately (Connor 1995).

The time between death and cremation or burial is the period known as *ngébag* (in Balinese, to guard), when the body is still in the family compound. Neighbors attend to the family, dropping by during the day and night with offerings of rice, coffee, or white cloth, and provide distractions for bereaved relatives. Music is also played here, often by many *gamelan*, including *gamelan angklung* and *gamelan gambang* (an ensemble of wooden-slabbed instruments, played with forked mallets. The deceased's family, in recognition of the support and help of their neighbors, provides food and drink throughout this important interval. On the morning of the cremation or burial, the body is washed, wrapped, blessed with holy water and offerings, and placed in a *wadah* (cremation tower). The *wadah*, mounted on a bamboo platform attached to long bamboo poles, is carried by family members, while the entire *banjar* forms a procession to escort the corpse to the cremation grounds (*kuburan*).

The importance of cremations for the Balinese should not be underestimated. A vast amount of scholarship has long existed describing these elaborate ceremonies, seemingly so different from those in the West, and various interpretations have been offered as to their meaning and significance to contemporary Balinese. Prominent among these is the belief in the very real connection, or, as Jean-François Guermonprez, an early historian of Bali, writes, the ongoing "partnerships that exist between the living and the dead" (in Warren 1991:57). A proper cremation restores and ensures cosmic order. Involving the family, *banjar*, and wider community in its elaborate series of rites, a cremation brings about the transition through which the soul breaks its material bonds and becomes fused with the collective ancestors worshipped in the home compounds and village temples.

The immaterial essence of the soul—what remains after cremation—is what is ultimately reincarnated and placed again, in material form, within its own community and descent group. The oldest male in the compound is responsible for mounting a cremation when someone in the family dies, a task that is both time-consuming and financially burdensome. Further, when a death occurs, all the men in the *banjar* must visit the house of the deceased for three days and nights, helping the family and providing distractions for the living. The family provides continuous servings of food, coffee, and water throughout this time, often further straining budgets. These practices, among many, are simply part of life, the normal, everyday practice of various local traditions that constitute *dharma* and have been in place for centuries.

The *Sekehe*

Sekehe simply means "group" or "club," a collective started by a few people in a *banjar* who share a common interest. *Sekehe* have long existed in Bali as a site for working together on specific projects. *Sekehe* rise and fall over time, some lasting only a few weeks, others for decades. As with a *banjar*, fees may be collected, leaders chosen, and meetings held, but unlike a *banjar*, members are free to come and go at will.

Most *banjar* have at least one *gamelan sekehe*, such as a *sekehe gong*, a group of musicians who play the *gamelan gong kebyar* (see Tenzer

2000:71–114), or a *sekehe angklung*, such as *banjar* Baturiti's *sekehe angklung* Taman Sari, the group I joined and played with during cremations. *Sekehe* membership and organization changes frequently, and a *sekehe* can be started or disbanded easily. (See chapter 6 for a discussion of the history and social organization of *sekehe gamelan* Taman Sari.)

The Development of Courts

Although the roots of village life go back for millennia, the conventional date in the mid-fourteenth century, as mentioned above, is regarded by most Balinese living today as the beginning of the island's modern history. In 1343, as documented in the many versions of the *Babad Dalem* (*Chronicle of Kings*), a text believed to have been written by a Brahmin attached to the eighteenth-century court of Klungkung (Hägerdal 1995:103–23), members of the powerful and expansive Majapahit Empire, the last remaining Hindu kingdom in eastern Java, entered Bali, forming a small colony in the western portion of the island. They eventually settled in the southeastern plains, an area already supporting a thriving rice-growing agriculture. By the end of the fourteenth century, Majapahit descendants had established a kingdom in Gelgel—today, a village in the province of Gianyar (see the map on page 14).

When members of the Majapahit dynasty relocated to Bali in the fourteenth century, it is believed that they brought with them an already centuries-old social and ritual structure based on the four-*warna* (color, caste) system, similar to that of India. This consisted of three upper strata (*triwangsa*): *brahmana* (priests), *ksatria* (warriors, noblemen), and *wesya* (merchants, craftspeople), who together comprised about 8 percent of the population; the remaining Indigenous population (about 90 percent) comprised the lowest stratum, *sudra* (farmers, workers). This ranked system was easily superimposed on local communities in Bali, especially in the south, as they were already structured on family lineage and clan ties.

Originally, the four-*warna* system referred to skin color, but soon became associated with occupation or profession. One was born into a family that was known for its skill at learning and/or ritual practice, fighting and/or governing, or trade and/or craft. Those whose families did not fit into this tripartite system were *sudra* (workers). Over the centuries, hundreds of subdivisions developed, mainly from differences between competing family groups, but the original four-part structure remained essentially intact (Eiseman vol. 2, 1990:28; Pringle 2004:22–27).

In the fifteenth and sixteenth centuries, as the *warna* system spread throughout much of Bali, some of the more isolated groups, not central to the expanding court culture or to the staple rice economy, resisted this ranked system, largely retaining their autonomy. These groups, known today as Bali Aga (Mountain People, Indigenous communities), are believed by some to have inhabited the island since the beginning of the common era (Pringle 2004:28–40). Others state that no evidence exists to support this, but that the Bali Aga continue to remain outside the *warna* structure and have never fully integrated into the post-Majapahit court culture (2004:10). Late in the sixteenth century the word "caste" (from the Portuguese) became the label used to refer to the system by outsiders (mainly Westerners). Caste was strictly defined by the Portuguese, and later by the Dutch in Bali, as being designated solely by birth (i.e., a clan).[6]

After the decline of the Gelgel court near the end of the seventeenth century, Bali fragmented into a multi-kingdom island, with Klungkung, in the southeast, as the most powerful. Eventually, nine independent kingdoms emerged. This period (c. 1600–1850) is often described by historians as a time of powerful, frequently warring kingdoms, with central power held by a few local rulers, Brahmin priests, and warriors attached to their courts, along with musicians, artists, puppet masters, builders, and others who entertained and provided ceremonial richness to court life. It is also during this period that visitors and immigrants, mainly from eastern Java and China, as well as a few Europeans—from Portugal (1512) and Holland (1597)—began arriving on the island.

With the rise and growth of centralized courts in the sixteenth through the nineteenth centuries, opportunities for musicians, dancers, and artists of all kinds flourished on Bali. Important genres, such as the dance-drama, *gambuh*, are believed to have developed during this time; later, new dance forms, such as *topeng* (masked dances) and *legong* (welcome dances), and the grand tradition of court music (*lelambatan*), played by the *gamelan gong gdé*, evolved, becoming staples within court culture, often fueling competition between families and kingdoms (Gold 2005:72–92). *Gamelan angklung* music, having developed largely outside the court system, continued to play for *banjar* cremations, often by the same musicians as those attached to the court.

Although Holland had already set up trade and established administrative footholds in Java and the western islands of the archipelago through its Dutch East India Company (VOC, est. 1602), it was not until the beginning of the nineteenth century that the Dutch began to take control of the administration of villages in Bali, working in tandem with local rulers and priests to create a nexus of power that controlled the island until 1949, the year Bali joined the newly independent Republic of Indonesia. Between 1902 and the Japanese invasion and occupation of Bali from 1942 to 1945, the Dutch, with cooperation from local rulers and priests, did much to strengthen the already-established caste and *banjar* system. In addition, the Dutch imposed taxes to help construct and maintain an infrastructure of roads connecting villages and districts and, among other things, installed a European-styled village bureaucracy that, in effect, resulted in today's dual governing systems.

A centralized, national system, *desa dinas*, controlled today by the Muslim-based government in Indonesia's capital, Jakarta, is responsible for national policies and laws that affect all twenty-seven Indonesian provinces; an older, more localized, Hindu-based governing system, *desa adat*, controlled by local *banjar* and village groups, oversees the massive irrigation systems and sets appropriate dates for temple ceremonies, weddings, and cremations, among many other things that regulate Balinese village economic and spiritual life.

Recent Political and Cultural Negotiations

When Indonesia became an independent country in 1945, various measures, long debated during the previous decades, were put into place to encourage the varied communities living on about 950 inhabited islands (out of about 17,500) to begin seeing themselves as part of a larger, unified, and modern nation-state. Adopting the Indonesian language (largely based on Malay); establishing universal education; consolidating power under the Guided Democracy and Pancasila policies of President Sukarno (1945–67) and President Suharto (1967–98); developing a self-sustaining tourist industry; curbing or eradicating dissenting groups; and other measures all resulted in a new and hopeful sense of a unified identity, as well as growing economic instability and political dissent.

Also occurring during this time (c. 1945–90) was an increased interest in Bali as an anthropological and ecological field site. Reconstructions of the island's history and culture resulted in various interpretations of its social and political history, including, most famously, those of Clifford and Hildred Geertz, who continued to position the Balinese within a hierarchic, status-occupied paradigm, based on fieldwork mainly with the *triwangsa*, the three higher castes—that is, with about 10 percent of the population. Among the many changes in the twentieth century, however, two are significant for our discussion of contemporary *gamelan angklung* ensemble, especially its music and performance outside the cremation context: (1) a reconceptualization and naming of Balinese spiritual practices, and (2) the patronage of Balinese "performing arts" seen through the twin lenses of secularism and tourism.

Hinduisms in Bali Today

If you ask a Balinese person today what religion he or she practices, the most common answer is, simply, Hinduism. Over the past century, however, the ritual practices of Balinese people have been variously labeled Agama Tirtha (Religion of Water), Agama Siwa (Religion of Shiva), Agama Bali (Religion of Bali), and Agama Hindu Bali (Religion of Balinese Hinduism, as distinguished from that of India). Again, as in much recorded history of Bali, many conflicting stories of Balinese Hinduisms abound, and interpretations vary widely depending on who is telling the story, when it is told, and for what purpose. Here, I wish to highlight important changes in Balinese self-identity and to establish a framework for contemporary spiritual and expressive practices that have affected contemporary village life and the music of *gamelan angklung*.

Michel Picard, in his 2012 article "What's in a Name? An Enquiry About the Interpretation of *Agama Hindu* as 'Hinduism,'" provides a good explanation of these changes, which I draw upon and summarize below. When the Dutch introduced European-derived administrative systems throughout the island in the nineteenth century, two significant cognitive and ideological changes were set in motion: First, in making a distinction between local practices, which they labeled *desa adat* (i.e., custom, ritual) and more widespread governing policies, which they labeled *desa dinas* (i.e., official, governmental), the Balinese had to consider, perhaps for the first time, dividing their activities into more or less Western-derived sacred and secular categories. Second, in attempting to spread their administrative system throughout the island, the Dutch, perhaps inadvertently, set in motion the idea that Bali was a unified island, thus blurring individual *banjar* distinctions and local practices. The notion of a more holistic category, "Balinese people," took hold and strengthened.

By the beginning of the twentieth century, a growing class of educated, relatively wealthy, and literate Balinese *sudra* began questioning the prevailing caste structure and the role of embedded Indian-derived ritual practices in legitimizing this system. At this time, the Balinese had no general term in their own language for their ritual practices; indeed, many *banjar* had their own local words for such practices, not necessarily shared with other *banjar*. Thus, they had "no generic name to designate that which would later become their 'religion' ... [that is], they had not yet singled out a set of beliefs and practices that could be demarcated from other aspects of their life in order to be labeled as 'religion'" (Picard 2012:130).

One significant outcome of these realignments led the Balinese to a moment of profound self-reflection on their own way of life in relation to a non-Balinese other. Never having had to make a clear distinction between traditional/nontraditional, sacred/secular, or local/universal, this process of self-reflection created a tension between a modernizing, reforming urge that moved toward sameness and unification (i.e., centralization, standardization, and nationalism), and a conservative urge that wished to preserve older systems of caste and social difference (i.e., separateness, autonomy, and locality).

Briefly, controversies arose from the meaning of the words *agama* (religion) and *adat* (custom, tradition). What, exactly, was a religion, as distinguished from a traditional practice? Preservers sought to retain the traditional Hindu caste system, where *agama* and *adat* were indistinguishable, favoring the name Agama Hindu Bali; reformers wanted to separate *agama* from the Hindu caste system, freeing and separately defining it as a religious practice, calling it simply Agama Bali. Reformers also wanted to standardize *agama*, moving it away from older beliefs in local gods and traditional practices, such as ancestor veneration, trance, and witchcraft, into a more modern monotheistic "religion" that could achieve the same worldwide recognition, status, and universalism as Judaism, Christianity, and Islam. In 1959, Agama Hindu Bali was finally recognized by the national council as the legitimate name of the religious practice.

Over the next twenty-five years, debate centered on how widespread or universal Agama Hindu Bali was. This debate resulted in various name changes for the religious practice, as well as for the Indonesian governing body established to oversee religious affairs throughout Indonesia. June McDaniel, in her article "Religious Change and Experimentation in Indonesian Hinduism," has documented that Sukarno's new state policies concerning religious practice were eventually spread through the religious curriculum of the public education system, so that Hinduism, a polytheistic practice, would now conform to fit the criteria set down by the government:

> One god was called the Almighty God (the other gods and ancestors were demoted to angels or other aspects of the one god), the Vedas and the Bhagavad Gita became the equivalent of the Qur'an or the Bible, and the Vedic sages or *rishis* became prophets. . . . There are currently various layers of Hinduism, which include folk Hinduism (local indigenous beliefs which are mixed with Hindu ones), Agama Tirtha (the religion of holy water, which emphasizes ritual and is largely Saivite), and Agama Hindu Dharma (which emphasizes ethics, philosophy, and social responsibility). These may be mixed and practiced simultaneously (2017:4).

Thus, today, although most people in Bali now use the simple term Hindu to label their own practice publicly, many, especially those still living and working in rural areas such as Kerambitan (and who continue to speak

Balinese), adhere, in practice, to older beliefs, to *banjar* differences, and to local gods without specifically naming what they do.

Changes instituted by the Parisada Hindu Dharma (PHD) have also affected *ngabén* practices, especially those concerning the question of immediate cremation or burial. Only Brahmin priests must be cremated immediately following death, so most families face this question at some time. Most scholars who study death rituals in Bali have seen this decision as based solely on caste affiliation or financial resources, but according to Carol Warren, many Balinese have long preferred short-term burial to immediate cremation, choosing to wait, sometimes for many years, to cremate the remains (Warren 1996:40).

Some say that the body has not decayed enough for cremation and must be buried for a time to avoid the corpse feeling the fire's heat. Warren interprets this preference as an example of the symbolic association of village soil with regeneration (1996:46)—as in the practice of burying the placenta of newborns at the home compound—further underlining the importance of place in the Balinese worldview. She further notes that, according to her informants, the Parisada Hindu Dharma organization has long wanted to standardize this process, "[b]ut, old people say that it is important to return to the place of origin—Ibu Pertiwi—the first element—earth" (I Suarsa 1985 in Warren 1996:48).

Constructing the Arts, Encouraging and Combating Tourism

In debating what to call longstanding, traditional rituals, and how to practice them, the Balinese had to consider the implicit division of their activities into sacred and secular realms. If there was a specific category of belief and behavior called *agama*, or religion, what was "not *agama*"? Over the early decades of the twentieth century, with its pull toward a democratized, Indonesian nation-state and the rise of tourism in Bali, a gradual shift occurred in the meaning and value of ritual offerings, especially musical expressions, as they were reevaluated in terms of aesthetic and economic potential, and ultimately reconceptualized as "art."

Although traders, missionaries, and others had been visiting Bali for centuries, 1908 marks the year that the Dutch colonial government opened an official tourist bureau in Java. By the late 1960s, the tourist industry had exploded, prompting the Balinese to question if their traditional culture had become diluted or compromised. A new policy called Cultural Tourism was introduced and modified over the next decade. Like the conversations concerning the semantic and practical boundaries of *agama* and *adat*, and constrained by difficulties in the translation of basic concepts from

Balinese, to Dutch, to Indonesian, Cultural Tourism resulted in a realignment of traditional ritual offerings (music, dance, puppetry, carvings, etc.) into categories of art, differentiated by their degree of sacredness.

As with the word "religion," no word existed in Balinese for "art" or "music." Words, borrowed mostly from Indonesian/Malay, such as *seni* (Indonesian, "refined art") and *karawitan* (Indonesian, *gamelan* music), and from European languages, such as *musiki* (Latin, muse, music), were used to label these new concepts. In 1971 a conference, Seminar on Sacred and Profane Dance, was held in Denpasar to determine which older, traditional dance forms could become more secularized and thus be used publicly and profitably as commercial tourist entertainment. Interestingly, purely instrumental music, such as the *tua* (old) *gamelan angklung*, *gambang*, and *gamelan luang* musics, were not considered here.

Initially, two categories resulted: *seni sacral* (sacred art) and *seni profan* (secular art). Criteria such as performance context, degree of sacredness, and association with some form of dance or narrative for these categories were adjusted somewhat over the next few years, ultimately resulting in the tripartite system with which most Balinese today are familiar: (1) *wali*: sacred dance, performed in the innermost courtyard of the temple, usually depicting a mythic and sacred narrative—for Balinese only; (2) *bebali*: ceremonial dance, performed in the middle courtyard, often presenting dramatic, court-related narratives—for Balinese and interested outsiders; and (3) *bali-balihan*: secular dances, performed in the outer court, or other public venues, often presenting shortened and adapted narratives from court-related dramatic forms as entertainment—for tourists (Picard 2012:66; Tenzer 2000:96–98).

Implicit within this new system was the underlying issue of patronage. Music and dance performances of all kinds, at least from the sixteenth to the nineteenth centuries, had been supported by the *puri* (court) and the *pura* (temple). Temple celebrations, such as *odalan*, had been mounted by villagers for centuries, and at the courts elaborate, large-scale dramatic events and competitions involving music and dance were often staged to glorify a specific ruler or to celebrate his link to a deified ancestor.

In securalizing and commodifying certain dance forms, patronage passed to audiences of outsiders in the form of commercialized "art." Picard makes the point that "once traditional (*adat*) practice [had been] secularized and converted into tourist attractions, [it] gained in aesthetic qualities what it had lost in religious prerogative, and eventually [became] celebrated as 'art' (*seni budaya*)" (2012:64). The result of this realignment of concepts was not, as predicted by some, the death of traditional performances; rather, it became a stimulus for new arts in the twentieth century, where large, urban institutions such as KOKAR, ISI, and the annual Bali

Arts Festival now provide contexts for training musicians and dancers, as well as venues for performances of new and experimental compositions.

Another outcome of these changes, well noted in the ethnomusicological literature on Balinese music, was the development of a historical narrative in which to frame the history of music and dance in Bali. I Nyoman Rembang (1937–2001), one of Bali's most important and respected teachers, composers, and instrument builders, developed, in the mid-twentieth century, a three-period historical framework for Balinese music that is now taught at the major arts schools (Tenzer 2000:149).[7] In doing so, Rembang lined up certain musical forms with historical periods. It is unclear what, if any, documentation he used to create his chronology, but it synchronized well with contemporaneous histories of the island that focused on the defining moment of the entrance of the Majapahit.

Tua (old period) musical ensembles and forms, according to Rembang, were created before the Majapahit era, that is, before 1343. *Madya* (middle period) musical forms were developed from c. 1500 to c. 1900, the time of the highly prestigious and competitive kingdoms stemming from the Majapahit Empire. *Baru* (new period) music began with the decline of colonialism and the rise of nationalism, c. 1880 to the present. *Gamelan angklung* and its cremation music, as well as a few other ensembles and genres, were placed in the *tua* category and are still commonly thought to be a part of an older, pre-Majapahit era.

Rembang's mid-twentieth-century classification of Bali's musical ensembles is based, in part, on the widely held assumption that today's Balinese are the inheritors of the great Javanese-Hindu culture, as brought to Bali in the fourteenth century, a culture that grew into the powerful, court-village structure of the fifteenth through nineteenth centuries. This story was promoted for various political, social, and economic reasons by many—Dutch colonizers, Balinese political and cultural leaders, Western visitors to the island—and grew in strength throughout the eighteenth through twentieth centuries, effectively dividing Bali into two distinct yet intertwined cultures: court and village.

Although this narrative has been seriously questioned by many scholars, until quite recently it has been embedded within many existing music histories of Bali, some of which we visit in the next chapter. Recent radical revisions of certain aspects of Balinese and Javanese cultural history have begun to reexamine the colonial processes and cultural interactions in greater depth, applying a bolder set of theoretical approaches and paying sharper attention to Indigenous Balinese and Javanese understandings of their histories.

CHAPTER 2

Gamelan Angklung Today

This chapter examines the many *gamelan angklung* ensembles and musics that exist today, describing their varying performance contexts and repertoires. First, though, it addresses two important issues: the first concerns the word *angklung* itself; the second and more significant issue concerns a lack of differentiation between the various contemporary ensembles and repertoires.

Throughout most of Southeast Asia and beyond, the word *angklung* refers to a shaken tube rattle, constructed of two to four bamboo tubes tuned to one pitch, sounded in octaves.[1] The tubes are inserted into a bamboo frame held together by rattan cords. As each *angklung* sounds only one pitch (in octaves), depending on the set of pitches used and the specific performance context, many players are required.

Shaken *angklung* rattles come in many sizes and have been used for centuries at rice harvesting ceremonies honoring Dewi Sri, the goddess of rice. These instruments are frequently used in processions, performing interlocking patterns that play, or elaborate, melodies. An ensemble of these instruments, especially those found in and around Sunda (West Java), is referred to generically as a *gamelan angklung* (Baier 1986; Wolbers 1986).

In Bali, however, this instrument is referred to as *angklung kocok* (shaken bamboo rattle), and its ensemble as *gamelan angklung kocok*, to distinguish it from the *gamelan angklung kléntangan* (bells), the ensemble that uses bronze metallophones and small pot-gongs (Hatch 2016). This ensemble, called *gamelan angklung* in Bali, is the subject under discussion here. Sometime in the past, the bamboo *angklung kocok* was part of, and lent its name to, the Balinese bronze ensemble and, although no longer used in most contemporary *gamelan angklung* repertoires, the histories

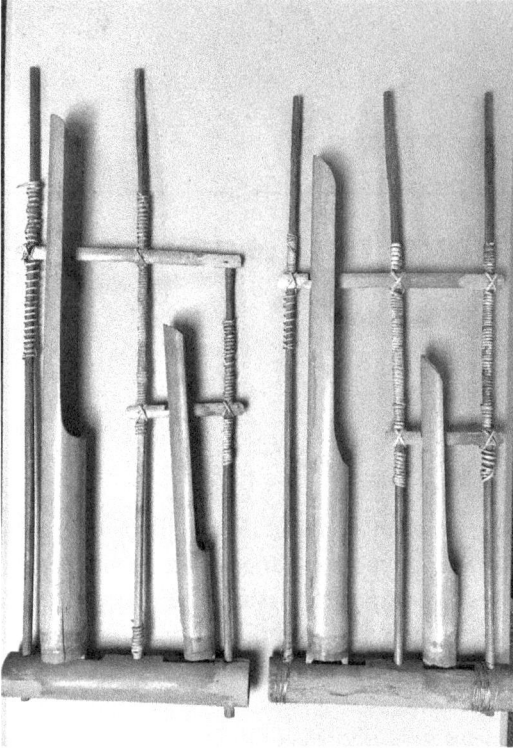

FIGURE 2.1 Two *angklung kocok*.

of these two ensembles are entwined. For purposes of clarity, the bamboo rattle ensemble will be referred to throughout this book as *gamelan angklung kocok*, and the Balinese bronze-keyed ensemble simply as *gamelan angklung*.

The more significant issue, however, concerns a lack of differentiation—among scholars and performers alike—between the distinct repertoires played by the bronze-keyed ensemble in different contexts and for different purposes.[2] Possibly beginning in the eighteenth century, the bronze-keyed *gamelan angklung*, used commonly for village cremations in Bali, was occasionally integrated into court and temple ceremonies; if a village lacked other ensembles, the *gamelan angklung* would play for all community ceremonies, including cremations.

When not playing for cremations, different repertoires were used and instruments added; performers played pieces adopted from contemporaneous five- and seven-tone ensembles, such as *gamelan gong gdé*, and later, from *gamelan gong ageng (gamelan gong)* and *semar pagulingan*, adapting them to fit the *angklung*'s one-octave, four-tone ambitus, and its bell-like timbre. Thus, new, borrowed repertoires of pieces that could be played in different contexts were created.

In addition, beginning in the mid-twentieth century, new pieces (*kreasi baru*) began to be composed specifically for *gamelan angklung*, mainly at schools such as KOKAR and, later, ISI. Especially popular were pieces that combined the four-tone range of this ensemble with the explosive, iconic *byar* and the breakneck speed of the interlocking sections (*kotekan*) of the *gamelan gong kebyar*. These new compositional techniques quickly grew into a subgenre, *angklung-kebyar*, composed mainly by faculty and students at KOKAR and ISI; today these pieces are regularly composed, taught, and performed at concerts and at the annual Bali Arts Festival, where highly skilled groups from all over the island compete for a place on the program.

Today, *gamelan angklung*, in its older, core form, and playing its own repertoire, is found solely at cremations; but in its expanded forms, with larger, more prominent gongs and drums, it is found throughout Bali performing in contexts of all kinds. Wayne Vitale, in the notes accompanying his 2014 recording *Gamelan Angklung: Bali's 4-Tone Bronze Gamelan Orchestra*, states that while this ensemble has "remained true to its fundamental

FIGURE 2.2 Part of the Institute Seni Indonesia (ISI), Denpasar campus.

obligation—to accompany Balinese-Hindu cremations—it has changed dramatically over the past century" (3–4), now playing for many other Hindu ceremonies, including temple and private *odalan*, tooth-filings, and weddings, for public competitions and concerts, as well as for cremations.

Thus, in addition to older pieces performed solely for cremations, where, as Vitale writes, "the repertoire is known and recognized by everyone" (5), at least three new repertoires for *gamelan angklung* have emerged within the last century:

1. pieces that have been adopted from five-, six-, and seven-tone ensembles and adapted to fit the four-tone, *gamelan angklung* range;
2. *angklung-kebyar* pieces, which are new compositions composed specifically for *gamelan angklung* that may incorporate iconic styles or gestures from *gamelan gong kebyar* music, including larger instruments, such as drums (*kendang*) and large hand cymbals (*ceng-ceng kopyak*); and
3. a five-tone cremation repertoire with an expanded range and ensemble now found mainly in the north of the island.

However, scholars of Balinese music who have mentioned *gamelan angklung*, from Jaap Kunst onward (with some notable exceptions below), have tended to gloss over these differences, seeing all *gamelan angklung* ensembles and repertoires as similar. What I wish to suggest here and throughout this book is that the music performed at cremations is an old and unique repertoire consisting of specific pieces played *only* at cremations, pieces with their own instrumentation, structures, and meanings. In fact, it was precisely this unique repertoire that first drew me to *gamelan angklung* music and inspired me to undertake this study. What follows is a closer look at today's varying *gamelan angklung* ensembles, beginning with the oldest, core ensemble used in cremation contexts. The discussion is then expanded to include newer *angklung* ensembles and repertoires that have developed, mainly over the past century.

Introduction to the *Angklung* Cremation Ensemble and Its Music

Although changes in the *angklung* cremation ensemble have undoubtedly occurred over the past centuries, the instrumentation, tuning, core style, and repertoire of cremation music have recently become somewhat standardized, especially in the south, and are so well known by their immediate communities that they are often taken for granted. Eliciting a kind of poignant, bittersweet sadness at cremations, these ensembles and their repertoires have become, for the Balinese, necessary audible symbols of death and reincarnation, less actual music than musically coded spiritual offerings for the spirits of the dead, as well as entertainment and distraction for the living.

As stated earlier, the men with whom I worked often found it odd when I wanted to discuss instrumentation, tuning, the name of the piece they were playing, or any other aspects of this music as music. From their perspective, I was weirdly preoccupied with seemingly irrelevant issues that had nothing to do with the significance or effectiveness of their performances. It appeared that it didn't matter *what* or *how* they played, but only *that* they played.

Here, I introduce the instruments and some of the basic characteristics of the cremation *gamelan angklung* and its repertoire, using *banjar* Baturiti's *gamelan* Taman Sari as a guide, while also cautioning that things may be (and often are) different in different *banjar*. Before moving on I present a recording of an entire *gending* (piece), "Capung Gantung" ("Hovering Dragonfly"), that I made during one of my recording sessions (not at a cremation), where the men played entire pieces for me to learn (December 8, 2007). This recording illustrates some of the basic musical structures that help define this repertoire (◁)) Recording 2.1, "Capung Gantung"). Below is a listening guide to help you along the way, showing the main musical events and when they occur, as well as some things to listen for.[3]

RECORDING AND LISTENING GUIDE 2.1 "Capung Gantung"

0:01–5:08	*Pemungkah*	
	0:01–0:25	**Cue:** *gangsa pemadé (ugal)*; listen for slowing tempo, *rincik* damp, and *kempur* (For more on specific instruments, see below.)
	0:25–5:06	**Section:** whole ensemble plays entire section: seven phrases of uneven length; section repeated eight times; tempo and dynamic cues given by *rincik*; *kempur* marks endings/beginnings of the sections; last two repeats marked by slower tempo
5:07–7:03	*Pengawak*	
	5:07–5:17	**Cue:** *gangsa pemadé (ugal)*; listen for *rincik* damp
	5:17–6:55	**Section:** played once; similar rhythmic pattern played on one pitch at beginning of some phrases; phrases have different lengths; tempo and pacing increase near end
7:04–end	*Pengiba*	
	7:00–7:11	**Cue:** *gangsa pemadé (ugal)*; listen for *rincik* damp and *kempur* (tawa-tawa comes in a little early)
	7:12–fade-out	**Section:** played sixteen times, using *kotekan ubit empat*; tempo and dynamic cues given by *rincik*; *kempur* marks endings/beginnings of the cycle; last repeat slows considerably

Instruments

There are eighteen instruments in the full Taman Sari ensemble, most within the *gangsa* family; the *suling* (flute) was played only occasionally.

DIAGRAM 2.1 Instruments of the *gamelan angklung* cremation ensemble, Taman Sari.

suling	two-octave range (or more); end-blown bamboo flute, using circular breathing
4 *gangsa kantillan*	highest *gangsa*; slab metallophone struck with a wooden *panggul* in the shape of a small hammer
4 *gangsa pemadé*	tuned one octave lower than *gangsa kantillan*; slab metallophone struck with a wooden *panggul* like that above
1 set of high *réong*	four small, bossed pot-gongs set in two cases; tuned to same octave as *gangsa kantillan*; struck with a stick-like *panggul*, whose upper half is tightly wrapped with thin rope
1 set of low *réong*	four small, bossed pot-gongs set in two cases; tuned to same octave as *gangsa pemadé*; struck with *panggul* like that above
2 *jegogan*	slab metallophone, tuned one octave below *gangsa pemadé*; struck with a padded stick-like *panggul*
1 *rincik*	small set of brass hand cymbals, attached to a wooden carving of a turtle
1 *tawa-tawa*	medium-sized bossed gong, held in lap, played with a padded *panggul*; used as a beat-keeper
2 *kendang*	small, single-headed drums played with a knobbed stick
1 *kempur (pur)*	tuned somewhat lower than lowest *jegogan* note; medium-sized hanging, bossed gong played with a padded *panggul*

Gangsa is now a generic term for musical instruments with bronze keys, which are strung together and draped over tuned bamboo tube resonators. The tubes are encased in carved jackfruit-tree boxes, illustrating local, traditional stories, and often painted gold and red, or varnished in a dark wood-brown color. *Gangsa*-type instruments are found in most Balinese metal ensembles; in the *gamelan angklung*, the *gangsa* family contains three sets of different-sized instruments (see the diagram above): *gangsa kantillan*, *gangsa pemadé*, and *jegogan*, together spanning a two-and-a-half-octave range.

FIGURE 2.3 *Gamelan angklung* Taman Sari playing at a *ngabén*.

Gangsa kantillan and *pemadé*, along with the two sets of *réong* (pot-gongs), play the higher, faster-moving layer of the music. The *jegogan* (from *jegog*, large) are the lowest and largest *gangsa* in the ensemble; they play the lower, slower-moving layer (*pokok*), sometimes called a "core" or "skeletal" melody in Western descriptions. Although the *gangsa* are doubled in octaves, no instrument in the ensemble exceeds four pitches (except the flute [*suling*], if present).

The two sets of small, bossed pot-gongs—*réong*—usually double the *gangsa*. The four pots in each octave sit in two cases and are played by two players (i.e., player one plays pitches 1 and 2; player two plays pitches 3 and 4). The gong (*kempur*, or, simply, *pur*) only plays to mark the end/beginning of a piece, and the small set of brass cymbals mounted on a carving of a turtle (*rincik*) is used for cueing and rhythmic animation. The hand-held *tawa-tawa* (a medium-sized bossed gong) is used as a beat-keeper and is held in the lap with one hand holding a padded *panggul* while the fingers of the other hand curl over the rim to help soften the sound. The drums (*kendang*) usually play soft, interlocking patterns at a continuous rate to "fill in" any rhythmic spaces. Finally, if a *suling* is used, it plays semi-improvised elaborations of the *pokok* over a two-octave range.

Dampening Techniques

Gangsa, once struck, are usually dampened. Three dampening techniques are used:

1. The ringing damp: a key is struck by the *panggul* held in one hand and rings out; then, at the same time as the *panggul* plays the next note, the other hand's forefinger and thumb come together under the first key, pinching it to stop its vibration; this effectively cuts the sound to allow the second note to sound alone;
2. The staccato damp: here the two-finger pinch comes immediately after striking the first key, before the next note sounds; this allows the fastmoving interlocking patterns (*kotekan*), as well as an occasional staccato note, to sound crisp and dry; and
3. The click damp: this technique, often used in slow movements of the cremation repertoire, creates a short "click" sound, as the strike and the pinch occur simultaneously.

Jegogan most often use the first technique, or in passages where there is little *jegogan* movement, the key is not dampened at all after striking, allowing the deep resonant sound of the instrument to die away naturally. *Réong* use a different technique altogether. Each player holds two *panggul* and, as indicated above, is responsible for two pots. Since there is no way to pinch a knobbed gong to stop the sound, each *panggul* strikes the knob twice in rapid succession: the first time sounding the note, the second time—more of a gentle pushing into the boss—stopping the note. This gets quite complicated during fast passages. *Rincik* (small brass hand cymbals) can play an open sound or damp immediately, depending on the passage and whether the instrument is being used as a cue or as a rhythmic animation. The *tawa-tawa*, *kendang*, and *kempur* are never fully dampened.

Pitch Set and Tuning

The *gamelan angklung* uses a unique set of instruments containing four bronze keys with no higher-octave key. For simplicity's sake, here they are numbered 1 2 3 4, based on their position in the row, with number 1 the lowest, but not necessarily the most important. Any of the four pitches can assume importance depending on which coincides with the *kempur*, but no modal system has yet been established for this repertoire. Pitches are sometimes syllabized by trained Balinese musicians using the following syllables: pitch 1 *neng*; pitch 2 *nung*; pitch 3 *nang*; and pitch 4 *ning*, although the men with whom I worked did not use these.

The gamut of this pitch row roughly encompasses a wide fifth (i.e., 650–750 cents in Western terminology) or slightly more than half an octave. Although all instruments in one *gamelan* are tuned to each other, there is no fixed, or standard tuning for this ensemble; the exact size of the outer and internal intervals can vary considerably from village to village, as can the relative register of different tunings, as each *gamelan* maker and each *banjar* has its own preferences for the *gamelan*'s ideal construction and sound.

Today, there is some disagreement as to whether *saih angklung* (the *angklung* pitch-row) belongs to the *slendro* modal system. Adopted from Java in the mid-twentieth century, the modal systems *slendro* and *pélog* are today distinguished by their internal intervals—both are essentially pentatonic. *Pélog*, which contains seven possible pitches, from which five are chosen, is characterized as having both narrow and wide internal intervals, while *slendro*, with only five possible pitches, is defined by its more or less equally wide intervals (see Perlman 2004; Herbst 2001; Wakeling 2010 for fuller discussions).

Very few *slendro* ensembles are found in Bali, but the most important of these is the *gamelan gender*, the ensemble that accompanies *wayang kulit* (shadow puppet) performances. This is discussed more fully in the chapters that follow, but for now, let us simply say that *saih angklung* is sometimes today referred to as *slendro*-derived, *slendro alit* (high, or small *slendro*), or *slendro kiring* (*slendro* with a missing tone [McPhee 1966:55]).[4] Finally, as in other Balinese ensembles, pairs of instruments in the *gamelan angklung* are not tuned to unisons, but are slightly off each other, creating the characteristic *ombak* (wave), that bright, shimmering "beating" that is unique to Balinese music.

Gamelan Angklung Gending

Although the cremation repertoire that I learned from the men of *sekehe* Taman Sari is discussed more thoroughly in later chapters, I introduce it here, describing its basic musical and structural features. The fifteen named pieces (*gending*) performed today by *gamelan* Taman Sari consist of one to four contrasting sections, each a separate and complete unit on its own, lasting from two to ten minutes depending on its tempo, structure, and how many repetitions are played in performance. During a cremation, a section from one *gending* is most often followed by a similar section from a different *gending*. Performances at cremations are thought to be offerings, not concerts; thus, the order of sections is somewhat random, based more on the ritual activities at hand and on the basic atmosphere or mood of the crowd than on a formal presentation, a topic discussed at length in chapter 9.

Most complete *gending* consist of three sections, an overall form perhaps borrowed from the earlier *madya* period court genres discussed in chapter 1: (1) *pemungkah* (head, or beginning, from *bungkah*, to open up, the term used to describe the beginning of a *wayang kulit* performance); (2) *pengawak* (from *awak*, body), a slow, main section that in *angklung* cremation music is often characterized by an initial rhythmic marker and asymmetric phrases; and (3) *pengiba*, a third, fast-paced section frequently using a specific kind of interlocking technique called *kotekan ubit empat* (interlocking spanning four keys, where pitches 1 and 4 sound together). Each section is introduced by a *gihing* (backbone),[5] which cues the beginning of the piece and its starting tempo. This cue is played by the *ugal* (head *gangsa*), often joined by another *gangsa* or *suling*.

The instruments of the *gamelan* essentially perform different densities of the piece they are playing. This has sometimes been described in the literature as stratification, or heterophony, where some sets of instruments may be responsible for a slower-moving structural contour (*pokok*), others for filling in or elaborating the *pokok*, and still others for cueing, animating, and marking the beginnings/ends of cycles. But this division is not conceptualized by all Balinese musicians, especially everyday performers, who tend to see all instruments in the *gamelan* as one unit rendering the piece together, described by Michael Bakan "as a solid block of music material" (1997:290), performed at different levels of density. Melody and elaboration are not separate "lines," or "voices," as they are conceptualized in Western music; they are simply more or less filled-in or active versions of the same thing. In fact, no Balinese word for melody exists in the context of instrumental repertoires, such as those of the *gamelan angklung*, although *lagu* (a word for sung melody) is sometimes used.

One other feature of *gamelan angklung gending* that is frequently mentioned in the literature is the often whimsical names they are given. These names, as McPhee notes in *Music in Bali* (1966), have nothing to do with the music itself, and a piece called one thing one day may have a completely different name the next day. The following entry from my field notes describes how a name was given to a *gending* during one of my meetings with *gamelan* Taman Sari.

November 25, 2007: I Learn a New Piece

Last Friday night's session was a humbling experience. I asked the ugal *player to teach everyone a brand-new piece and I wanted to be part of the process to see how he did it, so I joined in on a* gangsa, *instead of my usual* jegogan. *He began with the* polos *part of a* kotekan, *moving at lightning speed. Suddenly, he was teaching only me, and the others were shyly looking on, listening, and trying to get the pattern. I was, of course, pretty clueless, but within a few minutes, the other players had already figured out the* kotekan.

But the truly strange moment came at the end of the evening. I asked the ugal *player what the name of this new* gending *was. He looked blankly at me and then at the rest of the men. "Nama?" "Yes," I said, "its name. What do you call it?" Lots of mumbling from the men. I am standing there thinking, "Well, how do they know what to play if it doesn't have a name?" I must have looked a bit perplexed (read, "tense"). Finally, one of the men looked up, waving at me, and said, "Just call it 'Jumping Cricket'!" There was no name for this piece? He had just made that up? No name!?*

Newer *Angklung* Ensembles and Their Repertoires

As stated earlier, at least three other repertoires exist for the *gamelan angklung* ensemble today, often with the addition of larger drums, gongs, and cymbals. Underscoring the different styles and performance contexts for these musics, when played by *gamelan angklung* Taman Sari, different men participated in these performances. Other community members, also part of Baturiti's overall *sekehe gamelan angklung*, but not cremation performers, would participate here, wearing different clothes (temple, or concert dress), not the usual orange polo shirts and *kain* (a wraparound piece of colorful cloth) considered the uniform for cremations. Thus, the core *sekehe angklung* group of fifteen or so members was enlarged and subdivided when not playing for cremations. And, occasionally, when a core member was busy or ill, he would send a substitute to take his place. Everyone knew the music; if one did not, he could use the opportunity to learn it during a performance (more on this later).

Borrowed and Adapted Pieces for *Gamelan Angklung*

Adaptations of preexisting pieces, often taken from *madya* or *baru gamelan* genres, are common, and they frequently involve adding new, larger gongs and drums, and arranging one- or multiple-octave melodies by reconfiguring them for the *gamelan angklung*'s four-pitch range. This process involves frequent pitch alterations and octave substitutions to create new, perhaps diminutive, abstractions of the original pieces that can still be recognized by knowledgeable listeners.

"Tabuh Telu"

"Tabuh Telu" (Form of Three) is one of many musical forms associated with the largest and grandest Balinese *gamelan* ensembles of the past: *gamelan gong gdé* (ensemble of the great gong) and *gamelan gong ageng* (ensemble of the large gong), and provides an excellent example to illustrate how a piece in a certain form, originally intended for these large, eighteenth- and nineteenth-century ensembles, collapses in on itself to become playable on the instruments of the *gamelan angklung*.

The *gong gdé* was a popular ensemble during the height of the *madya* court period, when large-scale, extravagant musical performances were common displays of court power and influence. Using up to fifty or more players, with large gongs, drums, cymbals, extra-lower-pitched instruments, and *trompong* (a two-octave set of pot-gongs, usually played by one improvising musician), the *gong gdé* played an extensive repertoire of instrumental and dance pieces for rituals and ceremonies.

The *gamelan gong ageng* (known today simply as *gamelan gong*) arose in the nineteenth century when the power of the courts was waning. Almost as grand as its predecessor, but requiring fewer instruments and players, *gamelan gong* adapted genres from *gong gdé* repertoires. It was this ensemble, located in Payangon village, that played the "Tabuh Telu" that composer Colin McPhee eventually transcribed and used as the basis of one of the pieces in his set of three piano duets, "Ceremonial Music of Bali, for Two Pianos," composed in 1937.

"Tabuh Telu" originally took its name from the number of times a small, encased, bossed pot-gong (*kempli*) and a larger, bossed hanging gong (*kempur*) were struck in alternation, creating three metric units (*palet*) over the span of one sixteen-beat gong cycle (*gongan*), at the beginning of a *pengawak* (main, slow-moving section of a *gending*).[6]

DIAGRAM 2.2 One sixteen-beat *gongan* in "Tabuh Telu" with three *palet*.

Gong punctuation:	.	.	.	k	.	P	.	k	.	P	.	k	.	P	.	G
Beats:	1	2	3	4	5	6	7	8	9	10	11	12	13	14	15	16
Palet:				1				2				3				

This gong punctuation provided a repeated metric structure for the slow-moving *lelambatan* and faster moving *gangsaran*, two important genres played by both the *gamelan gdé* and *gong ageng* ensembles. "Tabuh Telu" has been adopted and adapted by many ensembles, but today one is most likely to hear a piece in this form played by a *gamelan gong kebyar*, the ensemble that inherited the essence of the old *gong gdé* through the instrumentation and musical structures of the *gamelan gong*.

"Tabuh Telu" at the Eastman School of Music

I had long thought it would be fun to present a concert featuring different versions of a "Tabuh Telu," including the one composed by Colin McPhee in 1937. In April 2017 I finally got the chance. At our final concert of the year, we played three different versions of this piece: one arranged for our gamelan gong kebyar (Sanjiwani), *one for our* gamelan angklung *(Lila Muni)—both arranged by our teacher, Nyoman Suadin—and McPhee's piano version, played by two Eastman School doctoral piano students, Brian Park and Hyoung Kim.*

Using McPhee's description of the gamelan gong ageng *and the* tabuh telu *form, taken from his book* Music in Bali *(1966:63–112), I explained to the audience how various adjustments had been made to the original form for the* gamelan gong kebyar, gamelan angklung, *and piano duet versions. Below are recordings of the improvisatory introduction* (ginneman) *and first two sixteen-beat* gongan (cycles) *for all three versions. (◀)) Recording 2.2, "Tabuh Telu," Introduction and* pengawak, *played by the Eastman School's* gamelan gong kebyar, *Sanjiwani)*

RECORDING AND LISTENING GUIDE 2.2 "Tabuh Telu," Introduction and *pengawak*, played by the Eastman School's *gamelan gong kebyar*, Sanjiwani

0:05–0:48	**Ginneman:** *ugal* and *suling* play improvisatory segments; no meter
0:48–0:56	**Cue:** *ugal, kendang*
0:56–1:04	Whole ensemble plays 8-beat phrase, ending with *gong*
1:05–1:14	**Cue to pengawak:** *ugal, kendang, gong*
1:15–1:25	**Pengawak:** Whole ensemble plays 16-beat *gong* cycle (*gongan*) using a *gegaboran gong* structure:

gong pattern:					p			K				p				(G)
beats:	1	2	3	4	5	6	7	8	9	10	11	12	13	14	15	16

1:25–1:35	Repeat
1:35–fade-out	Beginning of next phrase

Key to gongs

G   *gong*

p   *kempli*

K   *kempur*

The largely improvised introduction in the gong kebyar *version is played here by the* ugal *(a two-octave gangsa) and* suling, *not the* trompong *as in the older version described by McPhee. It stresses the two most important pitches found in the underlying layer* (pokok) *of this "Tabuh Telu." The* suling *and* ugal *play the same basic melodic gestures and ornaments, but the* suling *occasionally sharps the note or adds a slow warbling trill—a sort of wide* ombak *(wave)—on the long notes. In the main body of the piece, more differences emerge: (1) two sixteen-beat cycles are played here; (2) no* kempli-kempur-palet *are present; a different sixteen-beat gong structure,* gegaboran, *is used that repeats every phrase; and (3) the tempo, as defined by the* kajar *stroke (beat-keeper in* gong kebyar *ensembles), is considerably faster than it would be if played by a* gong gdé *or* gong ageng *ensemble.* (◀◎) *Recording 2.3, "Tabuh Telu," Introduction and* pengawak, *played by the Eastman School's* gamelan angklung, Lila Muni)*

RECORDING AND LISTENING GUIDE 2.3 "Tabuh Telu," Introduction and *pengawak*, played by the Eastman School's *gamelan angklung*, Lila Muni

0:00–0:29	*Ginneman* played by *ugal* and *jegogan*; improvisatory elements, no meter
0:29–0:37	**Cue:** *ugal*
0:37–0:47	Whole ensemble plays one 8-beat phrase, *kempur*
0:47–0:56	Cue for *pengawak*; *ugal*
0:56–1:07	**Pengawak:** whole ensemble plays 16-beat *gongan*, with no internal punctuation; the *kempur* sounds at the end of the cycle
1:08–1:19	Cycle repeats
1:19–fade-out	Beginning of next cycle

When you listen to the same portion of the piece played by the gamelan angklung, *even more changes are apparent. First, a completely different set of pitches is heard from the beginning: the four-tone* saih angklung, *not the five-tone* pélog selisir *(the most common mode in* pélog) *used in the* gamelan gong kebyar *ensembles. The introductory, unmetered solo is played here by the* ugal, *with the* jegogan *underlying important pitches. Here, the* ugal *is limited in its ability to sweep through the ten-note range of the* gong kebyar ugal *(let alone the* trompong *of the* gong gdé *or* gong ageng).*

The main body of the piece, as played by the gamelan angklung, *demonstrates the practice of note substitution so frequently needed when this ensemble borrows and adapts pieces from other ensembles. For example, pitch 5 in the* kebyar pélog *row does not exist in* saih angklung, *so pitch 3 substitutes for this note, creating a smaller, more constricted contour in the* pokok. *Finally, there is no gong cycle in the* gamelan angklung *version to mark smaller divisions of the phrases; the* kempur *alone is used here to signal the beginnings/ends of each cycle. (◀))* Recording 2.4, "Tabuh Telu," Introduction and pengawak *from "Balinese Ceremonial Music for Two Pianos")*

RECORDING AND LISTENING GUIDE 2.4 "Tabuh Telu," Introduction and *pengawak* from "Balinese Ceremonial Music for Two Pianos" (1937), by Colin McPhee

0:00–0:28	*Ginneman:* piano 1 plays improvisatory elements, no meter
0:28–0:35	**Cue:** piano 1
0:35–0:45	One 8-beat phrase played by both pianos with the final "gong" played as a sweeping arpeggio
0:45–0:56	**Cue:** piano 1
0:56–1:06	*Pengawak:* 16-beat cycle played by both pianos; *gegaboran* punctuation provided by low, chromatic chords
1:06–1:17	Cycle repeats
1:17–fade-out	Beginning of next cycle

There are some obvious differences from the previous two versions in McPhee's two-piano version of "Tabuh Telu." Perhaps the most important difference here is the use of two pianos. The piano's standard chromatic tuning is measured in equal, 100-cent intervals, and its extensive range seems to simulate the deep sonorities of the gong ageng. Cues used in the previous two versions are played here by the first piano and chromatics are used, especially to denote the low sounds of gongs and to simulate the Balinese distinctive tunings.

Although many aspects of these three versions of "Tabuh Telu" change, many also remain unchanged from their older, more stately ancestors: (1) the overall formal structure is similar: improvisatory introduction, repeated statements of a phrase, with a repeating gong structure; (2) the improvisatory introduction achieves its purpose in all three versions by highlighting the important pitches in the section to come; (3) sixteen-beat phrases/cycles are still used; and (4) the pokok is played within a one-octave range, and its basic contour, if not its exact pitches, is similar in all three versions. The instrumentation and musical gestures of the gamelan gong kebyar—closely related as they are to the older ensembles—make it fairly easy to play this "Tabuh Telu" in a way that would be recognizable to a modern Balinese audience; however, as the gamelan angklung is not related in any way to the massive court ensembles described above, and the two-piano version is essentially outside the realm of Balinese music altogether, more significant changes had to be made.

Kreasi Baru: Angklung-Kebyar

As mentioned earlier, since the late twentieth century, a new genre for *gamelan angklung, angklung-kebyar,* became an important showcase for this ensemble. Pieces, most often composed and performed at the Bali Arts Festival and other concert venues, combine the excitement and explosiveness of *gong kebyar* with the older, more familiar sounds of the *gamelan angklung.*

When he was a student at KOKAR-Denpasar in the early 1980s, our teacher, Pak Nyoman Suadin, was frequently asked to visit villages in the area to teach new *gamelan* pieces using a particular village's ensembles. One village he visited had a *gamelan angklung.* Rather than teach an old piece adapted from another, larger ensemble, Nyoman decided to compose his own piece, one in the new *angklung-kebyar* style, to teach to the village's children. He called it "Kelinci Nongklang" ("Jumping Rabbits" or "Rabbits Hanging Out"). He wanted to show how the *gamelan angklung* could adopt the more boisterous sounds of the *gong kebyar*, yet still retain the poignant sweetness of the village ensemble.

Unlike traditional pieces for *gamelan angklung,* whose whimsical titles are not related to the music, Nyoman deliberately chose "Kelinci Nongklang" as his title and based the music on his memory of chasing rabbits as a child. He wanted to evoke both the playfulness of children as they dashed after rabbits in the rice fields, and the cleverness of the rabbits as they escaped into the brush. As this was to be a piece composed in the new

FIGURE 2.4 | Nyoman Suadin.

genre, *angklung-kebyar*, Nyoman added the larger *gamelan kebyar* drums and gongs, creating a composition that captured the energy of the *kebyar* ensemble while also retaining the *rasa* (flavor) of the *angklung*. Below is a Listening Guide for the first two minutes of "Kelinci Nongklang." (◀ᵢ)) Recording 2.5, "Kelinci Nongklang")

RECORDING AND LISTENING GUIDE 2.5 "Kelinci Nongklang" (1982), by I Nyoman Suadin

0:00–0:35	**Cue:** *kendang*, silence; *kebyar*-like cue played by whole ensemble, *gong*
0:36–0:44	Cycle 1: 16-beat cycle, using *gegaboran* punctuation, played once as an introduction
0:44–1:53	Cycle repeated eight times; in first 8-beat segment listen for *réong* scuttling back and forth, like running rabbits; in second 8-beat segment listen for syncopated rhythms in the *réong* used to simulate rabbits jumping; tempo and dynamic cues played by drum
1:54–2:14	Transition; five 8-beat phrases with compressed *gong* pattern
2:15–fade-out	Return to earlier cycle

The Five-Tone *Gamelan Angklung*

In 1965, ethnomusicologist Ruby Ornstein was living in Bali studying the development of *gamelan gong kebyar* music and happened to travel to the north of the island near the port of Singaraja (see the map on page 14). There she encountered a five-tone *gamelan angklung*, an ensemble that had not been mentioned in the scholarly literature since 1937, the year of references from both Colin McPhee and Walter Spies to this new "transitional" set of instruments.[7] Here, Ornstein noted, the four-tone *saih angklung* had acquired an additional note and was now being referred to as *slendro* (sometimes *slendro alit*, or high/small *slendro*), essentially the same as the five-tone modal system used by the *gender wayang* ensemble to accompany *wayang kulit*, but pitched higher (1971).

Although still being used primarily for cremations, this new *angklung* ensemble was now able to play a variety of repertoires, including music from *wayang kulit* as well as other pieces traditionally associated with dance and narrative forms. Ornstein also noted that in addition to expanding the four tones to five, the northern *gamelan angklung* had also enlarged most of the other instruments, adding keys to the *gangsa* and *réong* to extend their ranges from one to one-and-a-half or two octaves.

Ornstein was able to show that these changes had developed in the 1930s based on an article by McPhee, published in 1937, where he first mentions this new form of *gamelan angklung*, stating, "We must now turn our attention to the new tendencies, which are rapidly invading the classical *gamelan [angklung]*. These include an expanded scale, developed instruments, new music, and a seeking after more original orchestration" (1937:344–45). Thus, it was the addition of another tone, one that would align the four-tone *saih angklung* with the five-tone *slendro*, plus the addition of actual keys, that extended the capabilities of the instruments to adapt pieces from other, more expansive repertoires such as *gong kebyar*. The additional size and weight of the instruments also made them less likely to be used for a cremation procession and perhaps more likely to be seen, set in place, at a public performance.

In addition, the northern *gamelan angklung* had also added instruments, such as larger drums and cymbals (*ceng-ceng kopyak*), to help with the more explosive sounds and energy of the *gong kebyar* and other repertoires. Even the *réong*—one of the defining features of the bronze-keyed *gamelan angklung*—was expanded to *kebyar*-like dimensions: up to twelve pots set in one case, played by four musicians, often using the *byar* style of playing—all hitting the boss of the pot together in one loud stroke, a technique also used by Pak Suadin in "Kelinci Nongklang."

An example of the five-tone *gamelan angklung* is included on Ornstein's recording *From Kuno to Kebyar: Balinese Gamelan Angklung*, which appeared in 2010. It was the first recording devoted entirely to *gamelan angklung* in all its forms. Thirteen tracks chart the changes in this ensemble from the time of McPhee's work (1930s) to the 1970s. Ornstein groups them as traditional (tracks 1–4), transitional (tracks 5–7) and *angklung-kebyar* (tracks 8–13), with examples from Sayan village where, in the 1970s, the *angklung* group still used the *angklung kocok*, thirty years after McPhee had left the island. This collection also beautifully illustrates *saih angklung*'s higher and lower pitch registers found in both the north and south.

Although a fifth key had been added to all the instruments in the villages Ornstein visited, it was rarely, if ever, used in the *jegogan*, the instrument carrying the lower layer in cremation music. If used at all, it usually appeared as a passing note between two more structurally important notes. Ornstein herself comments that one recording ("Lagu 3"), which does not use the fifth note at all in the *jegogan*, may have been adapted from a four-tone piece, and left intact as a reference to the four-tone *saih angklung* (2010:6).

Musical References to *Gamelan Angklung*

Another form of *gamelan angklung* music also exists. Not specifically a genre in and of itself, it consists of music played by other ensembles that reference the sounds of the *angklung*. Michael Tenzer discusses these references, which he calls topics (2000:166), defining them as "rhetorical devices used in musical passages that carry an affect recognizable by practiced listeners" (2000:454). One of these, the "stylistic topic," refers specifically to a style found in *tua* (old) ensembles, which, according to McPhee, Rembang, and others, had no association with the court, with dance, or with narratives, but which used instead certain characteristics associated with the *gamelan angklung* ensemble, such as its four-note set, *saih angklung*.

Citing an unusually clever, topic-saturated composition, "Wilet Mayura," composed in the 1980s by Wayan Sinti (with a passage contributed by Rembang), Tenzer discusses an *angklung* stylistic topic found in the first two phrases of the piece following the opening *byar* (see transcription on pages 398–410 in Tenzer 2000). The reference to *angklung* is in the *trompong*, an important instrument in the *gamelan gong kebyar* as well as older ensembles, which plays a four-tone passage, underlining a five-tone quotation from another early twentieth-century piece. Tenzer tells us that Sinti made a point of this stylistic feature, referring specifically to the four-note range of the *gamelan angklung* that appears in most of the two phrases (2000:413).

Embedded references, quotations, and borrowings are common in *gamelan* compositions, especially newer ones, and the knowledgeable listener—which, in the case of *gamelan angklung* cremation music, is everyone—will easily hear the reference and perhaps make an appropriate association. Thus, the features discussed here (*gamelan angklung*'s four-ness, its high register, bell-like quality, and association with cremations and musics of a distant, perhaps pre-Majapahit past) seem to mark this ensemble and its music—wherever it is heard—as a sounded symbol of an earlier, perhaps more sacred, time.

Finally, in a musical culture where borrowing, adapting, arranging, referencing, and even parodying musical characteristics are common practices, it is the merging of context, instrumentation, and music that truly defines a repertoire. A specific piece, normally used for a cremation, becomes, in a sense, a different piece, if large, *kebyar*-sized drums or two-octave *gangsa* are added, or if it is performed in the context of an *odalan*, even if the name of the piece and its basic shape remain the same. Thus, pieces that may sound alike in some way are not necessarily experienced as the same, or even as "different versions" of each other. In changing the context of their performance, or their instrumentation, they take on a different, sometimes opposite, affect and cultural meaning for the Balinese who experience them.

CHAPTER 3

Gamelan Angklung Scholarship and Its Legacies

Perhaps the first mention of an instrument known as *angklung* in Western scholarship was made by Sir Thomas Stamford Raffles (1781–1826) in his *History of Java* (1817). He writes, "In some parts of the interior, especially in the Sunda districts [of Java], the inhabitants still perform on a rude instrument of bambu, called the angklung. The Javans say that the first music of which they have any idea was produced by the accidental admission of the air into a bambu tube, which was left hanging on a tree, and that the angklung was the first improvement upon this Aeolian music" (vol. 1:527–28).

This quotation by Raffles sets the stage for an examination of the historical scholarship on *gamelan angklung* and for the particular direction it took in the works of Jaap Kunst (1891–1960), Colin McPhee (1900–1964), and subsequent scholars. Raffles is, of course, describing the *angklung kocok*, said to have originated in West Java (Sunda), and brought to Bali sometime in the distant past. How and when the *angklung kocok* came to Bali, how it became incorporated into and lent its name to the current bronze-keyed ensemble, however, remains in the realm of conjecture. That is, no artifacts or written documentation (standards used most often in Western scholarship) have emerged that establish the origins of this ensemble or its subsequent history.

This chapter briefly summarizes some of the Western scholarly literature on *gamelan angklung,* begun in the 1920s and 30s with the work of Jaap Kunst and Colin McPhee, which has continued to inform most of us in the West who study Balinese music. Beginning in the early twentieth century, with the drive to create and preserve a Balinese culture (a Dutch-promoted policy called *Baliseering,* or Balinization),[1] musicologists such as Kunst and McPhee began assembling a narrative framework for *gamelan angklung*'s origins and contemporary usage that could be consistent with other music histories being constructed in Bali at that time.

Early *Gamelan Angklung* Scholarship

Jaap Kunst, an early ethnomusicologist, and his wife, C. J. A. Kunst-van Wely, conducted fieldwork on Bali in the 1920s, devoting a chapter in their *De Toonkunst van Bali* (*The Musical Art of Bali*, 1924–25) to *gamelan angklung*. They dealt primarily with various instruments in the ensemble, describing, for instance, the evolution of the *réong*, as well as the *slendro* scale system, thought to have been derived from the pitch set found in the Balinese dance-drama *gambuh*. Unlike the *pélog* system, containing narrow and wide intervals, *slendro* was thought, in the Kunsts' time, to be a set of five evenly spaced intervals within the octave (i.e., 240 cents each, to equal 1,200 cents). The Kunsts and others, however, struggled without much success to find any ensemble that conformed to this ideal, and today this theory has been largely abandoned.[2]

Colin McPhee (1900–1964)

It is Colin McPhee's work on *gamelan angklung* that remains the most impressive and important. Although often in agreement with the Kunsts' assumptions, McPhee, in a variety of publications such as "Angkloeng Gamelans in Bali" (1937); "The Five-Tone Gamelan Music of Bali" (1947); a chapter in his book, *Music in Bali* (1966); and charming accounts of his revival of this ensemble, including the *angklung kocok*, for the boys of Sayan in "Children and Music in Bali" (1937) and *A Club of Small Men* (1948), charted the geographical and musical territory of *gamelan angklung*, as well as that of many other *gamelan* existing in Bali during the 1930s. This is where all those interested in Balinese music must begin. Carol Oja, McPhee's biographer, writes, "McPhee had been enchanted with *gamelan angklung* since his early days in Bali. It was a musical style at the opposite end of the social scale from that of *semar pegulingan*; it had no court connection at all but was rather the music of the village people, a 'folk orchestra,' as McPhee called it in *Music in Bali*" (2004:129).

Two distinguishing characteristics of *gamelan angklung* and its music seemed to especially delight McPhee, as he writes in his earliest publication on *angklung*:

> One is that the scale is unusual inasmuch as it consists of only *four* notes rather than the usual five; the other is that *all* the instruments are of exceptionally small dimensions. The drums and gong are almost miniature in size; the metallophones are unusually small and high-pitched,

extending generally three octaves up from a lowest note that varies from
e-flat to a b-flat below Middle C. . . . The high pitch of the gamelan,
the predominance of small metallophones, the smallness of the drums
and the special character of the scale all combine to give the sonority
of this gamelan a peculiarly sweet and aerial quality. Even the music
is of miniature proportions, compared with the extended phrases and
elaborate structures of the music for such gamelans as *Gong Gede* and
the *Semar Pegulingan* (*Djawa* 1937:323–24; old spelling retained and
emphasis in the original).

McPhee was also enchanted with the *angklung kocok*, the shaken bamboo rattle that gave its name to the bronze-keyed *gamelan angklung*. Iden-
tifying the *angklung kocok* as "ancient, certainly pre-Hindu" (1937:341),
McPhee classified the *angklung* ensembles he studied into three groups: (1)
old ensembles, such as those he saw in the remote villages of Karangasem
in eastern Bali, which used bamboo, wood, and bronze instruments, but
had mainly disappeared on the rest of the island by the 1930s; (2) classical ensembles consisting of a small, core set of bronze instruments that
performed specifically for cremations; and (3) modern ensembles that
used adopted and adapted pieces and various *gong kebyar* techniques and
instruments, as well as the newly developed five-tone ensembles in the
north that continued to play for cremations as well as in other contexts.

The old, remote ensembles found in Karangasem, although no longer
used today, are significant for an understanding of a possible history for
gamelan angklung. Larger and louder than the classical ensembles studied
by McPhee, these older *gamelan* included not only the core set of instruments found in the bronze-keyed ensembles today, but also four *angklung
kocok*, each tuned to one pitch of *saih angklung* and often decorated with
colorful feathers and small tinkling bells. In addition, the ensemble contained a *cingklik* (two-octave wooden xylophone); a *grantang* (two-octave
bamboo xylophone); a *trompong* playing improvisatory solos; and up to
five pairs of *ceng-ceng kopyak* (large cymbals used today in *beleganjur*
performance) playing interlocking rhythmic patterns. The size and scope
of these *gamelan* inspired McPhee to remark that the full ensemble was
reminiscent of the old *gong gdé* (1966:234–40).

One instrument, the *réong*, McPhee noted, was generally believed to
be the oldest instrument in all *angklung* ensembles, perhaps having come,
according to Kunst and his Balinese informants, from Java in the fourteenth century; further, as noted by Kunst, it was the only instrument
that had changed significantly since that time. Pictured in carvings from
the East Javanese temples Candi Ngrimbi and Candi Penataran (McPhee
1966:244; Ornstein 2010:6), the *réong* was first structured like a dumbbell,

with one pot fixed at each end of a pole for easy playing on the lap or for carrying in cremation processions. Wayan Ardika and Peter Bellwood suggest that bronze-forging technology was known throughout the area from about 150 BCE (Ardika and Bellwood 1991:221 in Herbst 2016:76, n. 128) and that the *réong* could be the oldest instrument found in today's *gamelan angklung*. This form of *réong* still existed in McPhee's time, as well as a newer construction in which two or four pots were encased in carved wooden boxes. What is especially interesting here is that, as McPhee notes (1966:235), the *réong* was sometimes still referred to by older villagers in the 1930s as a *kléntang* (bell) and its inclusion in the bronze *gamelan angklung*, many believed, was what provided the characteristic high bell sound to the ensemble.

Edward Herbst's accompanying notes to his monumental recording project *The Roots of Gamelan: The First Recordings* (World Arbiter 2016) provide an interesting perspective on the use of musical terms for *gamelan angklung gending*. In preparation for this project, Herbst returned to the villages where McPhee researched *gamelan angklung* to see if changes in instrumentation and musical forms had occurred since the 1930s. In Sidan (Gianyar Province, see the map on page 14), where McPhee had recorded the classical style of *gamelan angklung*, Herbst found that certain terms used today seemed to be unique to Sidan: "Rather than *kawitan* for the first section, musicians use the term *pamungkah* 'opening' (played by two *gendér*, *molos* and *sangsih*), followed by a *pengawak* 'body' of a composition. Some musicians in Sidan use the term *pengécét* while others do not, although many pieces do indeed have a fast, concluding section" (2016:8). Although we take up the question of a possible history for *gamelan angklung* in the next chapter, it is interesting to note that *sekehe* Taman Sari also used the terms *pemungkah* and *pengawak* to designate the first two sections of their *gending*, but chose the term *pengiba*—not the more common *pengécét*—for their fast, concluding section.

McPhee, like Kunst, and later, Mantle Hood, was also interested in developing some sort of unified theory of Balinese scales and modes and spent a great deal of time charting various *gamelan* tunings, intervals, and ranges; but he remained somewhat ambivalent about the origins of *saih angklung*. Thoroughly acquainted with the theoretical systems of *pélog* and *slendro*, McPhee could easily classify most Balinese ensembles he heard as *pélog*, albeit some with unusual tunings, while lamenting that only one gamelan was tuned to the *slendro* system—*gamelan gender*, for accompanying *wayang kulit*.[3]

The Balinese cultural experts with whom McPhee worked at the time considered all scales in current use to be derived from a "mother scale," a set of seven pitches (*saih pitu*) used, they believed, by pre-fourteenth-century ensembles as well as the *gamelan gambuh*, a post-fourteenth-century ensemble employing large end-blown flutes (*suling*).[4] *Saih pitu* became the defining set from which five pitches were extracted to create scales. This seemed to work especially well for the *pélog* system. Pitches were numbered from 1 to 7 but different five-tone subsets of these could only be determined when specific pitches were chosen from the seven and syllabized. McPhee writes: "[T]he impossibility of defining with finality the actual interval structure of any scale type is evident. . . . Seven-tone *pélog* is found to be a scale with no fixed interval structure, whose tones are nameless until some five-tone scale has been established. Five-tone *pélog* and *slendro* scales are found to be linked together by a common pentatonic solfeggio system, which can only serve, however, to indicate a tonal sequence and the relative pitch of the scale tones" (1966:55).

Saih angklung, though, remained an anomaly for McPhee. He knew that various musicians with whom he worked associated *saih angklung* with *slendro*, calling the ensemble *gamelan kembang kirang* (*gamelan* lacking a note [*dong*]). He dismissed this at first, however, writing in his 1937 article "Angkloeng Gamelans in Bali": "The *angkloeng* scale however, like the *slendro* scale used in the *wajang*, must not be considered as belonging to this system. It is essentially complete in itself; there is no feeling either in the scale or in the music built upon it of incompleteness or even of relationship to one of the pentatonic modes" (1937:327). Using the syllables as a guide, he continues:

> If we compare the nomenclature of the notes in the *angkloeng* scale with those of the pentatonic one, we find that the names of the notes (as denoting their relative positions) of the *angkloeng* scale do not correspond with those of the pentatonic. It would seem then that the *angkloeng* four-note scale is something to be considered quite apart— unrelated to the tonal systems contained in the *saih pitu*. The Balinese make the claim that the tuning is taken from that of the *gender wajang*—a five-note slendro—but there are certain discrepancies that make this hard to accept (1937:327).

He continues with the assertion that *saih angklung* is more closely related to the pitch set used by the *génggong* (the Balinese Jew's harp):

> What seems to me to be of more significance in understanding this scale from the Balinese standpoint is that it is considered for all practical purposes, identical to the four chief notes produced on the *génggong*, the Balinese Jew's-harp [by means of the overtone series]. The *génggong* gives the following series of notes, but the four central ones are chiefly

used to play *Angkloeng* music, and are named after the *Angkloeng* and although the internal intervals are not the same, the Balinese play the same music (i.e., the same pattern of notes) in either scale. Melodies on the *gamelan Angkloeng* are heard on the *génggongs*, and conversely the *Angkloeng* repertoire contains many pieces which, the Balinese state, have once been old *génggong* tunes (1937:327–28).

McPhee tried comparing *saih angklung* with both *pélog* and *slendro*, using actual tunings and various transpositions, but found no real correspondences between them. He did declare, however, that *saih angklung* was perhaps closer to *slendro*, as its internal intervals were all more or less wide, as opposed to those of *pélog*, which were both wide and narrow, and the syllables used for both ensembles were the same. Later, however, in the chapter on *gamelan angklung* in his 1966 book, McPhee began to agree more with his contemporaries, referring to this scale as "*slendro*-derived," based on the wider spacing of its pitches, which had become fairly standardized in the south; but he remained unconvinced that it was truly connected to the now codified *pélog/slendro* system or its syllabification.

When I first began studying *gamelan angklung*, and read McPhee's work, I was often overwhelmed (and confused) by these different tunings, scales, and intervals, frequently wondering if McPhee was simply noting village differences, or if he was interested in finding a "true" or "fixed" scale system that could be discussed as representative of all Balinese music— a project I saw as useless and unwarranted. Later, when reading Oja's biography of McPhee, I came upon this quote from a letter that McPhee wrote to his mother on December 20, 1949, describing the progress of his book, smiling as I read: "I'm in a state of deepest concentration, for I've picked apart and had to reorganize the whole chapter on Balinese scales. I'm not out of it yet and I mustn't let what I've almost got hold of slip. . . . I nearly lost my mind over this and may still do, but there's no use in getting panicky" (2004:163).

McPhee was also quite taken with the interlocking passages (*kotekan ubit empat*) he heard in the *gamelan angklung* repertoire, which he saw as different from others he had heard and which he felt were at the core of *angklung* music: "the constant interlocking of parts and the sudden rhythmic breaks that occur from time to time, maintain a steady tension throughout the music" (1966:113). He also suggested that the *kotekan* figures, often played by the *réong* in other ensembles were, in *gamelan angklung*, played by the *gangsa* along with the *réong*—for him, a relatively new practice.

Further, he remarked that the *angklung kotekan* was unusual, in that it was frequently divided into three parts in performance: *sangsih* (pitches

1 and 2); *polos* (pitches 3 and 4);[5] and a third middle part, *kilitan*: pitches 2 and 3, seen as a binder, and added in by performers so as not to "break the kotekan" (1937:254). Finally, McPhee makes a passing comment that *angklung kotekan* were reminiscent of rice-stamping—a practice done in ancient times by women to separate the outer husk from the inner grain, and still practiced at various ceremonies, such as weddings and cremations.

McPhee also called attention to certain formal structures he found in the pieces of the classical ensembles he heard in and around southeastern Bali. These he divided into two groups: (1) pieces with simple melodies played by *jegogan* (i.e., *pokok*) and elaborated by the higher-pitched instruments, which were relatively more even, metrically; and (2) those with the melody played by the higher instruments, where the *jegogan* aligned with the melody at certain times. These were generally freer metrically (1966:246).

Both types were characterized by flexible meter and a certain melodic freedom that McPhee likened to some compositions of the *gender wayang* tradition, writing, "They reveal a flexibility of form, similar to the compositions of the *gender wayang* repertory." McPhee continues in the endnote, "Indeed, many *angklung* gamelans include in their repertory compositions said to be 'drawn' (*ditaerik*) from the *gending pewayangan* [*wayang kulit*]. *Angklung* compositions, such as 'pemungkah' and 'lagu gender wayang' are based on four-tone ostinatos and melodic episodes taken directly from the *wayang* repertory—a practice showing how closely related the two scale systems are considered to be by the Balinese" (1966:246).

Finally, McPhee was frequently amused by what he saw as the charming, whimsical titles of the pieces he learned (when there were titles), citing names such as "Bathing Dragonfly," "Drunken Bird," or "Crow Steals Eggs," and referring again to the origins of *gamelan angklung* music in the *génggong*, stating, "[I]n spite of their graphic titles, such *gendings* listed here are purely instrumental compositions, in no way descriptive or associated with any texts. Many are said to have their origin in the simple folk tunes known as *gending génggong*, which are strummed on the *génggong*, or Jew's harp by boys and men all over Bali" (1966:255).

Tua (Old) Ensembles Revisited

Music of the *tua* period, according to Western and Balinese scholarship, consists of smaller, less elaborate ensembles than those developed later during the *madya* and *baru* periods. *Tua* ensembles are described as having fewer layers of sound, more metric and melodic freedom, and older pitch sets not necessarily corresponding to the contemporary *pélog-slendro* modal system. The presence of asymmetry, frequently cited in the literature, is thought to be characteristic of the music found among Indigenous, pre-Majapahit peoples and has been used as a cultural marker, distinguishing this older music from that of the traditions inherited from Java in the fourteenth century.

Associated mainly with the village, these ensembles are still tied to ritual and are imbued with spirituality, power, and, sometimes, magic. A categorizing system, originally proposed by performer-composer-teacher I Nyoman Rembang (1937–2001), discussed in chapter 1, described the *tua* category as including seven ancient ensembles: four sacred *gamelan*: *gambang, saron* (also called *caruk*), *luang* (also called *saron*), and *selunding*; and three others: *gender wayang, angklung,* and *gong bheri* (Tenzer 2000:149–50).[6] Tenzer remarks that Rembang's system was based mainly on technology, as all *tua* ensembles were constructed with ancient and plentiful materials long found in the area: bamboo, wood, and forged metal (bronze).

In the twentieth century, the division between pre- and post-Majapahit periods became a convenient and widely accepted marker of both the end of Indigenous prehistory and the beginning of modern Balinese history. This division, as noted earlier, set in place a basic understanding of the contemporary Balinese as inheritors of a high-Javanese culture through the Majapahit, with musical ensembles, genres, and basic musical structures that developed later in the *madya* (middle) period, for example, having evolved from Javanese models.[7]

Since, according to this telling, modern Balinese culture had started in the fourteenth century, what had happened before was not especially relevant to a growing sense of modern Balinese identity; and, as few written documents existed to provide insights into how the Indigenous peoples on the island had lived before the Majapahit, their ritual and cultural practices were seen as occurring in an unknown, distant past. Thus, over time, musical ensembles in the *tua* category gradually became imbued with mysterious and spiritually heightened qualities. The *selunding* ensemble, for example, with keys made from iron, is said to have magical, possibly dangerous, properties and is seldom played in public (Eiseman vol. 1, 1990:239; McPhee 1966:258).[8]

Most scholarship on *tua* ensembles is limited to the first four on Rembang's list. These ensembles were probably attractive to early researchers in part because they were the oldest and most highly regarded. They were seen as both sacred and magical; all were relatively rare in the 1920s and 30s; all were housed in special *balé* (pavilions); some had (and continue to have) restrictions on who could play or even touch them; all carried tremendous spiritual power (*sakti*); and all were said to have been given to the Balinese by gods who bestowed these gifts in times of economic or political crisis. Thus, they all occupied, and continue to occupy, a special and highly significant place in Balinese constructions of their cosmology and its relationship to a distant musical past.

These four sacred *gamelan* also share certain musical characteristics that are significant to our understanding of *gamelan angklung*: (1) they all use *saih pitu* tuning in five-, six-, and seven-tone versions; (2) their music is structured using only two textural layers (*pokok* and elaboration); (3) there is an absence of drums and gong punctuation; and (4) they all use unique and flexible melodic and rhythmic figures that do not fit neatly into the more fixed formulas of musics developed later.

Two other *gamelan* are listed in Rembang's *tua* category: *gamelan gender wayang*, used exclusively to accompany *wayang kulit*, and *gamelan angklung*, the ensemble that is the focus of this book. These two *gamelan* share some, but not all, musical characteristics with the four sacred *gamelan*. They are both considered "small," that is, they both use smaller and fewer instruments, as well as two textural layers (although divided somewhat differently), and their music is often described as asymmetric, both melodically and metrically.

One thing they do not share is their relationship to *saih pitu*. Although their origins, along with those of the sacred ensembles, are believed to be pre-Majapahit, repeated attempts by scholars to derive their tuning from *saih pitu* proved fruitless. What follows is a brief discussion highlighting both the importance of these musical characteristics (or lack thereof) for developing a coherent history of ancient and modern Balinese *gamelan* music in the twentieth century, as well as some possible explanations for why scholarship on *gamelan angklung* cremation music, and to some degree the music of *gamelan gender wayang*, is largely absent from this scholarly literature.[9]

Sounds of Oldness in *Tua* Ensembles

As suggested earlier, tuning systems and modes seem to have captured the imagination of early scholars working with Balinese music, an interest that has continued to the present.[10] The urge to construct an overall modal theory for both pre- and post-Majapahit musics seems to have driven much of this research, yet local tuning variations and differing terms used to identify pitch sets often proved frustrating. Early Western scholarship on the modal frameworks of the four sacred ensembles by Jaap Kunst and C. J. A. Kunst-van Wely (1925), McPhee (1966), Ernst Schlager (1965, 1974), Andrew Toth (1975), Danker Schaareman (1980), and more recently by Wayan Sudirana (2013) and Jonathan Stuart Adams (2021), for example, provides basic information on each ensemble's specific use of the pitches of *saih pitu*. In addition, the literature offers information on how many octaves (or half-octaves) are spanned; how modes are constructed from important pitches, pitch contours, and tonal centers; and how tuning schemes can be altered by the construction of the instruments or their *panggul*,[11] and so on.

Ultimately, scholars agreed that different versions, or modes (*patuan*), of *saih pitu* existed within the four sacred ensembles, as well as ensembles emerging in the *madya* and *baru* periods, that depended on how many tones (five, six, or seven) were used and on which tone sounded with the gong. They acknowledged that internal intervals varied greatly from village to village, and that the five pitches of any mode could be syllabized once the first tone was identified. This information validated the origins and importance of an essentially pentatonic modal system using both wide and narrow intervals, derived from *saih pitu*.

Saih pitu was associated with the *gamelan gambuh*, an ensemble using giant flutes (*suling*) that accompanied court dance-dramas. *Gambuh* modes were called *tekep*, meaning "to cover," which signified the covering of a hole to produce a note on the *gambuh*, and pieces were often named using the starting pitch in a particular *tekep*, as in *gending gambuh tekep ding* (piece in the *gambuh* repertoire starting on pitch *ding*). Although this system worked reasonably well for most ensembles, the vast majority of which were (and still are) tuned to *pélog*, it was less convincing in explaining the origins and workings of *slendro*, the modal system used in *gender wayang* and of the *slendro*-like tuning of the *gamelan angklung*.

Two explanations emerged: first, that *slendro*'s intervals were, like *pélog*'s, derived from *gambuh*'s *saih pitu*, a view held by McPhee (1966), Schlager (1965), and Hood (1966), among others. This theory positioned *gender wayang* as a true *slendro* and *gamelan angklung* as an incomplete one (*kembang kirang*), but still *slendro*. The second explanation posited that *gamelan gender wayang* and *angklung* used their own pitch sets that were older and not related to *saih pitu* (McPhee [1937] and Lisa Gold [1998], among others). Karl Richter, in his article "Slendro-Pélog and the Conceptualization of Balinese Music: Remarks on the *Gambuh* Tone System," goes as far as to say that *gambuh* had no influence whatever on *wayang* or *angklung* (1992:195). This question remains unsettled, although its urgency has lessened.

On the issue of layering, most scholars today have adopted the vocabulary of earlier researchers, such as McPhee, the Kunsts, Hood, and others, referring to Balinese music as layered, or as a form of stratified heterophony. According to this analysis, the music of *tua* ensembles has only two layers: (1) a lower, slower-moving, underlying layer (*pokok*); and (2) a higher, elaborative stratum consisting of medium-paced, tuneful sections, or sections of rapid interlocking. Both McPhee and Tenzer question if the underlying contours of *tua* ensembles can truly be called *pokok*, as this term is normally associated with the musics of the *madya* and *baru* periods. Lacking punctuating gongs, drums, or equal and repeated cycles, the musics of *tua* ensembles do not always fit easily into this more fixed structure.

McPhee uses the phrase "stress or reinforcement tones" (1966:246) for the notes in the underlying pitches of *tua* music, implying that the melody is driving the contour, rather than the reverse. Tenzer suggests that the different layers in *tua* musics are perhaps more embedded within each other, "often resulting in the . . . fore-fronting of melody elaboration and surface rhythmic details and contrasts" (2000:232–37). Further, as the lower layer of *tua* ensembles does not extend beyond one octave, this limits their melodic contour: "A melody that ends on its lowest pitch cannot be approached from below, a melody that ends on the highest cannot be approached from above, and only melodies ending in the middle of the scale could be centered in a melodic arch" (2000:173).

Tenzer's work on *tua* ensembles also provides a general discussion of asymmetrical structures, melodies, and elaborations found in *tua* musics, especially within the four sacred ensembles but not specifically within *gamelan angklung*. *Pokok* found in *tua* musics, Tenzer notes, are of irregular length, not always constrained by the regular, duple meters of *madya* musics, which are governed metrically by the colotomic gong structure. He states:

> Tua music is not *systematically* asymmetrical (if that were possible); it is simply less consistently symmetrical than court genres. Tua pokok are thus neither abstracted by other instruments nor conceived of as a succession of tones of specific hierarchical weights. The lack of these constraints leads to enrichments of the music's horizontal flow, often resulting in internal rhythmic variety, irregular meters, fractional beats and the fore-fronting of melody, elaboration, and surface rhythmic details and contrasts. . . . [Further], patterns of interlocking figuration in these gamelan are in many cases less formulaic than those in the court ensembles, as if conceived of integrally with the melodies rather than as stylistic patterns to be added on to them (2000:232–33).

The Legacy of *Gamelan Angklung* Scholarship

Katherine Elizabeth Wakeling, in her 2010 doctoral dissertation "Representing Balinese Music: A Study of the Practice and Theorization of Balinese Gamelan," cites three general assumptions underlying most histories and analyses of music in Bali: (1) the idea that today's Balinese music originated on Java, arriving with the Majapahit Dynasty in the late fourteenth century and remaining a repository of ancient Javanese culture and spirituality; (2) that the *gamelan gambuh*, a Javanese-derived ensemble brought by the Majapahit, was the source of many Balinese court-related and modern musical genres developed on the island in post-Majapahit times; and (3) that the *gambuh* produced a seven-tone set of pitches from which today's modern four-, five-, six-, and seven-tone *pélog* and *slendro* scale systems are derived (2010:32–40).

These three assumptions led early scholars to make various evaluative comparisons between Javanese and Balinese musics, where Balinese music was seen as an inheritor of Javanese greatness (through the Majapahit), a repository of ancient Hindu beliefs and practices (through India), and "behind" Java (and the West) in development of a coherent theoretical modal system (*slendro* and *pélog*). More recent scholarship has tended toward begging these questions, assuming their validity while hotly protesting their falsehoods.[12]

Since the Kunsts' and McPhee's groundbreaking work on *gamelan angklung*, other scholars, such as Tenzer, have occasionally referred to this ensemble and its music, but no serious study or verification of any historical assertions has appeared since their time. Until recently, other scholars of Balinese music have largely repeated the findings of the Kunsts and McPhee, such as the continued use (or nonuse) of the *angklung kocok*, the possibility that *saih angklung* is (or is not) derived from *slendro*, or whether the music is (or is not) simple, or "small."[13]

However, since the first decade of this century, four scholars have contributed much to this discussion. In addition to Tenzer's work discussed above, three new recordings of this ensemble have been made recently, each with extensive liner notes: Ruby Ornstein's *From Kuno to Kebyar: Balinese Gamelan Angklung* (Smithsonian Folkways 2010, recorded in the 1960s), cited in the previous chapter; part of Edward Herbst's repatriation project *Bali 1928, Vol. IV: Music for Temple Festivals and Death Rituals* (World Arbiter 2016, recorded in 1928 by Odeon); and Wayne Vitale's *Gamelan Angklung: Bali's 4-Tone Bronze Gamelan Orchestra* (Vital Records, Historical Recording Series 2014, recorded in 1992).

Ornstein and Herbst restate the Balinese assumption of *saih angklung*'s relationship to *slendro*, Ornstein suggesting that "*slendro* tuning is said to suggest sadness" (2010:7–8), while Herbst relates a conversation that he had in 2009 with composer and instrument maker/tuner Wayan Berata about the speed of the *ombak* (wave) between the male and female tunings of *gamelan angklung*'s *gangsa*. Berata agreed that the *ombak* in *gong kebyar* should be a fast eight cycles per second, but he preferred *angklung*, "most commonly associated with *slendro* and with music for death rituals such as cremation—to be in the slower six *ombak* per second range as it resembles a person weeping" (Herbst 2001:12).

Herbst also confirms that the reference to *saih angklung* as *slendro* with a missing tone had originally come into common use "in the 1960s through I Nyoman Rembang, I Gusti Putu Made Geria, and I Nyoman Kaler, all teachers at KOKAR in Bali, who had also taught at KOKAR in Surakarta, Java, where *saih gender* (for *wayang kulit*) and *saih angklung* had been taught as *slendro*." Herbst concludes with the statement that contemporary music theorists now (c. 2000) want to "steer away from *pélog* and *slendro* to emphasize the many differences in tuning" (2001:15).

Vitale's recordings are from *banjar* Beluran, Desa Kerobokan, near Kuta, in the southern part of Bali. The first four pieces, played by members of *Sekehe Angklung* Gita Kencana (Angklung Group, Golden Song), were remarkably similar in structure to the pieces I learned from *Gamelan Taman Sari*, as was the playful attitude Vitale describes among performers, where "there is no distinction between rehearsal and performance" (2014:14) (more on this in a later chapter).

In reading this literature, one can see that certain metaphors arose that have become tropes, that is, words or phrases carrying emotional meanings that help distinguish *gamelan angklung* and its music from others in Bali. Adjectives, originally coined by McPhee, such as "folklike," "simple," "airy," "miniature," and "whimsical," for example, have been used consistently by other scholars to describe this ensemble, perhaps inadvertently creating a picture of *gamelan angklung* that may owe more to Western sensibilities than to those of the Balinese. Of course, McPhee worked with Balinese informants, such as Madé Lebah, who may have provided some descriptive words, but McPhee also contributed his own understandings of this music based on assumptions he had as a Western-educated composer and performer living in the mid-twentieth century.

For example, his characterizations of *angklung* music as "folklike" and "simple" recall the nostalgic construction of the European "folk-tunes" of Western music's historical imagination, a trope made popular by Johan von Herder's (1744–1803) eighteenth-century concept of the *volk* and used later in evaluative comparisons with "classical" and "popular musics" (see Bohlman 1988). Further, McPhee's frequent references to the ensemble as "diminutive in size" (1937:323–24) seem to reveal not only a class consciousness, but also (perhaps implicitly) a dismissal of this music as not truly worthy of serious study—more like a puzzle to be solved than a true musical genre. And, although McPhee was both enchanted and amused by *gamelan angklung* music, devoting considerable time and scholarship to better understanding it, he never fully saw this music as "not-music," that is, as an aspect of *dharma*, or as an offering. Certainly, most Balinese would (and do) describe *gamelan angklung* cremation music as sad—it is connected to death and loss; sweet—it is high and bell-like; and small—it is sometimes carried, but no one I worked with ever described it as "whimsical," or "humble," or less important than the grand traditions of *gong gedé*, or *gong kebyar*.

Thus, it is no surprise that this ensemble would be under-researched by scholars, as it is largely associated historically with boisterous, playful, and even competitive ceremonies surrounding the growth and production of rice, and uses melodies and rhythmic patterns borrowed from other rice-related tools and entertainments, such as *génggong* and rice-pounding. Old but not sacred, revered but not grand, pleasant but not flashy, *gamelan angklung* is regarded as a remnant of an ancient, Indigenous culture now performed by untrained village musicians. Further, its tuning, not derived from *saih pitu*, its pitch set not fitting comfortably into the inherited five-tone *pelos-slendro* modal system, and its history not connected to any ancient texts, mythical stories, or dance-dramas, must have appeared to early scholars as an anomaly, and to researchers who followed as an afterthought.

CHAPTER 4

Three Possible *Gamelan Angklung* Ancestors

This chapter explores three ancient bamboo music/sound-makers that, along with *tua* genres discussed in chapter 3, appear to have a bearing on the origins and meanings of *gamelan angklung* cremation music today: the *génggong* (Jew's harp), originally carved from bamboo or from the stem of a sugar-palm leaf and played by young boys and men in the rice fields; the *bumbung*, a large, hollow, bamboo or wooden tube, used mostly by women to husk rice; and the *angklung kocok*, the shaken rattle introduced earlier.

None of these instruments or ensembles appear anywhere on Rembang's historical list of *gamelan*, as no one at that time considered them to be true music-makers, "music" having been newly defined as artful, entertaining, or ceremonial sound. They are discussed here because they are all ancient in origin, they are constructed from a natural material such as bamboo, and because most Balinese, including the men with whom I played, see a connection between them and *gamelan angklung*. Finally, all three share a defining feature: their four-tone-ness.

Three Ancient Four-Tone Music/Sound-Makers

Four-tone musical instruments and other sound-makers, especially those made from bamboo, have been common throughout South and Southeast Asia for millennia. Bamboo, a fast-growing grass, is found everywhere in the area and is used as a flexible, strong, and long-lasting material for building houses, constructing tools and weapons, weaving, and making water vessels. It's also used as a food source, and as a particularly resonant material for musical instruments and other sound-makers. In Bali, bamboo,

FIGURE 4.1 *Jegog* performance at the Bali Arts Festival, June 2007.
Made from bamboo harvested in Jembrana.

like rice, is regarded as indispensable to daily life, especially in rural areas where it grows quickly and to enormous heights and circumferences, as in western Bali (Jembrana Province).

The sections between nodes on a bamboo stem are hollow and, when dried and allowed to harden, produce a resonant sound thought by the Balinese to be both beautiful and effective. Tubes of different lengths, often closed on one end or with their top halves partially carved out, can be used in a number of ways. They can be mounted on horizontal frames and shaken, like the *angklung kocok*; lashed together and struck with mallets (*rindik, jegog*, etc.); blown (*suling*); placed inside carved wooden cases and used as resonators for struck bronze or iron instruments (*gangsa, jegogan*, etc.); breathed into (*génggong*); or pounded in a trough while husking rice (*bumbung*). Endo Suanda, a highly respected Javanese musician, writes that if one applies a European-derived value system that dismisses bamboo, "truly understanding the village philosophy and culture—the bamboo culture—of Indonesia will be difficult" (1995:1). Readily available, sturdy, and strong, bamboo musical instruments are possibly the oldest instruments known in Bali.

The *Génggong*

The Jew's harp is a musical instrument found in almost every world culture, easy to construct and carry (but not to play).[1] It is classified in the Sachs-Hornbostel system as a lamellaphone (an idiophone with a "tongue"). When constructed from one piece of bamboo, wood, bone, or other material, it is called an idioglot; when constructed from two pieces— a frame and a separate vibrating tongue—it is referred to as a polyglot.[2] An idioglot Jew's harp is held near the lips, while a polyglot is placed against the teeth.

Only one fundamental pitch is produced by the lamella, but when the open mouth, acting as a resonator, articulates certain vowel sounds, four clear harmonics (upper partials of the fundamental pitch) are produced. These harmonics correspond to numbers five through eight of the harmonic series (Morgan 2008:49). For example, if the fundamental pitch is G, the fifth-eighth harmonics would be B, D, F, G. The most common Jew's harp in Bali today is the *génggong*.

Probably developed from an older instrument, the *enggong* (Balinese, frog), the *génggong* today is carved from the rib of a sugar-palm leaf and is held in the left hand near the lips of the open mouth. At the right end of

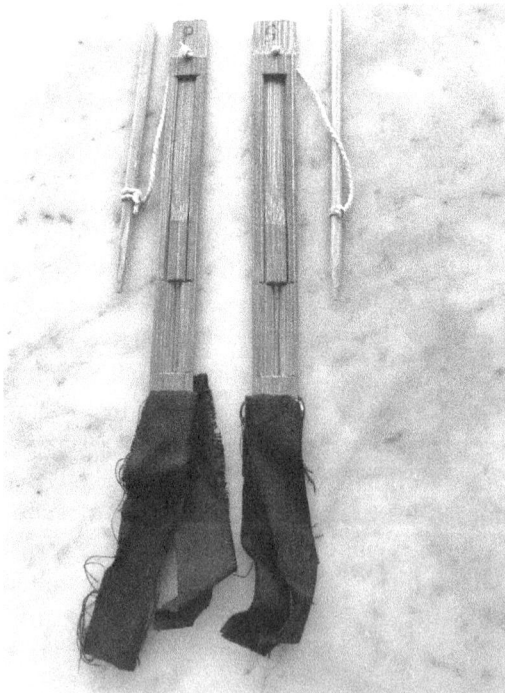

FIGURE 4.2 Two Balinese *génggong* (Jew's harps).

the *génggong* is a short string, rope, or ribbon that the player snaps with the right hand, causing the lamella to vibrate. While smartly snapping the cord, the player articulates the syllables Balinese musicians use to distinguish four pitches: *neng, nung, nang*, and *ning*, creating a set of pitches most Balinese villagers call *saih génggong*, which they also see as related to *saih angklung* (although the internal intervals may vary). To produce pitches 1 and 3, the player blows or coughs into the instrument, creating an accent; to produce pitches 2 and 4, the player inhales, producing a softer tone (Rai 2004:31); so, playing a *génggong* requires a quick succession of inhaled and exhaled breaths.

Making and playing *génggong* probably originated in the rice fields as an entertaining pastime and as an instrument used in courtship; it was either played alone, in pairs (as in courtship, by both men and women), or in a group of four or sometimes five, creating a *gamelan génggong* or *génggong-génggong* (Harnish 1998:754). When used in an ensemble today, *génggong*, like all Balinese instruments, are tuned in *lanang-wadon* (male-female) pairs, creating the characteristic Balinese *ombak*, or wave (Morgan 2008:52). The *lanang* (male, higher-pitched instrument) is considered the leader and sounds the four pitches that the Balinese associate with the *gamelan angklung*, while the *wadon* (female, lower-pitched instrument) can sound the lower *ning* and, occasionally, the "missing note"—*nong*—of the *slendro* scale (2008:53). Together, the two instruments have the capacity to play an entire five-tone scale with consistently wide intervals, as well as a low and a high octave. However, due to the constraints of the *génggong* itself, the lower *ning* and *nong* are seldom heard in the actual music. Thus, most Balinese players (and listeners) conceptualize this set of pitches, like *saih angklung*, as a four-tone row.

Since the 1930s other instruments have been added to the *génggong* ensemble to create larger performing groups. Today, the most active *sekehe génggong* exists in Batuan, where it accompanies dance-dramas, based on local adaptions of frog-prince stories. Here the ensemble consists of many *génggong*, accompanied by bamboo flutes (*suling*), drums, gongs, and other bronze-keyed instruments.

Deidre Morgan, a former graduate student at the University of British Columbia in Vancouver, Canada, conducted fieldwork on the Balinese *génggong* and noted that many of her informants claimed that the solo or paired instruments were far more popular before Indonesian independence, when "everyone played *génggong*." One elderly player stated that "while *génggong* is now used to accompany dance 'real *génggong*' is meant to be a purely instrumental ensemble" (2008:38). Thus, in its original form, the music of *génggong*, like that of *gamelan angklung*, was purely instrumental, never accompanying dance, poetry, or other narrative genres.

The association between *gamelan angklung* and *génggong* titles and tunes is clearly made by McPhee in his article "Children and Music in Bali" (1955), where he recounts the creation of a *génggong sekehe* in Sayan, the village where he lived, whose members included the young boys of the village. According to this account, McPhee enlisted the help of a teacher from a neighboring village who knew many *génggong* songs. The first meetings were spent without the instruments while the children learned to sing the textless *génggong* tunes, using vowels.

After a while, according to McPhee, the teacher began to expand the tunes by adding new sections where the four pitches of *saih génggong* were divided into two separate interlocking parts. This created an onbeat pattern sounding pitches 3 and 4, which McPhee called *molos*, and an offbeat pattern sounding pitches 1 and 2, which he called *sangsih*. He labeled this alternating, interlocking figuration *candétan*, a term he also used more generally to describe all forms of two-voice interlocking. Occasionally, he noted, the *molos* and *sangsih* would come together in a unison on pitch 3 (*ubit telu*), or play pitches 1 and 4 together, creating a vertical interval of anywhere from 676–770 cents (*ubit empat, ngempat*, "Bali fifth"), which seemed to pop out of the texture, creating cross-rhythms. (See more on this in chapter 7.)

Another clue that the musics of the *génggong* and *gamelan angklung* are related comes from Morgan's descriptions of the playing techniques used for executing *génggong* passages. Morgan makes a distinction between *candétan* (used for slower-moving melodies), which she defines as the sound produced only by exhaling, and *ócètan* (used for faster-moving, interlocking sections), which is produced by rapid in-and-out breathing. This distinction highlights the difference between slower-moving, more melodic, noninterlocking elaborations and faster, interlocking passages found in *gamelan angklung* cremation music, a topic that is more fully explored in chapter 7.

McPhee was also preoccupied, as we saw in the previous chapter, with Balinese scales, occasionally asserting that *saih angklung* and *saih génggong* were related to each other. In 2004, ISI-Director I Wayan Rai, then a graduate student at the University of Maryland, Baltimore County, wrote an article titled "The Scale of *Génggong* and Its Relation to the Four Tone *Slendro* Tuning System in Bali." In his article, Rai tested this assumption by using the fast Fourier transformation algorithm to analyze the four-tone scale frequencies of both the *gamelan angklung* and *génggong*, determining that although individual intervals between pitches were not entirely isomorphic, they were all wide—that is, more than 200 cents—and that the distance between pitch 1 and pitch 4 of both scales created a "Bali fifth." Therefore, there could be no doubt, Rai states, that these scales were not only related to each other, but also part of the (consistently wide-interval) *slendro* system, which, by the end of the twentieth century, theoretically included both a four- and a five-tone set. Although not as popular as it once was, the *génggong* remains a symbol of ancient Balinese culture, still used as a form of entertainment in the rice field or at a tooth-filing or marriage ceremony as a playful, even humorous, diversion for human, as well as nonhuman, audiences (Rai 2004:40).

Bumbung (Bamboo Tubes)

For millennia, villagers in Bali have traditionally used hollow bamboo tubes to remove the hard, brown, outer husks from recently harvested rice grains. Groups of up to ten or twelve workers, both women and men, participated. Working together in this way, they turned the tedious process of husking rice into an efficient, socially interactive, often pleasurable

FIGURE 4.3 Women playing stamping tubes at a wedding.

activity. Although still used occasionally by individual households today, this practice has long given way to a more modern, mechanized system, such as that described in chapter 1.

However, a ritual form of rice-pounding continues to take place, often in the context of ceremonies such as marriages, where it signifies the transfer of the bride to her new husband's family and *banjar*, and funerals, where it helps to ensure the sustenance of a community after the death of one of its members. Many scholars and *gamelan* performers today also believe that the interlocking rhythmic remnants of rice-pounding live on and are performed daily in the rapid, interlocking passages that characterize most contemporary Balinese music—*kotekan*. Early researchers of Balinese music, such as Colin McPhee and Ernst Schlager (c. 1896–1960), were fascinated by these performances, although the names and descriptions of this practice varied somewhat in their writings (Harnish 1988).

McPhee, in his *Music in Bali* (1966), for example, included a substantial description of this "lively percussion ensemble" in his "Appendix 1: Notes to Chapters" (1966:359–62). Under the title "Chapter 6, Rice-Pounding Music," he described *bumbung* of various lengths and thicknesses that were pounded on a carved-out wooden trough, with four workers (most often women) alternating precisely with their partners to create repeating rhythmic patterns. Sometimes an additional worker would hit the outside wall of the trough with her pole, providing a steady pulse to keep the others synchronized (1966:359).

On some occasions, McPhee witnessed larger rice-pounding ensembles where the women pounded their poles inside the trough to remove rice husks, while up to six men tapped syncopated, interlocking patterns with wooden sticks on the sides of the trough, or just inside the rim. Six players were usually needed to create "a full *kilitan* (binding together)" (1966:359–60). These patterns would change when one or more players dropped out and another would enter with a new pattern.

Frequently, the trough was placed on wooden slats, raising it a few inches from the ground, thus creating a resonating space, so that the patterns, notes McPhee, could be heard up to a mile away (1966:360). Further, because the pounding poles were of differing lengths and thicknesses, different pitches emerged from the pounding, creating a kind of melodic pattern; and, at times, one player might drop a pole with more strength, creating an accent that disrupted the flow.

McPhee provided drawings of various *bumbung* strokes, noting that one sounded like the "double knock of the *angklung*" (*kocok*) and another—a set of strokes executed by two players on the side of the trough—resembled the rapid interlocking and "filling in" (*kilitan*) of many *kotekan* patterns he heard. McPhee concluded his description with this: "Above the deep resonant tones produced by the rice-pounding poles, the animated polyrhythmic accompaniment clatters with timeless energy" (1966:362). Michael Bakan also notes that *kilitan* rice-husking patterns greatly influenced and were adopted by *gamelan gong kebyar*, *kecak*, and *beleganjur* ensembles (1999:66–68).

Ernst Schlager

It was the Swiss chemist, Ernst Schlager, however, who analyzed the interlocking rice-pounding patterns most extensively. Living and working in east Bali during the 1940s, Schlager was in contact with many scholars, such as Rolf Goris (1898–1965), who were interested in documenting the histories of the seven-tone sacred ensembles, especially their relationship to ancient Javanese sung poetry (*kidung*) (Wallis 1979). Transcribing hundreds of texts onto palm-leaves (*lontar*), Schlager showed how the metric and syllabic patterns of *kidung* were possibly related to the melodic structures of *saih pitu gamelan* genres.

Although McPhee and Schlager did not know each other personally (McPhee's work in Bali was done in the 1930s, Schlager's in the 1940s), it is probable that they knew at least some of each other's work. In *Music in Bali* (1966), McPhee cites Schlager's 1951 article "Bali," published in the first edition of *Die Musik in Geschichte un Gegenswart* (pp. 1110–15), as well as his article "Von Arbeitsrhythmus zur Bali" ("On Work-Rhythms of Bali"), published in a *Festschrift* for Alfred Bühler in 1965, and his book, *Rituelle Siebenton-Musik auf Bali (Ritual Seven-Tone Music on Bali)* (1976). Schlager cites McPhee's work, beginning with his earliest article in 1937 through 1966, the year of *Music in Bali*'s publication. Schlager's article and book were both published posthumously, so it is most likely that Schlager's editors added these references. Nonetheless, Schlager's work overlaps with McPhee's on the significance of rice-pounding, extending it far beyond McPhee's descriptions.

The most important work relevant to the study of *gamelan angklung* is Schlager's comprehensive analysis and classification of the interlocking rhythms of rice-pounding. His 1965 article, cited above, provides the beginnings of an analytic method that he expanded later in his book, outlining various kinds of interlocking patterns that existed in rice-pounding and how they could be used as melodic elaborations. Although he did not work specifically with *gamelan angklung*, some of his findings are relevant to this ensemble and its unique melodic and elaborating techniques.

Schlager, like McPhee, described a form of rice-pounding consisting of two distinct kinds of rhythmic patterns: (1) a regular pattern of alternating blows by four players over the span of two beats parsed into eight rapid pulses, called *tingkadan*; and (2) accompanying patterns of rapid rim-hits, played by an additional player, and organized over the same eight pulses, called *oncangan*. These rim-hits most often formed the following patterns: 3 + 3 + 2, 3 + 2 + 3, or 2 + 3 +3 (see below). Frequently, these two layers would be accompanied by a steady beat-keeping stroke, which Schlager called *kulkulo* (from *kulkul*, the hollow wooden tube used as a signal in the village, shown in Figure 0.1). Once started, the interlocking patterns would continue until someone dropped out (1976:36–7).

DIAGRAM 4.1 Simple *tingkadan* and *oncangan* patterns.

	Players:									
Tingkadan (alternating hits)	1	*				*				*
	2		*				*			
	3			*				*		
	4				*				*	
Oncangan (rim hits, 3 + 3 + 2 pulses)	5	+			+		+			+
Kulkulo (beats)	6	x			x			x		
Eight Pulses		x	x	x	x	x	x	x	x	x

Using these rhythmic models, Schlager applied them to specific elaborations used in the music of the four sacred *gamelan*, now dividing the four *tingkadan* strikes into two musical lines: *polos* and *sangsih*. When patterns were applied to four separate pitches, this resulted in what he called *kotekan katak ngongkek* (croaking frog *kotekan*), which had the singular property of simultaneous hits on pitches 1 and 4 (*ngempat*), creating accents whose pattern formed the most popular *oncangan* pattern 3 + 3 + 2. This, Schlager noted, was used almost exclusively in the music of *gamelan angklung* (1976:38 n.15). The importance of Schlager's work connecting rice-pounding rhythmic patterns to melodic elaborations and *kotekan katak ngongkek* within the cremation repertoire of *gamelan angklung* will be revisited later, in chapters 7 and 8, which are devoted to a closer examination of *gamelan angklung* cremation music.

Angklung Kocok

The popular shaken bamboo rattle, *angklung kocok*, was introduced in chapter 2, where it was discussed in relation to the old *gamelan angklung* McPhee discovered in the remote villages of Karangesam, as well as

McPhee's addition of this instrument to his classical *gamelan angklung* in Sayan. Here, we revisit the *angklung kocok*, beginning this time in Java, tracing its origin, its use in many different ensembles, and its possible journey to Bali.

Many theories exist concerning the origin of the word *angklung*. Aside from the possibility that the word is derived from the sound itself, other ideas have surfaced. Randal Baier, for example, states that some of the musicians he worked with in Sunda considered "the *klung* syllable to refer to the resonant quality of the bamboo sound, and they place *angklung* in a category together with other bamboo instruments, such as *calung* (a struck bamboo-tube instrument), *kunklung* (the bamboo stamping tube Balinese call *bumbung*), or *celempung* (bamboo-tube zither)" (1986:8). Or, that the word *angklung* comes from two Sundanese words, *angklung-angklung* (floating) and *klung* (the sound produced by the instrument itself), so *angklung* would be translated in Sunda as "the sound *klung* produced by lifting or floating the instrument" (1986:8). Baier further cites the Sundanese author Satjidibrata who, in 1950, proposed two other possibilities, "*ngadu angklung*, to batter useless thoughts back and forth; and *diangklungan*, to be flattered by someone so that one becomes loquacious, disclosing information that might better have been left unsaid" (1986:8).

The *angklung kocok*, although found today throughout much of Southeast Asia, is believed to have originated in Sunda as early as the seventh century. Jaap Kunst (1968:75) noted references to a shaken bamboo instrument seen on pre-Hindu stone carvings dated from about that time in Java, as mentioned previously. Baier, who conducted fieldwork in Kampung Cipining Village, in the Province of West Java (Sunda), among the Badui (Urang Kanekes) relates a myth told to him by the head of the *sekehe angklung kocok* there, describing why and how the shaken *angklung* was invented. Here is a summary of that myth:

> A devastating rice-crop failure in the village of Cipining threatened widespread starvation. The villagers believed that this failure occurred because the goddess of rice, Nyi Pohaci (Dewi Sri in Bali), was angry, claiming that the villagers had not entertained her sufficiently. So, the villagers tried playing a *suling* for her, and then a *karinding* (Sundanese Jew's harp), to no avail. In desperation, a young man from the village journeyed with some of his friends to a nearby mountain, where they cut down a large bamboo stalk and, when the bamboo was dry, the young man meditated in isolation and made an *angklung kocok*. He worked for forty days and nights, completing a full set of *angklung*, which he then used to teach his friends to play. When the boys returned to the village, the people held a ceremony and with the *angklung* playing, they begged

Pohaci to come back down to earth and she agreed. The rice began to grow strong and healthy, and the villagers were saved from destruction. The narrator concludes: "This spirit of frivolity, action, and festivity is precisely what Nyi Pohaci wants in order to bestow the earth with her favors. Essentially, a contract is established between Pohaci and the human world: her essence is imparted to the rice crop and humankind [only] if she in turn is consistently entertained and cared for at all stages of the agricultural cycle" (1986:9).

A variant of this myth, collected by Wim van Zanten in 1995, also from the Badui, describes Nyi Pohaci's descent from heaven and her marriage to the earth, with the *angklung kocok* ensemble playing tunes to entertain her and her children.

Following its presumed creation in Sunda in the seventh century or earlier, the instrument in various sizes, tuned to different pitches, and often combined with other bamboo instruments, singers, and dancers, took on a life of its own, spreading north into Sumatra, Malaysia, and the Philippines, as well as east into eastern Java, Bali, Lombok, and beyond. Some ensembles included multiples of four or more large *angklung* rattles tuned to a three-, four- and five-tone wide-interval scale, playing interlocking patterns accompanied by multiple small drums. At times, the ensemble would also accompany local songs, sung by young girls, or raucous mock-fighting displays performed by young boys.

Yet other *angklung kocok* ensembles incorporated large rattles and drums, as well as wooden and bamboo xylophones, double-reed instruments, dancers, clowns, and a *rengkong*—a bamboo pole carrying full rice bags that swayed and swished against the pole, creating various sound patterns. Baier concludes his survey with a basic description of the contemporary Sundanese *angklung* ensemble's character: "Trickery, spoof, mockery, and foolishness are [. . .] aspects of *angklung* performance that can be drawn from daily life. The ensemble carries with it the idea of a boisterous letting go, as if the loudness of an event in some way pulls the audience into a partnership between the performers and the purpose of the ritual" (1986:9). In Sunda, the *gamelan angklung* was and continues to be so central to life that it has become an iconic symbol of Badui identity.

Sometime in the 1930s a set of *angklung kocok* was constructed in Sunda that used a Western diatonic tuning. This became so popular throughout Indonesia, Malaysia, and other parts of peninsular Southeast Asia that it is now used, along with a chromatic set, in elementary schools and in competitions throughout the area to perform both Asian and Western songs (Perris 1971).[3] Some *angklung* sets are now hung from large horizontal poles and played by one player; and, in a recent article on new *angklung* developments, "Perkembangan (Instrument) Angklung" (2014), the author, Dinda Satya Upiah Bundi, states that from the 1990s onward, *angklung* ensembles have had a revival, with some now played by robotic technology (2014:21). Small *angklung* are now sold singly as souvenirs in tourist markets and an *angklung* decorates the back of the Indonesian 1,000-rupiah coin.

Another form of *gamelan angklung* in Java was studied by Paul Wolbers, who in his 1986 article "*Gandrung* and *Angklung* from Banyuwangi: Remnants of a Past Shared with Bali" discusses an *angklung kocok* ensemble found in the Regency of Banyuwangi, located on the eastern tip of Java. Part of the Majapahit Empire for much of its history, Banyuwangi was a lively trading center between Java and Bali, and goods flowed freely between the two islands for centuries. Wolbers describes the Banyuwangi *angklung* tradition as a lively entertainment (1986:71), highly competitive in nature, where young men showed off their musical and dancing skills. By the early twentieth century, the term *angklung* in Banyuwangi referred to both the shaken rattle and a two-octave bamboo xylophone (also called *caruk*) similar to the ancient Balinese *grantang*. The more modern *angklung* ensemble in Banyuwangi now includes both shaken *angklung* and various bronze-keyed instruments, drums, a double-reed, gongs, dancers, singers, and a two-octave bamboo xylophone; this ensemble is now called *gamelan angklung* Banyuwangi.

Wolbers states that in Bali, "the set of shaken *angklung* once played a role in the Balinese [bronze-keyed] *gamelan angklung*, which, because of its combination of bamboo and bronze idiophones, could be compared to the *angklung* orchestra from Banyuwangi" (1986:79). As further evidence for a link between these two ensembles, Wolbers cites the work of the Dutch composer Johann Sebastian Brandts Buys and his wife, who visited Banyuwangi in 1926, "where they heard an *angklung* group that was referred to as *Bali-balian* (in the Balinese way, i.e., used both bamboo rattles and bronze-keyed instruments)" (Brandts Buys 1926:207 in Wolbers 1986:78). Wolbers suggests that the ensemble known in both eastern Java and Bali as *gamelan angklung* was, at least in the 1920s and 30s, closely related despite differences in their geographic location, instrumentation, and performing contexts. It also appears that the term *gamelan angklung* had expanded in Java to include a two-octave, bamboo xylophone; thus, an ensemble called *gamelan angklung* could now mean—at least on Java—an ensemble with a set of rattles, or a bamboo xylophone, or both. It was probably this ensemble, or one like it, that McPhee saw in east Bali during the 1930s.

One final point: much of the information on the *angklung kocok* cited here comes from fieldwork done in the mid-to-late twentieth century in remote communities on Java and Bali among the Badui, living in the Province of West Java (Sunda); the Osing, from the Province of Banyu-wangi in East Java; and the Bali Aga, located primarily in the Province of Karangasem, in eastern Bali. McPhee (in the 1930s), Baier, and Wolbers (in the 1980s), and others have remarked that these communities were some-what separate linguistically, spiritually, and socially from other Javanese and Balinese peoples, in that they had all resisted, at some time in their history, religious conversion and other social changes to a certain degree, retaining many of their Indigenous, pre-Hindu, or pre-Islamic beliefs and practices. This seems to hint at the possibility that the *angklung kocok*, in its ancient form as simply a bamboo tube rattle, has become for these communities an embodiment of an older, more basic identity, and its use today in ceremonies such as rice harvesting or competitive dancing brings the hazy distant past to a living, performing present.

A Possible History for the *Gamelan Angklung* Cremation Ensemble

If we examine all the information presented thus far on the Balinese bronze-keyed *gamelan angklung* that is the focus of this book, we can immediately see many ways to construct differently intertwined histories. First, we must untangle some of the threads of this research by making a clearer distinction between the term *angklung*, referring *only* to the shaken bamboo rattle, and *gamelan angklung*, the term used here to refer to at least five distinct Indonesian ensembles and musics today, some of which were discussed in chapter 2.

Based on the research, the five different ensembles are as follows: (1) an ensemble of multiple bamboo *angklung kocok* and small drums, still found today in Sunda (west Java) and used for rice planting and harvesting; (2) an ensemble with multiple *angklung kocok*, a core set of bronze instru-ments, and a variety of other bronze, wood, and bamboo instruments found throughout Java and used for a variety of ceremonies; (3) an ensemble of multiple *angklung kocok* used since the 1930s throughout Indonesia and Malaysia, tuned to the Western diatonic and chromatic scales; (4) an ensemble with a core set of bronze instruments and any or all of the instruments mentioned above—but *without angklung rattles*, found today in Bali and used in a variety of ceremonies and secular entertainments; and (5) an ensemble with a core set of bronze instruments alone and *no angklung kocok*, found in southern and central Bali and used specifically for cremations. The fifth ensemble is the one of concern here.

A possible history thus emerges, one with many gaps to be sure, but plausible, given what we know so far. Other histories may also be plausible, but with an absence of documentation, all histories continue to remain largely in the realm of speculation. The bamboo *angklung kocok* probably originated in Sunda, possibly as early as 600 CE, as a musical instrument used in rice planting and harvesting ceremonies to entertain the goddess of rice and her children, thus ensuring a plentiful rice crop for the village. Over the centuries, the rattles spread throughout Southeast Asia, including Bali, perhaps expanding into large ensembles including supporting bamboo and bronze instruments and adding new performance contexts such as weddings, cremations, temple festivals, and youthful competitions.

At this point (c. 1000 CE?) these ensembles were probably known in Java as *gamelan angklung* as they still retained the shaken rattle. In the case of the Osing in Banyuwangi (East Java), a two-octave xylophone called *angklung Banyuwangi* now existed as a defining feature. We do not know for certain when the *angklung kocok* arrived in Bali, whether it formed an ensemble, as in Sunda, or was attached to an already existing Indigenous ensemble used in rice planting or harvesting ceremonies, or for cremations.

It was not until the end of the nineteenth century that travelers and scholars, mostly from Holland and Central Europe, such as Raffles, quoted at the beginning of chapter 3, noticed and wrote about these ensembles with a certain consistency. Stating that they still contained actual bamboo *angklung kocok* and played older rice-related music, Raffles observed that these ensembles were becoming more and more scarce and now were associated only with more remote communities that had resisted much of the cultural and ritual changes brought about by the spread of Hinduism, Buddhism, and Islam throughout the archipelago. At the same time, other ensembles still containing *angklung kocok* were flourishing in more secularized contexts, such as competitions and various early tourist venues.

In the 1930s, the *angklung kocok* seems to have had a revival with the change in tuning from the almost exclusive use of four- (in Bali) and five- (in Java) tone, wide-interval scales (by then called *slendro* in some places) to the Western diatonic, and later, the chromatic scales, where it became a vehicle for teaching simple Western-derived songs to schoolchildren throughout Southeast Asia. By the time Kunst, McPhee, and Schlager were working (the 1920s to the 40s), the *gamelan angklung* found in Bali and used for cremations now consisted of a small, core set of bronze instruments and still retained its original name, but no longer contained the rattles themselves, except in remote villages in Karangasem.

By the 1960s, two versions of this basic cremation ensemble existed in Bali: a northern ensemble with an expanded core of instruments, now tuned to a full five-tone *slendro* scale, and a southcentral *gamelan* with its original small core of instruments that retained its older four-tone *saih angklung*. This ensemble, adding larger drums, *ceng-ceng kopyak*, and other instruments, began to appear in more secularized contexts, playing adopted and adapted musics. Today, as we saw in chapter 2, many kinds of *gamelan angklung* ensembles exist in Bali, but only the small, core ensemble, without the shaken rattle, and its unique repertoire is used for village cremations.

The *gamelan angklung* of *banjar* Baturiti, Taman Sari, according to its current leaders, originated in the 1930s; and, from its beginning, the *gending* contained contrasting sections, the first two of which were, and still are, called *pemungkah* and *pengawak*. (See chapter 6 for more on this group.) These names were documented by McPhee in Sidan in the 1930s and Herbst in 2010. The original musician who first taught the men of Baturiti was from Denpasar, about halfway between Sidan and Kerambitan (roughly an eighteen-mile trek; see the map on page 14). Although traveling such distances was difficult in the 1930s, it is entirely possible that many of the *gending*, as well as their metaphoric sectional names, were known and used by the teacher in Denpasar and brought to Kerambitan. This could account for a general similarity of styles and naming found in the southcentral part of the island today.

Given this narrative, it appears that the bronze-keyed ensemble and the music used today for cremations in southcentral Bali developed from its associations with many ancient ensembles and performance contexts that predate the beginnings of modern Balinese history. Imbued with a certain celebratory spirit, yet used in the bittersweet context of death and loss, *gamelan angklung* cremation music provides a unique combination of lightness, sweetness, and sadness.

CHAPTER 5

Work for the Dead

From the beginning of my fieldwork, I realized that although I thought what we were performing at cremations was music, the men I played with did not see it as such. I had come to Bali after having played *gamelan* music for many years and had been trained throughout my life to understand certain structured sounds as music. The men I worked with—mainly farmers, builders, and *warung* (eatery) owners—understood that the sounds they made were "musical," in that they took the form of music, but what they were performing was not music, it was *dharma*—religious obligations to family, community, and ancestral deities based on unwavering and predestined laws. This was necessary for preserving order (*dharma*) at a time when not doing so could easily result in cosmic chaos (*adharma*).

Cremation was essential because it began the process of *samsara*, the Hindu cycle of death and rebirth, by freeing the soul from its body, purifying it through burning, and sending it on its path to the spiritual realm, eventually to return in a new material body. Rather than seeing their part in the cremation ritual as an artistic performance, the men of *gamelan angklung* Taman Sari regarded what they were doing as an essential responsibility, a primary obligation, one of many that assured that their position in a complex but interconnected cosmos remained fixed in its rightful place. In this chapter, we examine *gamelan angklung*, its music, and its presence at cremations from the perspective of *dharma*, that all-encompassing concept of social order and personal behavior that underlies the practices of Hinduism and Buddhism in Bali today. Let's begin with a brief return to the discussion of *dharma*.

Most researchers who study Hindu and Buddhist practices in Bali note that there is no adequate word in English that encompasses all aspects of *dharma*. Austin B. Creel, for example, writes: "*Dharma* refers to what one should do and why one should do it. *Dharma* means laws . . . enjoined patterns of behavior, but as Daniel M. Brown notes, 'dharma is more than particular laws, for it is what underlies law and creates law in the universe'" (Brown 1953:15 in Creel 1972:155). John Brockington, in his article "The Concept of 'Dharma' in the Rāmāyana," traces the meaning of *dharma* from its appearance in the Indian epic where it signified "tradition, especially family customs" (2004:655) to the present where it is more associated with religious practice and ethical behavior (2004:689–90). This change can be seen most clearly in Bali with the recent renaming of Balinese Hinduism to Agama Hindu Dharma, as discussed in chapter 1.

Dharma also carries with it the notion of specific time, place, and social identity, as illustrated in the well-known story of Arjuna and Krishna in the *Bhagavad-Gita*, a book within the Indian epic the *Mahabharata*. Arjuna balks at the idea of killing during war while Krishna argues that if Arjuna's *dharma* (his essence, his law) is that of the warrior, he must perform a warrior's right action (*karma*)—killing. Krishna further urges Arjuna to separate his predestined actions from his personal feelings about killing so that his rightful *dharma* can be acted upon and his caste position maintained. As Fred Eiseman writes, "Caste is the social codification of *dharma*. Caste lies outside, or perhaps deeper than political organization by governments" (vol. 1, 1990:24). Thus, people of different eras, social positions, genders, ages, and so on, have different *dharmic* obligations. *Dharma* is thus the essence of a specific individual living at a specific time and place, as well as the underlying essence of cosmic law that holds an individual, a group, and the universe together.

The cremation of a body upon death is one of the first of many *dharmic* obligations that must be performed to ensure that the soul travels on its path to reincarnation. A cremation in Bali is public—often playful, even raucous—involving the extended family, *banjar*, and village. For cremations among wealthy or royal families today, tourist buses often arrive with hundreds of visitors to observe and participate in the celebration. Other pre- and post-cremation stages involve more private and intimate family obligations, such as washing the corpse, holding a séance with a *balian* (local healer, spirit medium), taking offerings to the gods of major temples in the village, and constructing effigies that will ultimately reside with other spirits in the family shrine (*sanggah*) as deified ancestors. Each of these obligations is done to both purify and elevate the deceased's soul/spirit, as well as to strengthen the connections between the still-living, the deceased, the spirit world, and the new bodily materialization to come. "In reincarnation, the spirit ancestor reunites with the living through the grandchildren—children do this for their parents, and the deceased parents do this for their children's children—a complete system of reciprocity" (Hornbacher 2014:248).

What Happens at a Cremation?

A cremation in Bali usually involves three essential stages: preparation for burning the corpse (or its unearthed remains), the cremation itself, and the casting of remaining ashes into the sea. This process can last anywhere from a few weeks to decades. Below is a diagram showing some of the many activities involved in these three stages that would be enacted for a member of the *sudra* caste (about 90 percent of the population). Periods where our *gamelan angklung* would play are set in bold type. This list is not meant to be exhaustive, nor does it reflect any one individual family or community, but it does outline the basic activities expected of the still-living upon the death of a family member.

DIAGRAM 5.1 Cremation stages[1]

FIRST STAGE: Pre-Cremation
(Pre-cremation takes from one week to many years to accomplish, depending on family resources.)

A. Death

1. body washed and covered with oil or sandalwood paste;
2. body wrapped in white cloth;
3. effigy made, covered with coins and mirrors, and put on the chest of body;
4. body and effigy moved outside and blessed by priest;
5. many offerings made;
6. body moved Inside;
7. if not cremated immediately, body is wrapped in cloth and buried in *kuburan* (cemetery);
8. effigy washed and blessed;
9. effigy put in family shrine;

B. When ready to cremate (sometimes months or years later)

10. family seeks advice from *balian* (spirit medium) and holds séance;
11. family seeks advice on propitious day to hold cremation;
12. date is chosen;
13. family goes to *kuburan* and digs up what's left of the buried body;
14. family puts the body's remains in the shrine with effigy;
15. extended family, *banjar* members, neighbors start to help with offerings and food;

C. Three or more days before cremation

16. preparations accelerate;
17. **various *gamelan* hired to play around the clock at the home of the deceased;**
18. visits to the home compound begin;
19. men of the family start building the tower (*wadah*) and platform that will carry the corpse to the cemetery;

(continued)

DIAGRAM 5.1 (continued)

___

SECOND STAGE: Cremation Day

D. Morning of cremation (movement from compound to *kuburan*)

   20. *wadah* and platform completed;
   21. **gamelan angklung plays while family and village assemble;**
   22. body brought out of house and placed inside *wadah*;
   23. procession forms, with all holding a long piece of white cloth;
   24. **gamelan angklung splits; *réong* and *kempur* join with *ceng-ceng kopyak* (large hand cymbals) to form *beleganjur* ensemble; others go to the *kuburan* by truck;**
   25. procession to *kuburan*; carriers twirl the *wadah* and rotate around the field three times before settling near the center;[2]

E. Cremation ceremony

   26. people reassemble at *kuburan*, priest intones prayers;
   27. *wadah* arrives with body;
   28. priest blesses corpse with holy water; an effigy and offerings of flowers, money, clothing, pictures, incense, etc., placed on the body;
   29. **gamelan angklung reassembles and plays through the covering and burning of the corpse;**
   30. corpse is covered in white cloth and transferred to the pyre where it is burned;
   31. ashes collected;

THIRD STAGE: Post-Cremation
(Post-cremation takes place two or three weeks to decades later.)

   32. effigies made with ashes from the cremation, washed and blessed by priest at a *pancoran* (place where pure water flows);
   33. family goes to important temples in the village to make sure ashes are acceptable to higher gods;
   34. family casts the now purified ashes into the sea (or river); **angklung *réong*, *kempur*, and *ceng-ceng kopyak* play in beleganjur style;**
   35. holy water (sea water with ashes) taken back from the sea;
   36. family listens for the sounds of waves, which ensure that the spirit of the deceased has become purer;

F. Twelve or so days after cremation

   37. *nyekah*: effigies cremated to purify and elevate the spirit even further;
   38. ashes put in family shrine (*sanggah*) with ashes of other ancestral deities, and are tended to daily until time for rebirth, which can occur years or decades later;

G. Every year after death

   39. reunions with the dead on *Galungan* (once every 210 days) when souls are invited to earth for ten days to clear up any remaining issues with the still-living.

___

1. This chart is a distillation of many descriptions of Balinese *ngabén* found in the literature as well as observations based on my own experience. See especially Connor 1986, 1995; Warren 1996; Eiseman 1990.
2. Much has been written about the construction of large animal sarcophagi (for the wealthy and upper caste) and the twirling of the *wadah* through the village roads and at the cremation site. See especially Bakan 1999 for a complete description.

As a member of the *sekehe gamelan angklung* Taman Sari, I participated in over twenty-five cremations, most of which were held for Balinese *sudra*. Two cremations were held for the wives of former rajas (*kshatriya*); these occurred shortly after their death—more common for the wealthy and those of the Brahmin caste, so an actual corpse was immolated. I also observed a mass cremation, a ceremony held every thirty years, but our group did not play.

In most of the *sudra* cremations I witnessed, the deceased had died months (perhaps years) earlier and had been buried in a shallow grave at the *kuburan* until the considerable amount of money needed to hold a cremation was amassed (around US$5,000-$10,000 in 2008). What follows is a brief description of the bolded events in the diagram (numbers 17, 21, 24, and 29) that shows the contexts for *gamelan angklung* performances in which I participated or observed as a member of the *sekehe*. We revisit this in chapter 9, with further detail about the musical choices made during this time. I begin with a description of the importance of preparing for a cremation, as outlined in the first of the three stages.

Preparing for a cremation involves the entire community and serves to link the still-living family members and neighbors to each other, as well as to their territorial ancestral deities through the circle of reciprocity. "[T]he relationship between the living and the dead is one of mutual dependence. The living depend for their welfare on the dead, who have the power to curse, while the deceased rely on their surviving kin for successful apotheosis through the cremation and subsequent purification ceremonies" (Connor 1995:349). This connection between family, community, place, and deified ancestors creates a powerful solidarity (*patus*) that defines both individual and community identity. "*Patus* signifies the essence of community solidarity and mutual obligation. 'If you do not give *patus*, it means you are not bound (*iket*) together. *Patus* is what holds us all, the rope that is strongest. You could call it the fundamental law'" (Dewa Dani 1984 in Warren 1996).

How do preparations for a cremation begin? Upon death, the body is initially wrapped in cloth and laid in an enclosed area of the family compound where it may be covered in sandalwood paste and packed in ice or a preserving liquid such as formalin (Connor 1995). When a cremation is delayed, the remains of the body stay buried at the *kuburan* until the time comes for the cremation ceremony. An effigy—a stylized, fan-shaped figure representing the deceased—is constructed using artifacts belonging to the deceased (sometimes also coins and mirrors), and initially placed on the chest of the corpse, considered a spiritually significant part of the body, and then in a family shrine.

Once the body—considered an outward shell—is buried, it is the effigy that comes to symbolize the deceased's soul, the body having been successfully separated from its earthly existence. "Where the death and the immolation are separated by more than a few days, the remains of the effigy undergo another pre-cremation washing, which is more critical than the washing and enshrouding just after death, in that it prepares the now more purified person-spirit for the 'crossing over' into the realm of death" (Connor 1995:543).

Once preparations begin, they usually follow a similar plan: the remains and effigy are wrapped in white cloth and moved to an open area, where they are blessed with holy water by a priest, then taken back inside. Various offerings are made and family and *banjar* members who live away from the community begin to return home, bringing offerings of rice, coffee, and white cloth. Days before the cremation, the family begins preparing the enormous amounts of food that will be served to all visitors who come by to sit with and distract the bereaved. During this period the family usually hires one or more *gamelan* to play for visitors, and for the cremation itself. *Gamelan angklung, gambang, gamelan gender,* and other ensembles could, and often are, hired but *gamelan angklung* is the one usually deemed most desirable.

During the time I lived in Bali, Taman Sari was in high demand. I would be notified of an upcoming ceremony by one of the men in the group a day or so before, and I would be told when to meet the others at the *balé banjar* where the instruments were stored. Sometimes, especially in the early morning, my friend Nyoman—a young man who had inherited his place in the *gamelan* from his grandfather and father—would pick me up in his truck. Once at the *balé*, we (humans and instruments) would be blessed by the local priest (*pemungku*, who was also a member of our group), gather up the instruments, load them onto the back of Nyoman's open-bed truck, and drive to the *kuburan*.

If we had been hired to play in the evening before the actual cremation day, we would bring the instruments inside and set them up in a room near the home shrine, which now held the deceased's effigy. The priest would bless the *kempur* (medium-sized gong), and we would begin. At times, other ensembles would also be present, and we would play simultaneously in different parts of the compound. It was explained to me that the other *gamelan* were needed to "clear a path" for the sounds of the *gamelan angklung,* which were directed specifically at the deceased as well as the deceased's family (Interview, Nyoman Suadin, May 6, 2022).

I was also told that the bustling activities and sounds would help confuse the malevolent spirits that hovered around us. This would also help protect the remains as well as the visitors from harm. Women, and some men, would be preparing food, while other men would be sitting around gambling to pass the time—an activity largely frowned upon by the local police, but usually ignored at the time of a cremation. We would play, stopping every forty-five minutes or so for coffee and food—beautiful little rice cakes, or more substantial food, such as *gado-gado* (cutup vegetables and eggs, with peanut sauce). These breaks, like ones for a jazz combo in the West, were stipulated in a written contract that the head of Taman Sari and the head of the deceased's family had signed, and a lot of complaining was registered if they were not provided.

It was during these times that I became aware of the *sekehe*'s practice of learning while performing. As mentioned earlier, pieces would start that I did not know (i.e., were not part of the fifteen core *gending*). At times my partner, Pak Debet, would have some idea of what was happening, and I would follow him. At other times, he, as well as most of the others, would have no idea what to play and would listen carefully to the *ugal* player, laughing, talking, making mistakes, and generally fooling around until they caught on—usually after two or three attempts. Of course, I took much longer to catch on and was frequently the butt of good-natured joking. I initially called these "mystery pieces"; by the time I left, I had collected over thirty of them. Here is an entry from my diary from when I first realized what was happening.

October 14, 2007: Mystery Piece

Last night, from about 7:30–12:30, we played at a home compound. For some reason, the ugal *began playing a piece I didn't know and had never heard, and was new, even to the players themselves! This precremation ceremony was held at a home just behind the* balé banjar, *so we all walked there in the dark (precipitous paths, pitch blackness, no moon, or stars, slightly raining, path filled with obstructions, etc.). We set up outside, but the amplified singing and praying from inside the house was so loud we couldn't all hear each other, so there was a lot of jostling and shifting around. And it started to sprinkle on us a bit, so there was even more shifting.*

Anyway, there were lots of screwups, missed gongs, a whole section got lopped off because my partner didn't hear the right cue and I didn't know the piece; lots of laughing and good-natured goofing off. What was most interesting was that the guys sort of saw this as an opportunity to learn a new piece. When we made a lot of mistakes, for example, the ugal *would make us repeat the section a few times to get it better, like at a rehearsal (which they don't ever have), and there was some repetition of sections throughout the evening. Even during the long breaks, the* ugal, *Pak Rideng, and a few others, were learning new material from anyone who knew it.*

On the morning of a cremation, our *gamelan* would play outside the compound in anticipation of the arrival of deceased's effigy and remains that would be brought out into the open, while the men of the family and various helpers put finishing touches on the tower (*wadah*) and platform that would carry the corpse to the *kuburan*. During this time, members of the family and village would arrive to prepare for the procession. An atmosphere of busyness and excitement would surround these activities, reaching a peak when the tower and platform were lifted onto bamboo poles to be carried by family members to the *kuburan*.

At this point, the crowd would begin merging into a line, and our *gamelan* would separate into two groups: performers of the four-keyed instruments (including me), who would scoop them up and put them onto the truck, and the *réong* and *kempur* players, who would take one of their two pots and give the other to a partner. The now eight men playing the *réong* would join the drummers and gong players who had gathered to form a *gamelan beleganjur*—the loud, percussive ensemble that traditionally accompanies the body to the *kuburan*. The rest of the village would follow, each person holding a portion of a long bolt of white cloth, slowly weaving a path through the village. Meanwhile, we on the truck would drive to the site with the other instruments, set them up under the large banyan tree, and wait for the procession to arrive.

Prayers, offerings, and the immolation itself usually took a relatively short time to accomplish—often two or three hours. During this time, we would play a forty-five-minute set, take our break, then continue, playing a combination of sections from the core repertoire, as well as learning and practicing the new "mystery pieces." When the *ugal* cued "Jaran Nginjek" ("Runaway Horse"), number fifteen in the core *gending* (see Diagram 7.1 in chapter 7), we knew this was the last piece we would play. Essentially a long *kotekan ubit empat*, the *ugal* and *rincik* players would push us to an almost unplayable tempo and we would finish with a flourish of our *panggul* to signal the end.

Post-cremation ceremonies, which involve casting the remaining ashes into the sea (or any convenient natural water source), might or might not involve a full *gamelan angklung*. I attended one such ceremony, not as a performer, but as a member of the *sekehe*, where I watched, along with hundreds of other families and *banjar* members, a *gamelan beleganjur* escort the ashes to the water. The eight *réong* players, as well as the gong player in our *sekehe*, who had been a part of the procession to the *kuburan*, were now, weeks later, performing their final obligation to the deceased.

The Goals of Cremation: Purification and Elevation

Cremation in Bali is essentially about purification and elevation, two processes that must occur for the soul to safely travel from death to rebirth. Many of the activities referred to in the diagram above relate to these two processes. First, the body (or its effigy) must be purified with water and fire. This is believed to free the material body, elevating it not only from its earthly shell, but also from any leftover emotional attachments or unresolved resentments the person might have accrued during his or her lifetime. For example, item number 10 in Diagram 5.1 above refers to the practice of family members enlisting the help of a *balian* (spirit medium) to make sure that the spirit of the deceased is not angry with the family or that someone has not made a mistake in carrying out the first few activities after death.

Frequently, a séance is held, during which a medium confers with the still-hovering spirit of the deceased on behalf of the family and, speaking in the voice of the deceased, addresses any problems that might hinder the spirit's journey. Anthropologist Linda Connor and filmmakers Patsy Asch and Timothy Asch have studied this phenomenon extensively, collaborating on a series of DVDs that document these activities.[1] Working closely with a well-known Balinese medium, Jero Tapakan, who lived in Central Bali in the last half of the twentieth century, they documented, among other events, a family's visit to Ibu Tapakan and the ensuing séance. Here is a summary of that visit, taken from the film:

> The client's young son had recently died from typhoid (the doctor's diagnosis), but during the séance, the boy's spirit revealed, through the voice of the medium, that a female relative had been responsible for his death, through the practice of witchcraft. The boy's father confirmed this, citing evidence of the relative's jealousy over his newly prosperous household. The boy's spirit told the father to make many offerings to him (the son) so that he could take revenge on the offending relative. The father complied and was later gratified to learn that the relative had taken ill and had suffered injuries from a fall down a ravine (*Releasing the Spirits* 1991).

In working with the medium in the context of a possession séance, the family was able to both appease the boy's spirit and enable it to exact the proper revenge on the offending relative. Through this process, the boy's spirit was both purified—cleansed from any remaining earthly bad magic—and elevated—freed from the weight of its earthly responsibilities, and thus able to exact revenge without consequences. This having been done, the family was now able to resume preparations for cremation.

Purification and elevation also extend outward to others directly involved in cremation activities, such as those who touch a body or effigy, or those who are involved with cremation rituals. Anyone could inadvertently pick up something evil and carry it home, possibly contaminating the family or the compound. So, as part of a Balinese family, I was expected to engage in ritual washing when I returned home from a cremation event. All Balinese take at least two showers a day, one in the morning when they wake up and the other in the late afternoon before eating the final meal of the day. However, if one has participated in a cremation, further washing is required. Here is what I was told to do: Upon returning home from performing with Taman Sari at a cremation, I immediately had to fill a cup or a pot with water and toss it high onto the kitchen roof, taking a small handful of the dripping water and rubbing it into my hair. Then, I was to go take a long shower, washing all parts of my body thoroughly, especially my hair, because that was where evil spirits hid (Interview, Nyoman Suadin, June 4, 2007). I was further cautioned by many people about eating during the *gamelan*'s breaks. It was generally thought, especially if the deceased was not a member of one's *banjar*, that there was a significant possibility that he or she had been poisoned or had succumbed to a lethal form of witchcraft. Therefore, any food served at the deceased's compound could also be poisoned or somehow contaminated—so best not to eat, unless the leaders of the *gamelan* gave me the food (I did not always follow this advice).

Many other events in Diagram 5.1 indicate that obligations involving purification and elevation must be carried out many times and over many years. Recurring events include those in the First Stage involving the placing of effigies, bodily remains, and/or ashes in the family shrine. These activities further cleanse and elevate the soul to a higher and purer state. Completing the activities in the Third Stage signals that the deceased's remains are sufficiently spiritualized and etherealized to have been successful in reaching the status of deified ancestor. At this point, whatever is left is put in its final resting place—the home shrine where it joins with other deified ancestral spirits, to be consulted and attended to during the rest of the journey to rebirth.

Necessary Dyads

Many scholars have commented on aspects of Balinese cremations that seem at odds with Western conceptions of death, grief, possession, and pageantry, and it is beyond the scope of this book to go into detail on these discussions.[2] However, there are two important aspects of Balinese cremations that relate more directly to our study of *gamelan angklung*, its history, its necessary presence at a cremation, and the appropriate public performance of emotions such as grief. These relate to the dual realities that many Balinese live by: *sekala* (the seen world) and *niskala* (the unseen world), and to appropriate public behaviors alluded to above: *ramé* (busyness) and *sepi* (quietness, emptiness) that guide much of Balinese ceremonial and emotional life. These necessary dyads enable the immutable *dharmic* laws that hold the Balinese universe in place to be fulfilled with both good intentions and good outcomes.

Sekala and *Niskala*: Seen and Unseen Worlds

The Balinese universe is dependent upon the interaction between positive and negative forces, some that can be seen (*sekala*) and others that are unseen (*niskala*). "*Sekala* means what you can sense—see, hear, smell, and touch. *Niskala* involves that which cannot be sensed directly, but which can only be felt within. *Niskala* is a very personal matter, often difficult to articulate or, in some cases, hazardous to do so" (Eiseman vol. 1, 1990:127). Eiseman states that the Balinese are constantly aware of *niskala*, and "a major portion of their thinking and activities revolve around the existence of these forces and how they can best control and adjust to them" (vol. 1, 1990:127–28).

Both seen and unseen forces are responsible for individual, group, and cosmic imbalances, and only offerings and ceremonial performances such as cremations and *odalan* (temple festivals) can restore them to order. Five ritual categories (*panca yadnya*) exist to ensure that the proper balance between them is maintained: *dewa yadnya* (for deities); *bhuta yadnya* (for spirits and demons); *resi yadnya* (for the consecration of priests); *manusa yadnya* (for rituals associated with human life, such as those for childbirth, tooth-filings, and weddings); and *pitra yadnya* (for death, cremation, and reincarnation) (Vitale 2014:4). These rituals of devotion and offering, inherited from early Vedic practice, are still central to Balinese life today and, as we saw above, they connect the living with the dead in an ongoing circle.

Who inhabits the universe and what forces account for situations that are out of balance? Seen and unseen beings comprise five different, yet overlapping categories, arranged in order of sacredness: gods (highest, unseen); humans (seen); animals (seen); witches (*leyak*, seen and unseen); and demons (*bhuta*, sometimes *kala*, unseen). *Bhuta* are normal evil influences, responsible for lesser, noncatastrophic events, such as tripping at a crossroad or causing a computer crash (see my story below). These can be placated with small, positive offerings, such as rice or flowers, which contain high amounts of *sakti* (positive energy). Eiseman writes, "[Evil forces] are around all the time, and one cannot say when and where they might penetrate a weak spot and cause problems. The result is that offerings are made to just about everything imaginable" (vol. 1, 1990:133).[3] Even musical instruments, especially the gong, are regularly presented with small offerings before a performance. Below is an excerpt from my diary relating my own personal dealings with unseen forces.

"At the Pancoran," reconstructed from my diary entries of April 4–8, 2008

This morning I woke up to a message on my computer: "You have run out of storage space. Please transfer files." I had prepared for this, having brought many blank discs with me. What I was not prepared for was that, in transferring my files, I inadvertently deleted them! Yes—all the work I had done over the year was gone within an hour! Writing about this now cannot begin to get at the incredibly frightening, dismaying, sinking feeling I had when I realized this. I won't go into all the unpleasant details here, except to say that eventually—many days later—I recovered most of them. But at the time I was beside myself and spent the day desperately hunting for files.

By the end of that day, I was a total mess! Knowing that displaying emotions like anger, sadness, and frustration openly is not considered seemly in Bali, I decided to take a walk by myself to calm down (a practice also not common in Bali). The sun was setting, and I headed to the local pancoran, *a beautiful area with a natural spring that is considered spiritually pure. I had come here before in times of stress, and knew that if I sat here for a while, I would feel better. On the way, I said hello to one of my neighbors who had just left the* pancoran *after taking his afternoon shower and was on his way home.*

I sat quietly for about a half an hour and watched the sunset. I felt a little better and I started heading home. I passed Nyoman's parents' house and Ibu (his mom) was sitting outside on her stoop—unusual. She took one look at me, then jumped up and started saying something about Men Iluh and a flashlight. I had no idea why she was so excited. I walked up to Nyoman's house and through the gate. Men Iluh took one look at me and burst into tears! What?! She had never done this—what was wrong? She was visibly frightened and tried to hide her face, but she couldn't stop crying. I reassured her that I was okay and that I had only gone to the pancoran *to sit quietly for a while.*

Then I heard the whole story: The neighbor I saw leaving the pan-coran was so frightened and worried about me being alone in the dark that he ran over to Ibu's house and told everyone within hearing distance (quite a few people) that I was there; Ibu ran to Nyoman's house to find a flashlight and to get Men Iluh to come find me. But the batteries were dead and Men Iluh couldn't find any new ones, so she just sat there getting worried. When I finally showed up, she was so upset that she lost it. She told me that the pancoran, *like the* kuburan (graveyard), *is a really scary place, especially when it's dark. That's when the "other world" takes over, when the bad spirits come out to get you, and where black magic works. No sane person would stay at the* pancoran *alone at night without a light! This is physically and spiritually very danger-ous. I told Men Iluh that I was fine and that I wasn't afraid, and that although I understood her worries, I didn't actually believe in evil spir-its (uh-oh—bad ethno-moment), and that at home in Rochester I walk around all the time alone at night and nothing happens. She cried out, "Of course nothing happens! The spirits don't live in Rochester—they live here in Bali, and this is very dangerous!"*

The next morning and for the next four days, I was sick with "tummy trouble." I thought carefully about what I had eaten over the past few days. For the most part, I was eating and drinking the same things I ate and drank every day. But then I began to consider the possibility that my trip to the pancoran *had precipitated this. (I reasoned, "I don't know everything—maybe there really are evil spirits?") So, I went into the kitchen where Men Iluh was, and asked her, "Is it possible that I am sick because I went to the* pancoran *the other night all alone in the dark?" She laughed and said, "No—more likely that you ate something bad." (She is used to Americans asking crazy questions.) "But," I replied, "I'm eating the same things I always eat, so why am I sick now? You know, maybe I should take an offering over to the* pancoran *and ask the spirits to forgive me for offending them." "Good idea," she said, still looking skeptical.*

So, a few days later, in the late afternoon, Men Iluh and I put on our kains *and went to the* pancoran. *She was carrying a tray with many small and exquisitely beautiful offerings and some sticks of incense. We arrived and there was no one there. Men Iluh carefully scooped some water out of the wellspring and began the rituals. She went to nine separate places within the area, all the way to the very top, and repeated the same prayers, leaving one of the offerings in each (with incense). Every time she said a prayer, I took a piece of a flower and held it up to my forehead with my thumbs in the traditional prayer gesture. It was quite serious and—needless to say—I woke up the next morning completely cured!*

Leyak (witches), on the other hand, are more serious negative forces. The word *leyak* refers to both black magic (i.e., the negative use of *sakti*) and to the person who practices it. It is the only category of beings in the Balinese cosmology that are both seen and unseen. Witches emerge at night, taking over the bodies of ordinary, sleeping people. The *leyak* often changes form, turning into an animal, and wanders around, causing damage that can be seen, such as destroying crops, poisoning, eating babies, and causing illness or death (Eiseman vol. 1, 1990:135). *Leyak* frequently hide at crossroads, and visit natural springs and graveyards. More substantial offerings and ceremonies must be offered to protect against *leyak*. At times, a person afflicted by an illness believed to have been caused by a *leyak* will consult a *balian* for help, as we saw above in the story of the young boy who had died. Thus, *niskala* must always be respected to ensure that good and evil "can exist in dynamic equilibrium, so that neither gets the upper hand" (vol. 1, 1990:135).

Ramé and *Sepi*: Contexts for Living

Ramé and *sepi* are terms Balinese use to describe the basic feeling, or ambiance, of social situations. *Ramé*, usually defined as busyness, is a "desirable attribute of gatherings in the public sphere, such as marketplaces, shopping malls, movie theatres, and ceremonies. What may be unpleasantly crowded for a western visitor is often *ramé* for a Balinese companion" (Connor 1995:559). As Lisa Gold writes, "[T]he sense of ramé is of utmost importance: sonic spaces are filled with sound, physical space with people and movement, the air with incense, and the present with references to Bali's past" (2005:77). *Sepi*, on the other hand, describes an empty atmosphere of "quiet rest, if not boredom" (Hobart and Pujawati 2020:9).

Ramé and *sepi*, however, do not describe individual or personal feelings, "but rather [are] applied to certain social milieux. People participating in a context that is *ramé* are likely to describe their personal feelings as 'cheerful' or 'happy'" (Connor 1995:550). Those participating in a *sepi* situation are not necessarily sad but may become so if, in their quietness and introspection, they "think too much," that is, go so deeply into themselves that they lose conscious awareness of their surroundings and its potential dangers.

Unni Wikan, who has studied the emotional lives of Balinese, writes: "Sadness is linked with a complex array of concerns pertaining to magic or sorcery, morality, health, social compassion, self-esteem, and social control" (1990:22). *Sepi* attracts, but does not cause, sadness; it also attracts witches and demons, who prefer quiet places. "The sad fact of the world is that black magic abounds in ingenious forms, yet one must try not to feel-think about the matter. Thinking would create fear, and fear undermines the spiritual energy (*bayu*) needed to persevere and resist actual onslaught" (1990:87–88). Wikan highlights the common human state of brooding, of focusing too much on one's problems when one is sad, which can result in feelings of fear, vulnerability, or anger—states that can lead to various forms of bad behavior, illness, or communal harm.

Cremations, as we know, are often public, even commodified events. Work for the dead, especially that surrounding group preparations and procession to the graveyard; the twirling of the *wadah*; the simultaneity of sounds, sights, and smells at the *kuburan*; and the laughing, shouting, and occasional mock-fighting of the participants all suggest an atmosphere of abundant *ramé*. Michael Bakan, in his work on *beleganjur* (1999, 2016), the ensemble that proceeds with the body to the *kubaran*, describes the crucial importance of *ramé* at a cremation: often "generated by the cacophony of many *gamelan* playing simultaneously, *ramé* not only confuses the spirits but also strengthens the men who carry the *wadah* (1999:70)."

In such an atmosphere, weeping is generally discouraged, as sadness will spread and erode the wellbeing of the community (Wikan 1990:170). Distractions before and during cremations help the family to not give in to sadness: "It is bad if we express our sadness, for everyone will see and be sad and perhaps crying, too. It will be bad for all and very dangerous" (1990:147). Wikan further asserts that although Balinese, like all humans, feel sadness, what is problematic is thinking and acting on these feelings in public. She writes, "Balinese do not recognize feeling (*perasaan*) to be distinct from thought (*pikiran*), but regard both as aspects of one integral process—*keneh*—which is best translated as feeling-thought [and] both are in the realm of awareness" (1990:35).

Therefore, during a cremation, where one may be feeling sadness, it is crucial to "manage your heart" (*ngabe keneh*), that is, not to act on these feelings, but rather to distract yourself with positive thoughts for your family and community and for the spirit of the deceased. Thus, for the Balinese, a cremation is far more than a ceremony marking the death of a loved one. It is a multisensory event within a context of heightened emotions, wariness, and ambiguity, where succumbing to any intense emotion can have serious consequences. We revisit *ramé* and *sepi* in chapter 9, with a deeper discussion of both musical and social performance at a cremation.

CHAPTER 6

Work for the Community

The men of *sekehe gamelan angklung* Taman Sari consider the instruments of their ensemble and the music they play for cremations to belong solely to them. This sense of ownership is imbued with ideas about family, place, and groupness, essential elements in the concept of *dharma*. This chapter examines the central importance of these ideas in the face of the changing social and musical landscapes of the twenty-first century. We begin with the origins of the group, the ensemble, and the music, as a thrice-told tale.

Origin Stories

Origin stories, like myths, relate the essences, if not specific truths, of stories, as believed by the people who tell them. During my fieldwork in *banjar* Baturiti I heard three different versions of the origin of *sekehe gamelan angklung* Taman Sari. Rather than choose one to be the "real truth" (as in the Western sense of provable by evidence), I present all three and regard them, despite their differences, as all true in the sense that they all carry not only the truths as understood by their tellers, but also the truths of the fixed social, religious, and cultural positions their tellers occupy in the *dharma* of contemporary life.

The Paks' Story

The three leaders of the *sekehe*, Pak Rideng (head), Pak Wayan (secretary), and Pak Ketut (public relations) sat with me over many days relating their understanding of the origins of the group. Also present were two other players, Pak Marwi (sometime *ugal*) and Pak Madia (*ceng-ceng*), acknowledged by all to be the best performers in that they knew all the music and had been a part of the group since its early days. Here is a summary of this conversation:

The story of *banjar* Baturiti's *sekehe angklung* begins in 1922, when a group of men came together to form a cohort responsible for planting and harvesting rice. They worked successfully for three years, each year equally dividing the various tasks. After a time, they began to realize that they liked working together, so in 1925 they recruited more members and split into two groups: a planting group and a harvesting group. By this time there were about thirty members of the two groups combined.

Things were going so well that the men decided to build a musical ensemble to celebrate their friendship, so they harvested some bamboo growing nearby and built a small *tinglik* ensemble (a set of four or more instruments made from bamboo tubes [*bumbung*] strapped into a frame) to use for community dancing. Pleased with their efforts, they held a meeting and decided to build another ensemble that could be used by the community—this time, a more substantial, bronze-keyed one. But what ensemble? Every village around them was making the new *gamelan gong kebyar*—but they wanted something different, something older. They soon realized that no one in the vicinity had a *gamelan angklung*. Until then, they had been hiring an ensemble from Denpasar to play at their *ngabén*, so they decided to pool their resources and build a full *gamelan angklung*. They felt that having their own *gamelan* would ensure that they could always have proper cremations for their families.

However, the cost of constructing a *gamelan angklung*—forging and tuning the bronze keys, casting the pots and hanging gong, carving cases, and so on—proved to be too high, so in 1928 the men went to the royal palace to ask the Raja of Baturiti (Cokorda Ngurah Ketut 1906–39) to give them one of his gongs so that they could melt it down to make a *gamelan angklung*. The Raja agreed to give them one of his special gongs—one that contained a small amount of gold. But even more money was needed to complete the project.

The richest man in the village (apart from the Raja) was Anak Agung Wayan Raka, the grandfather of today's *banjar* Baturiti priest (Anak Agung Rai Winaja). He lived in a *jero*[1] near the palace, owned a great deal of land, and supported many *sudra* (workers). He asked each of his workers to contribute a small amount of their rice harvest to help pay for the *gamelan*'s construction, and then provided the rest of the money. Late in 1928, the group contracted a well-known *pandé* (blacksmith), Pak Sukana, from Klungkung to build the instruments. Pak Sukana tried many times to melt the king's gong, but the gong was too hard and would not melt. So,

FIGURE 6.1 *Gangsa kantillan (siem)*.

he prayed to the gods, telling them that if they helped him melt the gong, he would make a *siem* (a special *gangsa kantillan*) that contained gold.

Here, the men went on to explain why the *siem* is so important to the continued success of the group:

> The purpose of the *siem* is to absorb the combined sounds of many *gamelan* playing simultaneously at a ceremony, such as a *ngabén*. When all the ensembles play together, the sound can be overwhelming and become harmful—the multiple vibrations can break the instruments, especially the gong. The sounds fight with each other and fill up all the sonic space. For example, if we put a *tawa-tawa* on the ground and hit it, it will break—it needs space to sound and vibrate. When too many *gamelan* play at the same time, there is not enough space for the sounds to escape and resonate; so, the *siem* protects the bronze-keyed instruments and gongs from breaking, as it creates extra space for the combined sounds to escape. It acts somewhat like a bodyguard, protecting and preserving the metal bars of the other instruments in the ensemble. To this day, *banjar* Baturiti's *gamelan angklung* is the only ensemble in the area to have a *siem*, and members of the group credit this special instrument with much of their success and longevity. They use the *siem* whenever and wherever they play.

The *gamelan* was finished in 1929 and was called, at first, simply *gamelan angklung* Baturiti. The *sekehe* constructed a special *balé* for the ensemble at the home of the ensemble's sponsor. One of the members of the group had originally come from Denpasar and was familiar with some of the pieces known by the *angklung* group that had previously traveled to *banjar* Baturiti for cremations, so this is when they began their *sekehe angklung* in earnest.

In 1930, having run out of pieces, they contacted an *angklung* teacher in Denpasar who came to Baturiti for a week; the men practiced morning, noon, and night, learning the fifteen *gending* that ultimately became the core of the present-day repertoire. There are many other *gending* that they also play at *ngabén*, but these have been borrowed from other *angklung* groups that various members have visited and then taught to the group in Baturiti. The men of Taman Sari regard the fifteen *gending* they learned initially to be theirs, uniquely associated with their *sekehe* and *banjar*.

By 1931 the ensemble was well known in the area and played often for *ngabén* in and around Kerambitan. But the *balé* they had initially built with local coconut trees had begun to crumble and was no longer adequate to protect the ensemble, so in 1933 they built a more permanent structure with six stone pillars, which is the pavilion that is used today.

FIGURE 6.2 Original door of the *balé* set in stone wall.

FIGURE 6.3 Detail from the right edge of the door showing the date of its completion.

Around 1965 the group went back to the *pandé*, Pak Sukana, and purchased a larger gong for the ensemble. They already had a *kempur*, the medium-sized gong traditionally used with *gamelan angklung* at *ngabén*, but the men wanted to play different repertoires at different ceremonies, such as temple *odalan*, and for competitions now being held in their area. They also purchased larger drums, as most of these newly adopted and adapted repertoires called for a stronger rhythmic presence. The group itself had expanded somewhat and was now separated into subgroups, each of which specialized in a different repertoire. They also officially named the *angklung* group Taman Sari (Essence of a Flower).

In the early 1970s the ensemble was still privately owned and maintained by the original group of thirty members and Anak Agung Wayan Raka, its sponsor; and, although most of its members lived in and around the palace, they belonged to three different local *banjar*. In 1971 the first post–New Order legislative election under President Suharto (1921–2008) was held in Indonesia with ten parties participating. Government manipulation in the form of vote-rigging and redefining election rules, among other tactics, resulted in rioting in Kerambitan, where houses and rice storage areas were burned. The riots persisted until 1979, causing much hardship and bad feeling among and between the three local *banjar* in Baturiti.

Finally, members of *sekehe angklung* Taman Sari proposed a solution: why not sell the *gamelan angklung* to the players themselves? That way, all three *banjar* would together be responsible for the ensemble and its performances. The group wanted to help make the village safe again and thought this could be accomplished by having the instruments belong to the three *banjar* equally, rather than owned privately. They began to charge each family in the three separate *banjar* a small fee to support and maintain the ensemble and agreed to play free for all *ngabén* in the area.

Many of the men in the group today were part of this peace process, and they take pride in saying that it was in this way that *gamelan angklung* Taman Sari brought peace back to Baturiti. Today, there is a strict division of the players: ten from each of the *banjar* in the area. When they perform at a cremation, only members of the cremation group are permitted to play; when they perform for other occasions in the area (i.e., *odalan*, tooth-filings, etc.) anyone from any of the three *banjar* can play (summary of interviews with members of Taman Sari, September 19–21, 2007).

The Priest's Story

A temple priest, or *pemangku (mangku)*, is a lay member of the community who is responsible for maintaining the temple and officiating at local, everyday rituals. One of his or her responsibilities is to remain in contact with the ancestral deities, that is, with members of the community who have died and passed on into the realm of a familial god, or deified ancestor. *Pemangku* are not chosen from the Brahmin rank, but are often *sudra*, making their living by farming or similar occupations.

Pak Anak Agung Rai Winaja, the *pemangku* of the main Baturiti temple, has a special relationship to *gamelan angklung* Taman Sari. His grandfather was the original sponsor of the group—Anak Agung Wayan Raka. One day, according to Pak Winaja, his grandfather called the heads of thirty *banjar* families together and proposed that they construct "something beautiful—a *gamelan angklung*" (Interview, Pak Winaja, October 29, 2007). All the families agreed to help purchase the *gamelan* by giving a portion of their rice harvest.

Although neither Pak Winaja's grandfather, the original sponsor, nor his father had ever been a part of the *gamelan angklung*, just before his father died he told Pak Winaja to join the *sekehe*, to take care of the *gamelan*, and to play the instruments. And, although he had never played in the *angklung* ensemble and knew nothing about the instruments or the music, when his father directed him to join the group, "suddenly he could play without any trouble or practice" (Winaja interview, October 29, 2007). That is when he became the temple's *pemangku*.

Pak Winaja has been with the group since the big gong was made in 1966. At that time, the thirty members of the original group again contributed a portion of their rice harvest, and they purchased the gong from

Pak Sukarna, the original *pandé*. Pak Winaja confirmed that after 1966 the group, sometimes with different players, was now able to perform outside the cremation context—at *odalan* and for other ceremonies—as the new, larger gong enabled them to play different repertoires that required a stronger gong presence (Winaja interview, October 29, 2007).

The Raja's Story

In August 2007 I was playing with the group for a cremation held at the local *kuburan* in *banjar* Wani, and I noticed a man walking through the crowds whom everyone seemed to know and revere. It was the way the people moved their bodies in relation to his that seemed to indicate deference. Nyoman, who had not yet left for Rochester, rushed over to inform me that this man was the former Raja of Kerambitan, and that the cremation was being held for one of his relatives. The Raja caught my eye, smiled, and came over to say hello. What follows is a summary of what happened next.

October 18, 2007: "The King and I"[2]

The Raja, Cokorda Anglurah Tabanan, has invited me to the palace to tell me the story of how gamelan angklung *Taman Sari came to* banjar *Baturiti. We drive to the palace, and I enter the outside court with the Raja. He speaks excellent English and tells me that he is a Bali guide, something he now does professionally and diplomatically. His large compound, housing five separate families, is absolutely beautiful! Hanging stone baskets of flowers, dripping vines, solid gold, and hardwood carvings everywhere, with many (invisible) servants in attendance. He leads me into the third courtyard (the personal, family area) and invites me to sit and have some coffee.*

The Raja gives me a book he has put together explaining the history of his family. Here are the basics: His family entered Bali in the early 1600s as part of the Majapahit Empire and established a court in Klungkung Province (east of Tabanan). This family site in Baturiti was built around 1850, and his private quarters were rebuilt in the 1950s. He is 78 and is a twin. His mother is still alive at 98, after having had eleven children (!); his father was born in 1895, his grandfather born about 1860, and his great-grandfather, around 1830; the Rajas had many wives and hundreds of children. During the seventeenth century, his family area in Klungkung was vast, with many specialized communities existing within it, such as pandé *for making iron, gold, and* gamelan *instruments.*

FIGURE 6.4 The three palace courtyards.

Here is the story of how his family first came to Baturiti from Klung-kung and how the gamelan angklung *was made, a story he heard from his mother (Interview, Cokorda Anglurah Tabanan, August 7, 2007): His family originally came from Desa Tihingan, which was the center of arts and culture in Klungkung Province around 1800, especially known for* gamelan *performances. The Raja of Klungkung at the time became angry with some members of his family because of a "mistake behind the curtain"³ so he punished the transgressors by "sending them to the West (i.e., Tabanan), where all the mosquitoes live."*

He banished the family to Baturiti, along with many of the lower-caste communities that they had been supporting at their court. When they all got to Baturiti, the great-grandfather, who was the head of the family, took stock to determine just who had come with him. He discovered that a gamelan *maker had come with the others and commanded him to make the* gamelan angklung, *as it was the most important ensemble used for cremations.*

The instruments of Baturiti's gamelan angklung *originally belonged to his family. The ensemble was constructed around 1850 and was used in the palace for cremations until the 1960s, when he gave it to the community. The decorations on the* angklung *instruments include real gold. Two ensembles were made at that time that included gongs made with gold: a gamelan gong gdé for lavish court performances, and a gamelan angklung for cremations. He said that in the early days, when it rained, people would come from all over to visit the gongs and scoop up the water, thinking there was a little bit of gold dripping down. His father gave the gamelan angklung to the people in the 1960s and eventually it ended up in the present-day balé banjar.*

Here is a story Cokorda Anglurah Tabanan told me of an early gamelan angklung composer. This clever man who composed many songs would frequently invite other gamelan teachers to visit and teach him new gending (pieces). But, one day, after a long time between visits and with no money to pay, the composer went to the rice fields and "accidentally" heard another angklung group practicing a song. He "borrowed" (air quotes provided) the song and returned home to teach it to his group. The original owner of the tune heard about this and came to Baturiti demanding payment. The composer's response? "Where's the proof that I didn't make this up myself? Ha, ha, ha!"

It was then that I learned another meaning of the word sari (which I thought only meant "flower"): it also meant money placed at the top of the flowers in an offering. I think this was a not-so-veiled message to me: give money to the Baturiti angklung group so they can teach you and keep going to learn new music. Finally, he related the story of how he managed to scrape up the money to cremate his own father properly: he had to sell a golden statue of a bull in Jakarta to a Chinese antique art dealer because he was so poor, but his father ended up having a perfect cremation on September 30, 1966, for which the Baturiti gamelan angklung played (Interview, Cokorda Anglurah Tabanan, August 18, 2007).

Although these three stories differ somewhat in their specifics, the essence of how the *gamelan angklung* began and developed over the span of a hundred years is there. A group of farmers (or the Raja), with the help of a wealthy sponsor who was living close to the palace and (probably) close to the Raja, decided to commission the construction of a *gamelan angklung*. Why this particular ensemble? Because they realized that no other *banjar* in the immediate area had one, and, as it was so important to the ritual of cremation, they felt it was the right thing to do for the community. Things were beginning to change in Bali: political and social negotiations were underway (see chapter 1), negotiations that would eventually lead to Indonesian independence and to massive land reform, where the former workers of the land (*sudra*) would be given portions of the land belonging to the Rajas. From the perspective of social and religious behavior, each group of actors in these stories was doing the right thing by performing the right action, based on caste, time, and place.

In addition to being a template of right behavior and intention, the principle of *dharma*, as stated earlier, also incorporates context in the form of *varna-āśrama-dharma*, the "duties appropriate to one's group (*varna/ wangsa* in Bali) and one's period of life (*āśrama*)" (Creel 1972:157). Time of life refers both to one's own lifetime and to the specific time in which one lives, so that in the context of early to mid-twentieth-century life in Bali, building a *gamelan angklung* and providing a service to one's community would be seen as fulfilling one's *dharma*, or essential character.

One possible (perhaps simplistic) interpretation of these actions might be that for the Raja and his wealthy friend, *dharma* was performed by initiating the idea and providing the money to build the *gamelan*; for the workers, *dharma* was performed by contributing rice to the project and playing the music. And for the priest, *dharma* took the form of becoming a member of the ensemble, as well as its custodian. Thus, the individual and social order remained in place, despite the political instability of the era and the different social positions of the actors. All participants were compelled to obey their own *dharma*, or essential nature, fixed by birth and place in time, as to ignore this would invite chaos. "Men have different natures and abilities, and their social duties correspond to this fact. To defy one's *dharma* is to go against the grain of one's nature. Further, since the universe is a vast congeries or a symphony of *dharma*, . . . to be out of step with the universe [is to] invite disaster" (1972:157).

Organization of *Sekehe Gamelan Angklung* Taman Sari

Since its beginnings the *sekehe* has been tightly organized, with those men most interested in maintaining the group acting as its informal leaders. Around 2000, this practice began to fail, so the group called a general election and Pak Rideng, Pak Wayan, and Pak Ketut were chosen to lead the group. Originally, these men were to serve for three years, but they have been repeatedly reelected because they have proven to be honest (they keep careful watch over the money they are paid for *gamelan* performances) and they enjoy their jobs. The group watches them closely and if they remain honest and are not lazy, they will be reelected again. "If you're lazy, you're out!" (Interview, Pak Rideng, October 29, 2007).

Pak Rideng has been the head of the *sekehe* for over ten years. He takes the requests for cremation performances and is responsible for calling the men together for a meeting. Pak Wayan is the secretary and acts as the official bookkeeper, noting down all fees and paying the performers for their work. He also has the responsibility for maintaining the instruments, which are refurbished and repainted on a regular basis. Pak Ketut handles public relations, alerting the members when a cremation is approaching and overseeing the moving of instruments (Interview, Pak Ketut, October 29, 2007).

Although these three men are the administrative heads of the group, they are not its musical leaders. All members of the group acknowledge three men—Pak Madia (*ceng-ceng*), Pak Riyus (*kendang*), and Pak Marwi (*ugal*)—as the official teachers and caretakers of the music. All three have played with the group for decades, having inherited their positions from their fathers, all of whom were part of the original group of men who first came together to form the *sekehe*. All have participated in other local *gamelan* and in the many changing performance contexts that have emerged since the mid-twentieth century.

Pak Riyus, for example, is known throughout the village as an expert dancer and, although in his eighties (at the time of my fieldwork), still teaches dances to members of the *gamelan gong kebyar*, *barong*, and *gamelan angklung-kebyar* groups in Kerambitan. The other two often participate in local and regional dance performances, so their music-dance expertise extends to many performance contexts outside cremations. However, they all regard *sekehe gamelan angklung* Taman Sari as their primary group, their main responsibility to the community and to their fathers who entrusted them with this knowledge and duty.

Pak Marwi, the *ugal*, has the additional responsibility of teaching the core fifteen pieces to newcomers and any new pieces that he has learned from other *gamelan angklung* performers in the area. As he says, "I'm the smart one—I know all the pieces" (Interview, Pak Marwi, November 11, 2007). It was his father who first learned this repertoire from the original teacher brought in from Denpasar in the early 1920s. As a young boy, he would accompany his father to rehearsals and cremations, easily learning the pieces, and in 1952, when he was twenty-five, he replaced his father, gradually becoming the acknowledged music expert. Now, when a dispute arises, or when a player forgets a passage or veers off in a different direction, it is Pak Marwi who decides the right course and all eyes are on him.

The *sekehe* earns enough money to pay the performers a small wage, to provide snacks, and to maintain the instruments and uniforms, which for cremations (when I was there) consisted of individual *kains* (wraparound cotton batik fabrics), bright orange polo shirts, *saputs* (aprons), and hats. If a cremation is held in Kerambitan, they will charge 200,000 rupiah (about US$18 in 2008) for a four- or five-hour performance; if held outside the village, the charges double.

Three time slots are available: 7:00 a.m. to 12:00 noon; 1:00 p.m. to 6:00 p.m.; and 7:00 p.m. to midnight. These times correspond to three separate cremation performances discussed in chapter 5. The nighttime slot takes place for a few nights before the cremation. The ensemble plays inside the house while family members prepare the corpse for cremation. Many people from the community pass in and out of the house all night to pay respects to the bereaved family and to distract them from their sadness, and large amounts of food and coffee are offered to visitors. As mentioned earlier, many different *gamelan* are often present and some form of gambling might be going on in a back room, all done to protect the corpse from evil spirits and the family from despairing.

The morning time slot is used while the corpse is being washed and wrapped in white cloth and the final touches are put on the *wadah* that will carry the corpse to the cremation site. The *gamelan* sets up just outside the house and plays while the men work on the *wadah* and while the villagers gather for the procession. Again, food and drinks are provided to visitors, whose numbers can range into the hundreds. The afternoon slot is used for the actual cremation ceremony in the *kuburan*. Again, many *gamelan* are likely to be present here and the overall atmosphere is one of intentional busyness, or *ramé*.

The *sekehe*'s primary responsibility is to its own community, so if an outside and a village performance happen to coincide, they will play for the village. Any money that is earned is distributed as follows: 20 percent goes to the temple, another 60 percent or so goes into the bank, and the remaining money is used for snacks and maintaining the instruments. After six months, they split what is left among the players. Further, the men made clear that the most important attribute that was expected of any group member was commitment. They stressed that group effort was mandatory; all must work together, with no whining. If a person missed a performance that he had agreed to in advance, he must pay a fine; and, if a person does not show up three times in a row for a job without a good reason, he is thrown out of the group.

At the time of my fieldwork, there were only twenty-five core members in the group—they were down five members. Luckily, many others in the village also know the music and could fill in when needed, but the three leaders worried that they would not find new members, especially among the young, most of whom, they said, do not like the music. They then told me that they were happy I had come along and wanted to play. I would be the twenty-sixth member. What follows is an account of my induction ceremony (and audition) taken from my diary:

August 4, 2007: Induction Ceremony

Last night was my induction ceremony into the sekehe gamelan angklung *at* banjar *Baturiti.*

Nyoman and I arrived at the banjar *about 6:30 p.m. and, except for the priest, we were the first ones there. Pak Rideng and Pak Wayan arrived, Pak Rideng sounded the* kulkul, *and others slowly trickled in until about 7:00 p.m., when about twelve men had shown up. The two Paks led Nyoman and me up many steps to a high room in the temple where costumes and other performing paraphernalia are stored; in the center of the room was a highly decorated shrine.*

We sat on the floor and the priest went toward the altar and began intoning prayers. He prayed that all would go well with my project and that we would learn much from each other. After the priest prayed, he blessed us with holy water and we put a smidgeon of rice on our foreheads, a small piece of flower behind our right ears, and it was over. There were flowers everywhere and many sticks of incense burning throughout. It was very solemn and moving and I felt honored to become an official part of the group.

We came back downstairs to the performance space and about fifteen men were there now, sitting at their instruments ready to play for me. I didn't realize that they were going to play, but I guess they wanted to do something to mark the occasion, too. The head of the village, Pak Ketut, was also there and Nyoman and he spent some time introducing me and explaining the nature of my project. Then they

FIGURE 6.5 Just after my induction ceremony, August 4, 2007.

asked me if I wanted to play (!); I wasn't sure if I would know any of the pieces. To be a good sport, I said I would play jegogan. *Everyone smiled as I took my place. We were all hoping for the best; I was just hoping that my partner knew what he was doing! We started to play and somehow I followed my partner, who was a very sure player (most of the time), and since the* jegogan *moves slowly, I was easily able to play with him.*

Everyone was greatly surprised that I could play the pieces. They were amazed that a person from America knew their music and the technique of playing. I didn't really know the pieces, but I knew the basic structures and was able to imitate what my partner was doing well enough to simulate knowing. The only mistakes I made were the ones he made! Nyoman said later that everyone was going to enjoy playing with me, but they just couldn't figure out how an old white lady from America knew their gamelan angklung *pieces! I told Nyoman how grateful I was for his help and support and that I was just happy (and relieved) that I hadn't embarrassed him. I had passed my audition successfully.*

It was great. We played for about an hour and a half, and I just followed along. All the pieces were from the cremation repertoire, and since I am proposing that they play with me every week, the three head Paks are seeing this as an opportunity for the group to learn some new pieces. So, part of the money I am giving them will be used for hiring some other gamelan angklung *teachers to come to Baturiti to teach new (old) pieces to the group. (This never materialized, although we did learn new pieces from the* ugal.*)*

On the way home Nyoman and I stop at the warung *and talk a bit. I tell him how much I have wanted to do this, how for decades my imagination about all those early visitors to Bali (Kunst, McPhee, Hood, etc.) has grown, and how this experience has connected my love for that early ethnomusicology and for performing music together in a really meaningful way. He says he understands, but I'm not sure even I understand!*

Joining, Learning, and Rehearsing

Most of the men in *gamelan* Taman Sari, as noted above, have inherited their positions in the *sekehe* and have known the core repertoire since childhood. Occasionally, a new member is recruited from one of the three *banjar* in the area. When an instrument becomes free, the group meets and determines who has the most ability or experience among the three *banjar* in the area, always trying to keep the ten—ten—ten division between the three as established in the early 1970s.

Some are chosen because they have shown an interest in the group while attending a cremation. They are often attracted by the opportunity to work in a longstanding *sekehe* that carries such an important responsibility. One man, Pak Gung Rantang, though, told me that he had had no special interest in the group before he joined, and that no member of his family had ever played in a *gamelan*. He had joined because the head of the *banjar* had come to him saying that at seventy, he had to assume more duties appropriate to his age. Which would he rather do—become the new head of the *banjar* or join the *gamelan angklung*? He figured playing in the *gamelan* would be easier. He had been playing with the group for three years and still does not know all the music (Interview, Pak Gung Rantang, January 10, 2008).

The men do not rehearse the music they play outside the context of a cremation. Indeed, meeting with me every week so I could play and record the core repertoire was something of a lark for them. They loved playing together, enjoyed the treats I provided during breaks, and had good laughs at my expense when I asked "crazy questions" or misinterpreted something. But, as they played together all the time and knew the pieces in the core repertoire well, they did not need to practice.

Many of the men I worked with commented on the difficulty of the music, which they attributed to the use of the four-note *saih angklung*. There were so many pieces, and many sounded alike; interlocking sections were too fast to learn easily; and the tunes were hard to remember. Although difficult, they said, *saih angklung* was also beautiful, providing a different feeling (*rasa*) from other *gamelan* pitch sets. They saw the sound of their ensemble as *manis* (sweet), *klasik* (classical), and *tua* (old)—not as *keras* (strong, harsh, loud), the word they used for the more popular *gamelan gong kebyar*. To provide an example of this feeling, one of the men (Pak Wira) began to sing the slow-moving second section of "Capung Gantung," illustrating its initial gentle rhythm.

The Importance of Groupness

Many of the men told me that the most satisfying and meaningful aspect of their membership in the *sekehe* was playing together with the others, many of whom had been lifelong friends and associates. One man, I Nyoman Nadra, said that when he attempted to learn a new piece, he could only do so if the other members of Taman Sari were there. He had tried learning a piece from another *gamelan* but was unable to do so because, he said, *gamelan* Taman Sari did not own the song and learning it on his own would separate him from his peers.

I also experienced this sense of groupness early on in my fieldwork. I was trying to learn the fifteen *gending* as quickly as I could, listening over and over to my recordings and trying to play along. It occurred to me that if I could find one person (maybe Pak Riyus or Pak Desek?) to work with me alone this would help. After all, other ethnomusicologists who had been in Bali had worked alone with master teachers. So, I approached Pak Rideng and asked him if this would be possible. He said he would talk to the group.

A few days later he came to my house to let me know that finding a person to help me was not possible. Why? Because the group itself was the teacher, not the individual; choosing one individual such as Pak Riyus or Pak Desek to work with me alone would go against the primary value of their group—its groupness—in that this would place one individual over the others. It was at this moment that I began to understand the major differences between professional Balinese musicians working at institutions, such as KOKAR and ISI, and local *banjar* members in relation to how they understood what they were doing. And, more importantly, I began to understand my own implicit assumptions about what *I* was doing. Was this music or not?

A final aspect of groupness became apparent when many of the men talked about their fear that the combined efforts of their *sekehe* to fulfill their obligation to the community through performing at cremations would be lost because the younger generation was moving away from the village and from the longstanding values of village life. Pak Dewa Berata expressed this worry to me in an email: "Today, more and more *angklung* [groups] play *kebyar* and the *angklung rasa* (feeling) of sadness is getting *hilang* (lost), little by little" (Dewa Berata, January 3, 2019).

It was not the music that was getting lost, he assured me, it was the *rasa*—the feeling that he had experienced since his childhood in Sidan (Gianyar), when he had listened to his local *gamelan angklung* at cremations, and how that feeling had connected him to his father. Being surrounded by the primary groupness of his *banjar*, and experiencing the *rasa* of sweet-sadness, as delivered through the medium of (what Westerners call) music had remained with him throughout his life. He, along with many of the members of *gamelan* Taman Sari, expressed the hope that this tradition would not die.

CHAPTER 7

Gamelan Angklung
Cremation Music Today

This chapter examines the Taman Sari cremation *gending* as a unified body of work. The cremation repertoire, although belonging to *banjar* Baturiti, is also known widely throughout south and central Bali, thus representing a broader distribution than their local name suggests. I became aware of this as I worked with the men and traveled with them to other *banjar* in and around Tabanan, where we often encountered other *gamelan angklung* groups performing at cremations. Most of them were playing the same or similar pieces to the ones I had learned from Taman Sari. It turned out that during the eighty or so years since the beginning of the *sekehe*, many other *angklung* cremation groups have appeared and the Baturiti players have been frequently called upon to teach their pieces to new groups. New pieces, picked up by members of these younger ensembles, are in turn passed along to the men of Taman Sari as extended repertoire, so that a large, circular network of performers and *gending* has emerged.

The term *gending* is commonly used in Bali to describe a complete, often multi-sectioned piece of instrumental music; here, it refers to a piece of music containing from one to four separate sections, which the men of Taman Sari referred to as *seksi*. All sections are complete units on their own and are not often related to each other in this repertoire. They all begin with a cue (*gihing*),[1] usually played by one or two *ugal* (leaders) on the *gangsa*, and end with a *kempur* stroke.

The fifteen *gending* in the Taman Sari repertoire are all named, mostly with whimsical titles like those noted by McPhee and others. However, individual sections within a *gending* are not named, but their order within the *gending* is indicated either by number (e.g., "Tambun," *seksi dua* ["Tambun," second section]) or by widely known Balinese terms, metaphorically described, as in many other genres, with parts of the human body: first section, *pemungkah* (opening, head); second section, *pengawak* (body); and third section, *pengiba* (feet), each with its own musical form and character.[2]

The Taman Sari Cremation Repertoire

As a body of work, the cremation repertoire contains an astonishingly varied and creative set of pieces. Diagram 7.1 shows the fifteen *gending* and their sections, as they were taught to me.[3] There are forty-two sections contained in the fifteen *gending*, but as ten are repeated, there are thirty-two different sections in total: twelve *pemungkah*, seven *pengawak*, eight *pengiba*, and five sections I call hybrids, sections that contain a relatively equal portion of two section-type characteristics, which often alternate.

The sections in Diagram 7.1 do not always correspond to the tripartite organizational scheme found today in many other genres. More formally called *kawitan-pengawak-pangecet*, and first developed during the *madya* (court) period of Balinese music history (c. 1700–1900), this structure continues to be associated with classical ensembles of that period, delineating various musical forms, tempos, and associated feelings. Michael Tenzer writes:

> The *kawitan-pengawak-pengecet* tripartition (introduction, slow-tempo main body, and faster conclusion, KPP) was originally applied to *lelambatan* in *pegongan* and *pegambuhan* repertoires. [This form] does not address scale tone or melody in the music at all; instead, it sketches an ordering of cycle types and points only to their dimensions, tempi, and, implicitly, their affect. As an archetype the KPP is a narrative framework. . . . In this narrative, sacred time in the *pengawak* is flanked by the preparatory gateway of the *kawitan* and the more human manifestations of that sacred time in the *pangecet* (2000:354–56).[4]

The fifteen *gending* in the Taman Sari repertoire are only roughly organized in this way. Although all sections were given metaphorical names by Pak Rideng, not all *gending* contain three different section-types. Some, for example, contain two or three heads and no feet; some sections are combinations of heads, bodies, and feet; and, beginning with "Bapang" (number 7 in the diagram), you see the start of repeated sections taken from other *gending* that appear to have been added to correspond to the three-part organizational scheme presented above. "Bapang," for example, contains two *pemungkah* (the first one being the same as that from "Tungtung Tangis") and a *pengiba* (taken from "Sekar Jepun"); "Lutung Loncat" has three *pengawak*, and the *pengiba* is a repeat of the *pengiba*

DIAGRAM 7.1 The fifteen *gending* in the Taman Sari *gamelan angklung* repertoire. (For complete recordings of all fifteen gending, see accompanying website.)

Gending Name	Section A	Section B	Section C	Section D
#1 Santun (Politeness, Giving)	Pemungkah	Pemungkah	Pengiba	
#2 Tambun (Belonging Together)	Pemungkah	Pengiba		
#3 Katak Ngongkek (Croaking Frog)	Pemungkah	Pengawak	Pengiba	
#4 Tungtung Tangis (Forever Weeping)	Pemungkah	Pengawak	Pengawak/ Pengiba hybrid	
#5 Capung Gantung (Hovering Dragonfly)	Pemungkah	Pengawak	Pengiba	
#6 Sekar Jepun (Japanese Flower)	Pemungkah	Pengawak	Pengiba	
#7 Bapang (an eight-beat pattern)	Pemungkah (4A)	Pemungkah	Pengiba (6C)	
#8 Lutung Loncat (Jumping Monkey)	Pengawak	Pengawak	Pengawak	Pengiba (2B)
#9 Prebangsa	Pemungkah (6A)	Pengawak (6B)	Pengawak	
#10 Capung Manjus (Bathing Dragonfly)	Pengawak/ Pemungkah hybrid	Pengawak (4B)	Pengawak/ Pengiba hybrid	
#11 Sekar Gadung (Gadung Flower)	Pemungkah (6A)	Pengawak (6B)	Pengiba (2B)	
#12 Cerukcuk Punyah (Drunken Bird)	Pengawak/ Pemungkah hybrid (10A)	Pemungkah	Pengiba	
#13 Alis-Alis Ijo (Green Eyebrow)	Pemungkah	Pemungkah	Pemungkah/ Pengawak hybrid	Pengawak
#14 Jangkrik Ngibing (Dancing Cricket)	Pemungkah/ Pengawak hybrid	Pengawak (10C)		
#15 Jaran Nginjek (Runaway Horse)	Pengiba			

from "Tambun"; and "Alis-Alis Ijo" contains two different *pengawak* and two *pengawak-pemungkah* hybrids.

Thus, although the pieces in the *gamelan angklung* cremation repertoire heard today were most likely adapted to a three-part narrative sometime during or after the *madya* period, they did so only partially. Unlike *lelam-batan* genres, which were conceived as three-part forms from the beginning, the different *gamelan angklung* section-types probably originated from already existing repertoires as short, single units, each with its own characteristic feeling, but not linked together to create a larger form.[5] Over time, they were probably strung together to create complete *gending*; or some of the sections heard today were composed later and entered the repertoire during the *madya* or *baru* periods, strung together to comply with new, more standardized forms. More evidence for this idea lies in the context of a real-time cremation; the three contrasting sections in a *gending* (even when they exist) are seldom played in order. This is discussed more fully in chapter 9.

In *lelambatan*, the three section-types were distinguished by length, tempo, and character, with tempo being perhaps the most important as a marker of affect. Tenzer recalls a personal conversation with Madé Lebah, master musician and teacher of Colin McPhee, who told him, "*Lelambatan* are for the gods, but the *pengawak* has the most godly feeling. In the *pan-gecet* we bring more of our own feeling to the music" (Lebah, personal communication, in Tenzer 2000:356). Thus, the three-part form became the norm at the *gending*-level of court compositions, but not at the *gending*-level of village cremation music, which remained more flexible.[6]

Rasa

Each section-type in the Taman Sari cremation repertoire is thought to be a musical expression of a *rasa* (feeling, flavor, mood). The concept of *rasa*, stemming from Vedic philosophy, is an essential component of Indian, and to some extent, Indonesian aesthetics.[7] Applied to the pieces in the repertoire under discussion here, *rasa* refers to the general feeling or character of a section-type, as well as to its performance context—here, a cremation.[8] As in *lelambatan*, a typical cremation *gending* consists of a beginning, perhaps calm, moderately paced *pemungkah* (called *kawitan* in *lelambatan*), a slow, deliberate, thoughtful, and wandering *pengawak*, and a fast, filled-in *pengiba* (*pengecét*, in *lelambatan*).

Placing these affects into the context of a contemporary cremation provides not only a general atmosphere of bittersweet sadness, but also a sense of oldness, as suggested in chapter 5 by Lisa Gold, in her understanding of *rameé*. This is communicated through various musical features that, over time, have taken on a deep emotional significance as affective topics. Some features, such as two-layered tonal textures and asymmetric phrasing, are associated with all genres in the *tua* (old) category. Others, such as the use of uneven phrasing, fractional beats, tuneful elaborations, flexible *kotekan empat*, and the presence of *saih angklung*, are uniquely characteristic of this genre. That is not to suggest that these musical gestures necessarily stand for specific emotional responses in a listener, but that the music, its context, and its communal performance combine to enable these emotions to rise to the surface.

Sounds of Bittersweet Oldness

The sounds of bittersweet oldness are communicated musically through a combination of musical structures and forms, the most important of which are discussed below: varying textures, flexible meters, inconsistent phrase lengths, and the high register, bell-like sounds of *saih angklung*, which add the flavor of sweetness. These characteristics are not only the most important musically but are also the most relevant to the men with whom I worked, and to the musical analyses that appear in the following chapter.

Varying Textures

Although I use the standard terms *pokok* and elaboration here to describe the two strands in this repertoire, the difference between them is not always clear. Translated from Indonesian as "basic," "fundamental," or "tree trunk," the term *pokok* has been used for centuries to describe a series of low, slow-moving musical contours often preserved on *lontar* (palm-leaf manuscripts) to help performers remember or reconstruct pieces (Tenzer 2000:33 n.14). In Western scholarship on Balinese music, *pokok* is often referred to as a skeletal or core melody and its elaboration as a filling-in or embroidery.

In the *angklung* cremation repertoire discussed here, the upper layer is often a singable melody, and the lower layer is sometimes *pokok*-like, or more fluid, frequently changing its rate of movement in relation to the beat, a characteristic consistent with other *tua* musics. Even McPhee, as suggested earlier, was unsure if the term *pokok* could even be used to describe some of the lower layers in *gamelan angklung* pieces. He used the terms "support" or "reinforcement tones" to describe their character, implying that the lower layer may have been added to the original *génggong, suling,* and/or *wayang* tunes that he believed constituted the primary sources of *angklung* music. And he used the presence or absence of a *pokok* as the defining feature of two types of *angklung* pieces he heard, stating: "Two different types of *gending* may be distinguished: a, those in which a simple basic melody—the *pokok gending*—is sounded by the *jegogans*, while *genders, kantils,* and *réongs* unite in continuous accompaniment; and b, compositions in which the melody—the *lagu* or *gending*—is played by the smaller metallophones and *réongs*, while the *jegogans* merely underline the melody at intervals" (1966:246).

In distinguishing between these two types of composition, McPhee asserts that "a melody" can lie in either the lower or upper region, without clearly defining "melody." Nor does his explanation cover the entire range of musical interactions between the two layers found in this repertoire.

POKOK   I define *pokok* here simply as the lower, slower layer, and elaboration as the higher, often more active one. Three *pokok* styles thus emerge, each of which is associated with a different section-type and is differentiated by its relationship to the beat, a constant *tawa-tawa* presence marking the pulse. I have labeled these styles "standard" (one *jegogan* tone per two beats, found mainly in *pemungkah*),[9] "support" (one tone per any number of beats, up to twelve, found most often in *pengawak*, after McPhee), and "ostinato" (one tone per beat, found mainly in *pengiba*). (◀)) Recording 7.1, Standard *Pokok*; Recording 7.2, Support *Pokok*; Recording 7.3, Ostinato *Pokok*) Below are some suggestions for listening.

RECORDING AND LISTENING GUIDE 7.1 Standard *Pokok*: First four phrases of "Sekar Jepun," *pemungkah*

0:00–0:29	**Cue:** two *gangsa pemadé* play through section; listen for the *rincik* cue at the end
0:29–0:34	**Phrase 1:** 8 beats; listen for the *tawa-tawa* playing 2 beats for every *jegogan* tone
0:34–0:38	**Phrase 2:** 8 beats, variant of phrase 1
0:38–0:42	**Phrase 3:** 8 beats, repeat of phrase 2
0:42–0:46	**Phrase 4:** 8 beats, variant of phrase 2
0:46–fade-out	Beginning of phrase 5

This recording was made at a cremation, so there is some background chattering.

RECORDING AND LISTENING GUIDE 7.2 Support *Pokok*: First four phrases of "Tungtung Tangis," *pengawak*

0:00–0:05	**Cue:** one *gangsa pemadé*
0:05–0:18	**Phrase 1:** 8 1/2 beats; notice the rhythmic marker at the beginning of phrase; one *jegogan* note per phrase; *rincik* follows rhythms of the *gangsa* and *réong*
0:18–0:30	**Phrase 2:** 8 beats
0:30–0:41	**Phrase 3:** 8 1/2 beats; repetition of phrase 1
0:41–0:52	**Phrase 4:** 8 1/4 beats; variation of phrase 2
0:52–fade-out	Beginning of phrase 5

RECORDING AND LISTENING GUIDE 7.3 Ostinato *Pokok*: Two cycles of "Tungtung Tangis," *pengiba*

0:00–0:05	Cue: one *gangsa pemadé* to *rincik*
0:05–0:35	Cycle 1: one 8-beat phrase, repeated seven times. Listen for *rincik* cue in sixth repeat
0:35–0:43	Cycle 2: one 8-beat phrase, repeated twice. Listen for *rincik* cue on second repeat
0:44–end	Cycle 1

ELABORATION   Elaboration styles also differ in their relation to the beat, with the most common being "simple," designating two divisions of one beat and "filled-in" four divisions.[10] Listen again to Recordings 7.1 and 7.3 above. Concentrate on the upper layer played by the *gangsa* and *réong*, and notice its movement in relation to the beat, played by the *tawa-tawa*. In Recording 7.1 one beat is divided by two; in Recording 7.3 one beat is divided by four.

NONINTERLOCKING ELABORATION: *NGEMPAT*   Both *gangsa* and *réong* play the elaboration, but their playing techniques differ. The eight *gangsa*—four *pemadé* (lower octave) and four *kantillan* (higher octave)—are instruments with four keys, each instrument played by one person. However, *gangsa* are not only divided by octaves but also by what they play in a particular section or passage. In slower-moving sections, such as *pemungkah* and *pengawak*, the elaboration is executed mostly in unisons and octaves.

However, when the elaboration moves to pitch 1, the *gangsa* divide into two groups, with one group striking pitch 1 and the other striking pitch 4 simultaneously.[11] This creates a vertical interval called *ngempat*, derived from the Balinese word *empat* (four), signifying the span of the interval, including its outer notes. Thus, when playing a unison passage, all *gangsa* share pitches 2, 3, and 4, and only diverge when the elaboration moves to pitch 1. Below is a diagram of the first sixteen beats of the *pemungkah* from "Santun," which uses a simple unison elaboration and six instances of *ngempat* (bolded). (◀ Recording 7.4, *Pemungkah* initial phrase-group from "Santun")

Interlocking Elaboration: *Kotekan Ubit Empat*

Réong, on the other hand, are constructed from two sets of four pot-gongs, each set separated by an octave. In *gamelan angklung* Taman Sari, the four pots in each octave are also divided and set in two boxes, each holding

DIAGRAM 7.2. First sixteen beats of "Santun," *pemungkah*, with *ngempat* elaboration style.

gangsa kantillan	3 2	3 2	3 2	4 2	3 2	4 2	3 2	4 2
gangsa pemadé	3 2	3 2	3 2	1 2	3 2	1 2	3 2	1 2
jegogan	3		2		3		4	
tawa-tawa	x	x	x	x	x	x	x	x
beats	(16)	1	2	3	4	5	6	7

gangsa kantillan	3 3	3 3	3 2	4 2	3 2	4 2	3 2	4 2	3
gangsa pemadé	3 3	3 3	3 2	1 2	3 2	1 2	3 2	1 2	3
jegogan	3		2		3		4		3
tawa-tawa	x	x	x	x	x	x	x	x	x
beats	8	9	10	11	12	13	14	15	16

two pots (i.e., four boxes in all).[12] Unlike *gangsa*, two players per octave are needed, one responsible for pitches 1 and 2 (*polos*, "basic") in one box and the other for pitches 3 and 4 (*sangsih*, "different"), in the other, with no pitches shared. This creates an interlocking texture called *kotekan* (see more below). Thus, *réong*, unlike *gangsa*, are always divided into *polos* and *sangsih*, and always creating interlocking patterns over four notes, no matter what section-type they are playing, or how fast the tempo.

In sections such as *pengiba*, where the elaboration is filled in (four divisions to the beat) and the tempo is quite fast, *gangsa* also divide into *polos* and *sangsih*, and, like *réong*, create *kotekan*. Many kinds of *kotekan* exist,[13] but the most common in cremation music is called *kotekan ubit empat*. *Ubit-ubitan*, or simply *ubit*, indicates a specific kind of interlocking, where *polos* and *sangsih* play their own independent parts and where certain pitches coincide. So, *kotekan ubit empat* signifies an interlocking passage played over four notes, where no pitches are shared and where pitch 1 and pitch 4 coincide, creating *ngempat*.[14] Thus, in fastmoving sections both *gangsa* and *réong* are divided. In performance, some Taman Sari *gangsa* players switched back and forth between *polos* and *sangsih* when one section or the other seemed to weaken.

Below is a recording of the sixteen-beat *pengiba* from "Santun" and a diagram of its first half (eight beats). The diagram shows the *polos* and *sangsih* divisions, as well as a repeating cross-rhythmic pattern (in parentheses) that results from *ngempat* over two beats (eight pulses; dots indicate rests). Each two-beat (eight-pulse) segment creates the cross-rhythmic pattern: 3 + 3 + 2 for a total of four segments. In the recording, the whole sixteen-beat cycle is played four times, then fades out. Although I have not provided a diagram of the second half, the cross-rhythmic patterns continue throughout.[15] (◁⑴) Recording 7.5, *Pengiba* from "Santun")

DIAGRAM 7.3 *Kotekan ubit empat* (interlocking over four notes), from "Santun," *pengiba.*

		(3 + 3 + 2)	(3 + 3 + 2)	(3 + 3 + 2)	(3 + 3 + 2)
sangsih	(4)3 4 . 3 4 3 . 4	3 4 . 3 4 3 . 4	3 4 . 3 4 3 . 4	3 4 . 3 4 3 . 4 3
polos	(1). 1 2 . 1 . 2 1	. 1 2 . 1 . 2 1	. 1 2 . 1 . 2 1	. 1 2 . 1 . 2 1 .
pokok	(3) 1	3	4	
tawa-tawa	(x) x x	x x	x x	x x
beats	1 2	3 4	5 6	7 8

It was this pattern that Ernst Schlager, cited previously, noticed in the interlocking rice-pounding that he heard women play in the 1940s. Calling it *katak ngongkek* (croaking frog), he likened it to the specific *kotekan* patterns he heard in *gamelan angklung* music. Occasionally, the men of Taman Sari would add a third strand to the *kotekan* where a small group would play only pitches 2 and 3 to ensure that the interlocking remained tight.

Although *pengiba* is the only section-type that commonly uses *kotekan ubit empat*, this elaborative technique also appears in other section-types when an internal cycle is present (see below), or at the end of a section where the elaboration becomes more filled-in as the lower layer moves closer to the *kempur*. But, even in *pengiba*, where *kotekan* is expected, the players often alternated between this technique and a noninterlocking texture, a characteristic that sets *angklung* cremation music apart from other *tua* genres and more modern *angklung* compositions. (See Tenzer 2000:242–44.)

There are seven *pengiba* in this repertoire, plus two *pengiba* hybrids. Three of these use a combination of *kotekan ubit empat* (interlocking over four) and unison (noninterlocking) passages. Below is a recording and Listening Guide for the *pengiba* from "Capung Gantung." It clearly illustrates a combination of *kotekan* and unison passages with *ngempat*. The *pengiba* is twenty beats long, with phrase one lasting twelve beats and phrase two, eight beats. I have divided the second phrase into two short segments of four-and-a-half and three-and-a-half beats, corresponding to the movement of the *jegogan*. The two phrases together give the whole *pengiba* a lilting, off-kilter feel. The full *pengiba* is played here three times before fading out. It is difficult to hear the *sangsih* part at the beginning of this recording, but it gets easier as the cycle repeats. (◀ᴺ)) Recording 7.6, *Pengiba* from "Capung Gantung")

RECORDING AND LISTENING GUIDE 7.6 *Pengiba* from "Capung Gantung"

0:00–0:13	**Cue:** *ugal*
0:13–0:29	**Phrase-group:** two uneven phrases; standard/filled-in, unison and *kotekan empat*
0:13–0:22	First phrase: 12 beats
0:22–0:29	Second phrase: 8 beats (4 1/2 + 3 1/2), *kempur*
0:29–0:56	Two repeats; *suling* enters near end of first repeat
0:57–fade-out	Beginning of third repeat

The alternation between *ngempat* and *kotekan ubit empat* also results in an important sonic difference. In both instances the outer pitches (1 and 4) are struck simultaneously, but in a *ngempat*, the remaining pitches (2 and 3) are shared, thus strengthening the melodic, perhaps more singable property of the simple elaboration style. In *kotekan ubit empat*, pitches 2 and 3 alternate between *polos* and *sangsih*, creating a continuous interlocking stream of more equally weighted notes that functions less like a melody and more like a sonic embroidery.

Tenzer suggests, in looking back from the perspective of the *gamelan gong kebyar*, that *kotekan ubit empat*, and other interlocking elaborations (not used in the cremation repertoire), probably derived from music of the *tua* period, went into decline during the *madya* period, and reappeared during the *baru* period where they developed new, more formulaic, stylized forms, and took on a lightning speed in performance. However, he continues, "For the absorption to take place from *tua*, sources had to be simplified [in newer genres] to facilitate combination with the colotomic meters and melodic symmetries of *madya* gamelan" (2000:213). What we find in the *gamelan angklung* cremation repertoire today are, perhaps, the remnants of those more flexible and elastic complexities that were, in times past, present in their more nascent forms.

Symmetry and Asymmetry

The interplay between symmetry and asymmetry has long been a defining feature of *tua* genres and appears here in all three section-types. Often in tandem with each other, symmetric and asymmetric passages together

provide a rich context for formal ambiguity, a defining feature of cremation *gending*. Not constrained by the punctuating gongs of court, dance,
or narrative genres, *gamelan angklung* music provides the perfect sound-
scape for the celebratory, bittersweet, and sometimes outwardly playful
atmosphere of a Balinese cremation.

All but three of the thirty-two different sections contain an odd number
of phrases, and many contain phrases of different lengths, thus qualifying
them as asymmetric, at least at the section level. Most sections, however,
contain smaller internal regions, or areas, that are often quite symmetric
in structure. (See chapter 8 for examples.) Another common characteristic
of this repertoire is the seemingly random presence of fractional beats
creating *gongan* (the distance between two gong strokes) that add up to
63 1/2 or 59 1/4 beats, for example. Fractional beats, however, are not
improvised addons, but rather are considered a normal part of a phrase's
length, and they are found in all section-types.

Internal Forms: Phrase-Groups, Internal Cycles, and Links

Colin McPhee was casually vague in his description of how *gamelan angklung* pieces were constructed, writing in *Music in Bali*, "Each [section]
has its own shape, not too different from the others, but organized in its
own special way. Chains of short melodic sections are interwoven with
syncopated linking passages; ostinatos with figuration accompaniment are
introduced for contrast" (1966:252).[16] Below, I both clarify and expand on
McPhee's description, providing a closer look at the variety of different
episodes within sections and, in chapter 8, examine the specific ways they
are woven together in each section-type.

PHRASE-GROUPS   Phrase-groups are defined here as areas constructed
from at least two phrases that are related, that is, are repeats or variants
of one another, adhere to a similar texture or textural pattern, and come
to a definite end. Phrase-groups of various kinds and characters occur
in all sections and can be constructed from metrically even or uneven
phrases. Beginning phrase-groups establish an initial tempo, texture, and
character/mood for a section, which become points of departure for new,
often unrelated material. Phrase-groups occurring in the middle or near
the ends of sections are sometimes variants of previous material.

Below are two recordings illustrating beginning phrase-groups.
◀ᴏ)) Recording 7.7 is taken from the *pemungkah* of "Tambun" and comprises

two similar eight-beat phrases, which end with a short, accented cue on pitch 1. 🔊 Recording 7.8 is the beginning of the *pengawak* from "Lutung Loncat." It consists of three phrases of differing lengths.

RECORDING AND LISTENING GUIDE 7.7 *Pemungkah* Initial Phrase-Group, From "Tambun"

00:00–0:06	**Cue:** *ugal: gangsa pemadé;* listen for *rincik* cue at end
00:06–0:28	**Phrase-group**
0:06–0:12	**Phrase 1:** 4 beats, standard *pokok,* filled-in elaboration; repetitive four-note figure in elaboration
0:12–0:18	**Phrase 2:** 4 beats
0:18–0:23	**Phrase 3:** 4 beats, repetitive figures
0:24–0:28	**Phrase 4:** 4 beats; internal rhythmic cell (see more in text below) at ending, accented by *rincik*
0:28–fade-out	Beginning of next phrase-group

RECORDING AND LISTENING GUIDE 7.8 *Pengawak* Initial Phrase-Group from "Lutung Loncat," A

0:00–0:06	**Cue:** *ugal:* two *gangsa pemadé*
0:06–0:45	**Phrase-group:** three slightly expanding phrases; notice rhythmic pattern played at beginning of phrases
0:06–0:18	**Phrase 1:** 8 beats + a tiny breath
0:19–0:31	**Phrase 2:** 8 1/2 beats + a breath; repeat of first phrase with an added note at end
0:31–0:45	**Phrase 3:** 10 beats, divided by the *jegogan* into two smaller units: 7 + 3 beats
0:45–fade-out	Beginning of new phrase-group

Phrase-groups can be quite varied and often contain surprises, such as alternating texture changes, as in the example below of another *pengawak* taken from "Lutung Loncat." 🔊 Recording 7.9, *Pengawak* initial phrase-group from "Lutung Loncat," A)

RECORDING AND LISTENING GUIDE 7.9 *Pengawak* initial phrase-group from "Lutung Loncat" C

0:00–0:05	**Cue:** *ugal, rincik* cue
0:05–0:54	**Phrase-group:** five phrases
0:05–0:15	**Phrase 1:** 6 1/2 beats; *pengawak* texture (support *pokok*, filled-in elaboration)
0:16–0:27	**Phrase 2:** 8 beats + breath; *pemungkah* texture (standard *pokok*)
0:27–0:39	**Phrase 3:** 8 beats + breath; *pengawak* (support *pokok*)
0:40–0:46	**Phrase 4:** 6 1/2 beats; *pengawak*, repeat of phrase 1
0:46–0:54	**Phrase 5:** 8 beats + breath, *pemungkah*, repeat of phrase 2 (standard *pokok*)
0:54–fade-out	Beginning of new phrase-group

INTERNAL CYCLES   Internal cycles are often short, repeating episodes that sometimes act as links between larger areas and at other times are more substantial, becoming extended phrase-groups of their own. They occur most often in *pengawak*, where they act as a contrast to the more inconsistent meter and phrase lengths. Many internal cycles are eight to sixteen beats long and resemble short *pengiba*, in that they are constructed with a standard *pokok* and a filled-in elaboration, sometimes using the technique of *kotekan ubit empat* in performance. In some ways, they resemble vamps in jazz—short patterns that repeat many times before moving on to new material.

Below is a recording of the beginning of the *pengawak* from "Capung Manjus," with an internal cycle placed in between two *pengawak* phrase-groups. Its steady eight-beat meter, punctuated by the *kempur*, provides a sharp contrast to the more flexible *pengawak* phrasing that surrounds it. (◀))) Recording 7.10, *Pengawak* internal cycle from "Capung Manjus")

RECORDING AND LISTENING GUIDE 7.10 *Pengawak* internal cycle from "Capung Manjus"

0:00–0:07	**Cue:** *ugal, rincik*
0:07–0:29	**Phrase-group:** two phrases
0:07–0:18	**Phrase 1:** 9 beats: 5 duple beats about 50 bpm + 4 triple beats at about 60 bpm
0:18–0:29	**Phrase 2:** 8 1/2 beats; variant of phrase 1 without triplets; internal ending cell; *rincik* cue
0:29–0:38	**Internal Cycle:** one 8-beat phrase with an internal ending cell
0:38–1:20	Six repeats of cycle, each gaining speed; *rincik* gives cue for last repeat
1:20–fade-out	*Pengawak* texture and phrasing reappears, but now at a faster tempo

LINKS Links are passages that connect phrase-groups, internal cycles, or other material. They are usually constructed from small fragments taken from the upper layer of a preceding phrase. Some links are quite short—perhaps only one or two beats long—while others can span six or more beats, creating a passage of multiple syncopations, such as the following from the *pengawak* of "Sekar Jepun." (◀)) Recording 7.11, Long syncopated link from "Sekar Jepun," *pengawak*)

To conclude this discussion of the important musical building blocks found in this repertoire, here is a recording of an entire *pengawak*, which contains an initial phrase-group, two differently constructed internal cycles, and a short link. The Listening Guide shows the breakdown of the section and its internal units, illustrating how creatively and seamlessly the various parts are integrated into the total fabric of the work. (◀)) Recording 7.12, *Pengawak* from "Tungtung Tangis")

RECORDING AND LISTENING GUIDE 7.11 Long Syncopated Link, from "Sekar Jepun," *pengawak*

This example is taken from the ending of the *pengawak* and fades in during an 8-beat internal cycle. The syncopated link occurs at 0:12–0:17; it connects the internal cycle and the two ending phrases. This was recorded at a cremation.

RECORDING AND LISTENING GUIDE 7.12 *Pengawak* from "Tungtung Tangis"

0:00–0:07	**Cue:** *ugal*
0:08–0:52	**First phrase-group:** four 8-beat phrases, marked by changing *jegogan* tones; phrases three and four are variants of phrases one and two
0:53–3:22	**Internal cycle 1:** five phrases of different lengths (cycle ends/begins on pitch 1)
0:53–1:03	**phrase 1** (8 beats)
1:03–1:10	**phrase 2** (6 beats)
1:10–1:17	**phrase 3** (6 beats)
1:17–1:27	**phrase 4** (8 beats)
1:27–1:36	**phrase 5** (8 beats)
1:36–3:22	cycle repeats three times
3:22–3:45	**Link** (begins like another cycle repetition, three uneven phrases)
3:22–3:28	**phrase 1** (6 beats)
3:28–3:40	**phrase 2** (10 1/2 beats)
3:40–3:45	**phrase 3** (6 beats)
3:45–4:08	**Internal cycle 2:** two 6-beat phrases repeated two times
3:45–3:50	**phrase 1** (6 beats, starts on pitch 2)
3:50–3:56	**phrase 2** (6 beats, starts on pitch 1)
3:56–4:08	cycle repeat
4:08–fade-out	repeat

Saih Angklung: The Added Flavor of Sweetness

Saih angklung, the four-tone row of pitches used for cremation music, is most often referred to as sweet (manis), due to its high register and bell-like sound. Wayne Vitale notes that saih angklung also evokes associations with rice planting and harvest activities, such as rice-stamping, rice offerings, and the place one plants rice (2014:5). Further, this set of pitches is generally regarded as a remnant of a pre-Hindu musical past, performed not for court or concert audiences, but for local village rituals. Because this pitch set and its village-based tuning has historically remained close to home, hearing it connects one to family, ancestral shrines, deified ancestors, local banjar, and village—in other words, specific place, perhaps the most powerful component of Balinese identity.

This is somewhat bolstered by the Balinese spiritual world, where musical tones are associated with, among other things, Hindu gods, colors, and mood (Tenzer 2000:33–39). The Prakempa, a Balinese text associated with gamelan music, probably written in the eighteenth or nineteenth century, orders ten musical tones into two series of five: the Panca Tirtha, Five Holy Waters (also called pélog) and the Panca Geni, Five Holy Fires (also called slendro). The slendro set, which most Balinese musical experts see as related to saih angklung, is closely tied to Ratih, the goddess of love. Thus, slendro also carries with it the connotation of love, grace, and femininity, and when syllabized, uses the softer "n" (not "d") as its first letter (i.e., neng, nung, nang, ning), as in other slendro genres. If one accepts that saih angklung is related to slendro, then the following attributes would apply to each of its notes:

DIAGRAM 7.4 Saih angklung pitches and associations.

Syllable	God	Character
neng	I Swara	niskala (unseen/scary)
nung	Wishnu	feminine/graceful
nang	Siwa	aggressive
ning	Brahma	majestic

Gamelan angklung cremation music certainly predates the Prakempa and the codifying urges of the nineteenth and twentieth centuries, so it is unlikely that this system is completely relevant to saih angklung, or to other tua genres (except in the abstract). However, the use of this pitch set in the context of cremation music, with its evocation of oldness, sweetness, and sadness, does in large part connect to this system, if not formally.

As discussed in chapter 3, *saih angklung* has long baffled scholars attempting to analyze it within the *pélog/slendro* system. But is it a coherent system as a four-tone row? And does it contain modes? As in most pitch sets, one tone carries more weight than the others, sounding with the *kempur*, or coming to rest on a strong beat. Theoretically, any of the four pitches of *saih angklung* can act as a *kempur* tone. If one considers *saih angklung* to be part of the five-tone *slendro* system, with one tone missing, then two forms of *slendro* are possible, distinguished by genre, gamut, and register: the five-tone *slendro*, associated with *wayang kulit*, and the four-tone *slendro*, associated with *gamelan angklung* (Lisa Gold, personal communication, July 29, 2023).

Thus, the different systems are labeled here in relation to each other not as descriptions of their *modus operandi*. There has been no such discussion in the literature concerning different modes in *saih angklung* or in the music of *gamelan angklung* (nor in *gender wayang*); but, if one considers *saih angklung* to be an independent scale, not associated with the *pélog/slendro* system, then an examination of its four-ness as a complete set might yield some insight into how such sets operate within the different section-types.

In my work with *gamelan angklung*, I have come to believe, along with McPhee (in his earlier work), that *saih angklung* is its own, independent, four-tone set, not historically connected to the *pélog/slendro* theoretical system imported from Java in the mid-twentieth century. Therefore, I do not see *saih angklung* as having been derived from a parent scale, such as *saih pitu*, that scale associated with *gambuh*; and, although syllables derived from *saih pitu* exist, as shown above, and are often used by trained Balinese musicians and teachers to identify specific *pokok*, the men of *gamelan* Taman Sari did not know or use them, so I have not included them here.

The question of mode, however, is trickier. Generally, mode is defined as a tonal hierarchy whose pitches create formulaic contours and predictable tonal centers. In Bali, musicians often use the word *jalan* (road, or a system of roads) to indicate which set of pitches to use and *ambah* (via, by way of [McPhee 1966:38]) to indicate how to use them, that is, how to create the specific tonal path of a piece, a mode, as in *modus operandi*.

In the music under discussion here, pitches 3 and 1 are the most important; of the thirty-two different sections in the repertoire, sixteen begin and end on pitch 3 (50%) and thirteen on pitch 1 (about 40%). Pitch 3 can be approached from both below and above, giving its arrival at the end of a phrase or section the most flexibility. Pitch 1, though, can only be approached from above, so this limits its use somewhat. Pitches 2 and 4, as *kempur* tones, are largely avoided in this repertoire: pitch 2 is used only once as a *kempur* tone, and pitch 4, only two times. Thus, pitch 3 seems to be the most common tonal center, with pitch 1 being an important contrasting area.

More important than the frequency of certain notes or their specific use in melodic contours, however, is the sense of mode that the men of Taman Sari communicated to me through various metaphors that captured the essential sound of the ensemble for them. Like most Balinese musicians, when they referred to *saih angklung* at all, which was rare, they simply meant that set of pitches and specific tuning belonging only to their own ensemble. In other words, though there might be other four-tone pitch sets, and other *gamelan angklung*, none contained the precise intervals, register, or timbre of their *saih angklung*, with its high-pitched range and fast *ombak*.

There were two other central associations to *saih angklung* that seemed to be important to the men of Taman Sari: mood and place. The men of Taman Sari (as well as many others) often referred to their cremation music as *manis* (sweet)—a reference to its high, four-note register and to the use of the bell-like *réong* and airy *suling*. One man stated that the music was so gentle (*halus*) that hearing it helped him go to sleep at night (Interview, I Nyoman Nadra, September 9, 2007). Another stressed the importance of learning the cremation pieces only from members of his own *sekehe*, and only face to face, because the group itself carried the special feelings of home, comradery, and safety that were lost when he learned music from others or from cassette tapes (Interview, I Made Bagiarsa, November 19, 2007). One man associated the sounds of the music with his father, who had also played in the ensemble, telling me that when he played at a *ngabén*, he could sense his father hovering around him (Interview, I Nyoman Budiarta, August 8, 2007). Thus, mode was far more meaningful to the men of Taman Sari as a set of notes that, when sounded, encouraged familiar associations and moods, not a theoretical system of note placement and weight.

The general feeling-flavors conveyed by *gamelan angklung* cremation music can be best described as a blend of bittersweetness and familiarity within an overall context of oldness. Two-part tonal textures, asymmetrical meters and phrase, and flexible *pokok*/elaboration interactions, combined with the sweetness of *saih angklung* and the familiar groupness of cremation performance, create a powerful emotional mix unique to this repertoire.

CHAPTER 8

Flow-Paths

While initially learning the pieces in the *angklung* cremation repertoire, I was often struck by how differently each section-type unfolded and how a beginning character or feeling could seamlessly slip into another with a change in texture or phrase length, or a well-placed syncopation. During my time with *gamelan* Taman Sari, I most often played *jego-gan*—the instrument usually carrying the steady, relatively slow-moving underlying layer, but I mainly listened to the higher *gangsa* and *réong*, with their frequent changing textural relationships to the *jegogan*, noting their pacing in relation to each other and to the beat, and I often used these changes in pacing as guideposts to help me remember where we were in a section.

Unlike many contexts outside Bali, where students are taught *gamelan* music through the process of aural chunking[1] (thus never hearing the whole piece until all parts are known), I learned the music in the opposite way, from repeated start-to-finish playings, much as the Balinese do, where I had to make sense of the whole myself. This required a different set of memory skills from those I was used to: rather than adding chunks together to create the whole, I had to divide the whole, using my own system, to create meaningful chunks. Using these chunks, I eventually created internal aural maps to guide me along the way.[2]

As I went along, probably the most difficult task was parsing sections into discrete phrases, a task Tenzer refers to as "speculative . . . yielding ambiguous results" (2000:233). Indeed, it was not always easy to determine the beginning or ending of a phrase or where it belonged, especially in a music characterized by inconsistent phrase lengths and a small range. So, I used the following criteria to make my decisions: a phrase had to be at least four beats long, adhere to a similar texture throughout, and come to a clear end, coinciding with a *jegogan* or *kempur* stroke. However, even with these criteria, some of my decisions were more or less arbitrary, based on my own sense of pacing within a specific musical context.

What has always captivated and delighted me about this music has been its ambiguity, inconsistency, flexibility, and elasticity. It was these often unexpected anomalies that were the most important elements of this music for me and ultimately led to the ways I began to think about the music analytically. In this chapter, I examine how each of the section-types is constructed, concentrating first on a section-type's defining stylistic features and then, on how these features unfold. First, I discuss how and why I developed this analytic method. And, even though I eventually transcribed the pieces into standard Western notation, I continue to experience them aurally, in terms of sound maps, or aural paths, using changes in flow as guideposts along the way.

I define flow here simply as the perception of musical movement relative to a fixed beat.[3] Flows change throughout most pieces of music, creating paths of movement and stasis. For example, a segment of music with a constant standard *pokok* and a filled-in elaboration will have a different feeling from one with a supporting *pokok* and simple elaboration, even if the tempo is the same. What that feeling is can be codified into descriptive categories, such as fast/busy or slow/calm, but I am more interested in the changes themselves than in classifying them.[4] While learning the pieces, often in the rapid-fire setting of an actual cremation performance, I began to chunk different segments when I heard a change in texture, or a metric variation; for me, these were the two most important changes in a section's style and character, and hence a change in its flow.

Analytic Basics

When I returned home, I began to diagram these pieces, creating flow-paths to show how they unfolded in each section-type, and I use them here, along with recordings and Listening Guides to illustrate my points. The Listening Guides, as you have already seen, provide specific information about the recorded example and are meant to help you while you listen. The title at the top of each Listening Guide gives the name of the *gending* from which the section is taken and its section-type. The Listening Guides show a breakdown of the different segments and their timings; how many phrases there are in each segment; how many beats there are in each phrase; and the section's changing textures as it moves along. Changing textures are indicated in the following form: *pokok* style/elaboration style (e.g., standard/filled-in, or support/simple, etc.; see chapter 7). If no textural information is given, this means that the phrases continue as before.

Below the Guides, I provide simple flow-path diagrams that visually represent the overall structure of the recorded examples and come closest to the internal, aural maps I used to learn and remember the music. The diagrams are divided into flow-areas, visually identified by shapes and sizes: open and closed parentheses signify the opening cue; a phrase-group, as defined in chapter 7, takes the form of a box or rectangle; an internal cycle is represented by a circle; a link by a double-headed arrow; a single, independent phrase is represented by a straight line; and a carat (^), an especially important *rincik* accent or cue. The changing borders of the rectangles and circles indicate areas of uneven phrases or fractional beats. Here is a key to the symbols I use in the diagrams, some of which will be defined and illustrated further below:

DIAGRAM 8.1. Key to symbols used in flow-paths

Symbol	Meaning
( )	cue
▭	phrase-group
◌ ◯	internal cycle
⟷	link
—	solitary phrase
∧	*rincik* accent
:‖	repeat
⊙	gong

To illustrate, I present the *pemungkah* from "Katak Ngongkek," below. This *pemungkah* comprises six, similar eight-beat phrases, which I have organized into three phrase-groups of two phrases each, based primarily on slight changes in the underlying layer. This could easily have been organized as one, six-phrase phrase-group, but I have divided it here according to the chunks I used in learning it. This is a short and simple *pemungkah* with repeated and slightly varied phrases. (◀)) Recording 8.1, *Pemungkah* from "Katak Ngongkek")

RECORDING, LISTENING GUIDE, AND FLOW-PATH 8.1 *Pemungkah* from "Katak Ngongkek"

0:00–0:22:	**Cue:** Two *gangsa pemadé (ugal)* play a slightly ornamented version of the entire section, ends with *rincik* and *kempur*
0:22–0:51	**Section:** Whole ensemble plays six 8-beat phrases, standard/simple
0:23–0:33	**First phrase-group:** two 8-beat phrases; second repeats first
0:33–0:42	**Second phrase-group:** two 8-beat phrases: variations of phrases 1 and 2
0:42–0:51	**Third phrase-group:** two 8-beat phrases: variations of phrases 3 and 4, with syncopations to *kempur*
0:51–1:16	Section repeats
1:16–fade-out	Section begins to repeat but fades out at the end of the fourth phrase

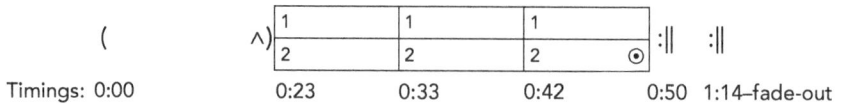

(	∧)	1	1	1		:‖	:‖
		2	2	2	⊙		

Timings: 0:00   0:23   0:33   0:42   0:50   1:14–fade-out

The flow-path visually represents the essence of the section's flow structure: three equal segments of music with the same number of phrases, the same phrase lengths, and no substantial change in texture or meter. What follows is an examination of the three main section-types in this repertoire, using recordings, Listening Guides, and flow-paths to illustrate my points. At the end of the chapter, I compare flow-paths to see if any similarities and/or differences occur in the ways the three section-types unfold.

Pemungkah Flow-Paths

Pemungkah (heads) are beginning pieces, felt as introductory, carrying no intense or deep feeling. Many are tuneful enough to be sung. Most *pemungkah* flow-paths, like that of "Katak Ngongkek" above, consist of short phrase-groups, some linked together by syncopated passages or internal cycles. Of the twelve *pemungkah* in this repertoire, most use a standard *pokok* style (one *jegogan* note to two beats). Five of the twelve use a simple elaboration (two divisions of the beat) and their beginning tempos rarely exceed 70–80 bpm.[5] The remaining seven use a filled-in elaboration (four divisions of the beat) and a starting tempo of about 40 bpm. The different subdivisions of the beat in the upper layer, combined with different tempos, create a similar metric-feel of moderate walking for all twelve.

The five *pemungkah* with simple elaborations are perhaps the most straightforward and tuneful of all section-types in this repertoire. Most contain an odd number of phrases, but all begin with phrase-groups; and many include fractional beats in some phrases that momentarily disrupt the walking sensation. Short and relatively monotextured, their elaboration layers are slow and tuneful enough to be sung, hinting that they may have originated as *génggong* or *suling* melodies, as McPhee has suggested. Further, all five of the simply elaborated *pemungkah* share similarly structured opening material. Three of the five, those from "Santun," "Katak Ngongkek," and "Sekar Jepun," share the same eight-beat opening, perhaps hinting at a common original source.

Despite the relative simplicity of *pemungkah* using this kind of elaboration, *pemungkah* phrase-groups can be quite varied. The opening nine-phrase *pemungkah* from "Alis-Alis Ijo," for example, comprises three phrase-groups, the second of which uses the animating feature of an ostinato *pokok*, with a three-feel in the elaborating layer (highly unusual). Here is the recording, Listening Guide, and flow-path for the first three phrase-groups of "Alis-Alis Ijo." (◀) Recording 8.2, *Pemungkah* from "Alis-Alis Ijo")

RECORDING, LISTENING GUIDE, AND FLOW-PATH 8.2 *Pemungkah* from "Alis-Alis Ijo"

0:00–0:04	**Cue:** one *gangsa pemadé (ugal)* to *rincik* cue
0:05–0:19	**First phrase-group:** whole ensemble: two 8-beat phrases; support/simple
0:19–0:23	**Link:** one 10-beat phrase of increasing elaborative activity
0:24–0:32	**Second phrase-group:** three 4-beat phrases at a slower, broader tempo; ostinato, with three-feel
0:32–fade-out	**Third phrase-group:** three 8-beat phrases; support/simple, ending cell (see below), *kempur*

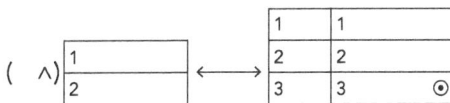

Timings: 0:00   0:05   0:19   0:24   0:32–fade-out

Here I use different-sized rectangles to show the phrase-groups' relative sizes: the height of the rectangle visually indicates how many phrases there are in each phrase-group, and the width shows how long the phrases are, relative to each other. For example, phrase-groups three and four, above, contain one more phrase than phrase-group one; and the phrases in phrase-group two are half as long as those in groups one and three.

The seven *pemungkah* using a filled-in elaboration style are generally longer and their phrase-groups are more structurally related to each other than those using a simple elaboration. They also make use of what I call "holding patterns" and "ending cells," features not found in their counterparts. I define holding patterns as one-beat units, repeated in the elaboration over four beats, where the *pokok* oscillates between two pitches.[6] They are of two kinds: (1) four onbeat units, each containing four notes that repeat over four beats (Diagram 8.2); and (2) five shifting units, each containing three notes, which repeat and shift in relation to the *pokok* over four beats (Diagram 8.3). The second kind provides a passage of shifting accents that eventually resolves on a strong beat.[7] Occasionally, these two holding patterns are combined to create an eight-beat segment.

DIAGRAM 8.2 Onbeat, four-note holding pattern.

elaboration	2321 2321 2321 2321 2			
pokok	2	3	2	
beat	x x x x x			

DIAGRAM 8.3 Shifting, three-note holding pattern.

elaboration.	.212 3123 1231 2312 3			
pokok	2	1		
beat	x x x x x			

Ending cells are essentially formulaic cues, used frequently in *pemungkah*. They, like holding patterns, are also of two kinds: The first, a section-ending cell, is one that literally ends a section, such as an upward flourish to pitch 3, as in "Alis-Alis Ijo," above, or a downward fall to pitch 1 (Diagram 8.4). They are used almost exclusively in filled-in *pemungkah* and in *pemungkah*-like regions found in other sections.

DIAGRAM 8.4 Section-ending cell.

For pitch 3				var. 1232 (3)
elaboration	2112	3123	2132	1312 (3)
pokok				
beat	x	x	x	x	x
For pitch 1				
elaboration	1312	3132 (1)		
pokok	3		1	
beat	x	x	x		

The second type, phrase-group ending cells, occur internally, where they mark a clear ending of a phrase-group; these are performed on one note in the elaboration and are always accompanied by strong accents created by the elaborating instruments and *rincik*, using a click damp, as in Diagram 8.5:

DIAGRAM 8.5 Phrase-group–ending cell.

	^^^	^
elaboration	.333	3
pokok		3
beat	x.	x

The *pemungkah* from "Tambun" beautifully illustrates the use of both kinds of ending cells, as well as both kinds of holding patterns, and short syncopated links. The recording presents the whole section three times. Unlike the flow-paths of the previous two examples, this one contains phrase-groups with phrases of unequal length (phrase-groups three and four). These are visually represented by the jagged right sides of the boxes. (◀) Recording 8.3, *Pemungkah* from "Tambun")

RECORDING, LISTENING GUIDE, AND FLOW-PATH 8.3 *Pemungkah* from "Tambun"

0:00–0:08	**Cue:** *ugal* and *rincik* cue using click damp
0:09–0:29	**First phrase-group:** two similar 8-beat phrases, standard/filled-in, holding pattern in the second phrase, internal ending cell (first time only)
0:30–0:48	**Second phrase-group:** two similar 8-beat phrases, with onbeat and shifting holding patterns, internal ending cell
0:48–1:16	**Third phrase-group:** three phrases (8 + 8 + 12 beats) with alternating holding patterns and short syncopated links, internal ending cell; tempo increases
1:16–1:34	**Fourth phrase-group:** two phrases of unequal length (10 + 8 beats) with alternating holding patterns and syncopated links (no *kempur* at end)
1:35–2:39	Repeat of whole section, with internal ending cells filled in
2:39–end	Repeat

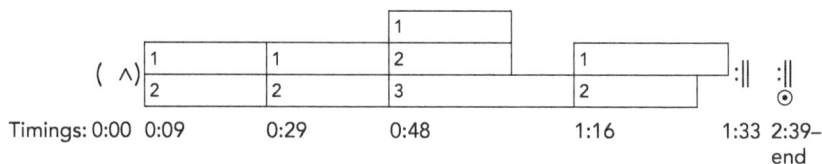

Timings: 0:00 0:09   0:29   0:48   1:16   1:33 2:39– end

A final example of a filled-in *pemungkah* illustrates the internal cycle. An internal cycle, as defined in chapter 7, is a cycle inserted within a section. Internal cycles often contain short phrase-groups of their own. All section-types in this repertoire are cyclical, in that they are meant to be repeated from beginning to end many times in performance. Embedding a cycle within an already-cyclical form creates a set of cycles that, in this repertoire, have their own independent repeat structure. That is, the entire section may only be repeated two or three times in a performance, but the internal cycle may be repeated eight or more times within each overall repeat.

This elasticity is important as it mirrors that of the ritual itself. As discussed more fully in chapter 9, timings in a cremation ceremony are flexible. Perhaps more (or less) time might be needed for grandchildren or *banjar* members to say a final goodbye to the deceased; or the burning of the corpse might take a long time in one instance and less time in another. Musical elements such as short sections and flexible repetition structures are necessary, as they can be easily adjusted to a specific context.[8]

The following sixteen-phrase *pemungkah*, taken from *gending* "Tung-tung Tangis," contains a thirteen-phrase internal cycle. The cycle is flanked by a one-phrase introduction and a two-phrase ending. It is possible that this *pemungkah* began as a thirteen-phrase cycle and an introduction and ending were added later. Phrases in the cycle have different numbers of beats, forming segments of contraction and expansion. I have indicated these differences with a multisided circle (an "irregular" circle). The entire *pemungkah* is played only once in this recording, but its internal cycle of seventy-four beats is played three times. (◀ᵈ) Recording 8.4, *Pemungkah* from "Tungtung Tangis")

RECORDING, LISTENING GUIDE, AND FLOW-PATH 8.4 *Pemungkah* from "Tungtung Tangis"

0:00–0:07	**Cue:** *ugal* (you can hear my voice at the beginning)
0:08–0:22	**Introduction:** one 8-beat phrase: standard/filled-in; internal ending cell
0:23–1:42	**Internal cycle:** thirteen phrases in three phrase-groups and one ending phrase
0:23–0:44	**first phrase-group** (starts on pitch 3): two 8-beat phrases, internal ending cell
0:44–0:58	**second phrase-group:** three 4-beat phrases
0:58–1:37	**third phrase-group:** seven phrases 6, 4, 6, 6, 6, 4, 6 beats
1:37–1:42	**fourth phrase-group:** 8 beats, internal ending cell
1:43–2:42	Cycle repeated; starts on pitch 3
2:43–3:32	Cycle repeated; starts on pitch 3
3:33–end	**Ending:** two 8-beat phrases, the second of which is syncopated In both layers, *kempur*

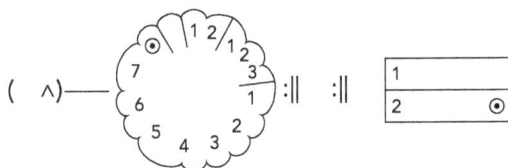

Timings: 0:00   0:08   0:23   1:43 2:43 3:33–end

Pengawak Flow-Paths

Pengawak, as we have seen, are distinctly different from *pemungkah*; they also contain the most changeable musical features. *Pengawak* (body) are conceptualized as substantial, intense, or "godly" (Lebah, in Tenzer 2000:356). Their inconsistent phrase lengths, combined with slow tempos, often give *pengawak* a feeling of expanding and contracting, like deep breathing. At times, a *pengawak* support *pokok* closely follows the syncopations and other rhythmic ambiguities of the elaboration; at other times, an internal cycle appears using a standard *pokok*. The continual repetition of the internal cycle in a *pengawak* creates a metric, textural, often lulling regulation, in contrast to the meandering unequal phrasing found elsewhere in *pengawak*.

All *pengawak*, as noted previously, begin the same way with a defining rhythmic cell played by the elaborating layer on one pitch of *saih angklung*, followed by a short, more animated *pemungkah*-like phrase. Often, these phrases form the beginning of an internal cycle. Below is a recording, Listening Guide, and flow-path for the *pengawak* from "Prebangsa." This *pengawak* contains an internal cycle of seven phrases of unequal length, some of which use fractional beats and/or breaths. It is comparatively short (nine phrases), including the seven-phrase internal cycle and a more animated and unrelated two-phrase ending. (◀ᴵ) Recording 8.5, *Pengawak* from "Prebangsa")

RECORDING, LISTENING GUIDE, AND FLOW-PATH 8.5 *Pengawak* from "Prebangsa"

0:00–0:07	**Cue:** *Ugal*	
0:08–1:34	**Internal cycle** (seven phrases)	
	0:08–0:36	**first phrase-group:** two phrases: 10 + 9 1/4 beats, support/filled-in
	0:37–1:02	**second phrase-group:** two phrases: 10 + 10
	1:02–1:34	**third phrase-group:** three phrases: 10 + 10 + 9 1/4
1:34–2:33	Cycle repeated	
2:34-3:30	Cycle repeated; last phrase becomes first phrase of ending	
3:30–end	**Ending phrase-group**	
	phrase 1: 9 1/2 beats, syncopation	
	phrase 2: 6 beats, to *kempur*	

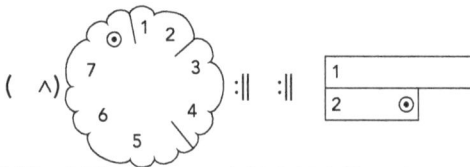

Timings: 0:00   0:08   1:34 2:34 3:30–end

The *pengawak* from *gending* "Lutung Loncat" also contains an internal cycle with fractional beats, as well as other elements that contribute to its metric flexibility. Each phrase is a different length, and syncopation in the support layer is prominent. The tendency here seems to be a deliberate avoidance of phrase regularity, meter, or symmetry, with the musical flow taking on more of the flexibility of everyday or declarative speech.

Some *pengawak* are constructed using alternating phrases with markedly different textures, such as the *pengawak* from "Sekar Jepun," seen below, where textures associated with *pengawak* and *pemungkah* alternate, although not to the point of hybridity. This *pengawak* also includes a short internal cycle and phrase-groups with changing lengths, illustrating the *pengawak* tendency to also avoid a fixed structure. ((◀)) Recording 8.6, *Pengawak* from "Sekar Jepun")

RECORDING, LISTENING GUIDE, AND FLOW-PATH 8.6 *Pengawak* from "Sekar Jepun"

0:00–0:06	**Cue**
0:06–0:25	**First phrase-group:** two 8-beat phrases; support/filled-in
0:25–0:41	**Second phrase-group:** two 8-beat phrases; variation on first phrase-group
0:41–0:55	**Third phrase-group:** two 8-beat phrases; phrases on second phrase-group
0:55-1:19	**Fourth phrase-group:** four uneven phrases
	phrase 1: 10 beats
	phrase 2: 6 beats
	phrase 3: 8 beats
	phrase 4: 8 beats
1:19–1:47	**Internal cycle:** one 8-beat phrase, standard/filled-in, played six times (*kempur* ends on pitch 1); the last time shortened to 5 1/2 beats
1:47–1:52	**Link:** 7 3/4 beats, highly syncopated
1:52–end	**Fourth phrase-group:** two phrases of unequal length
	phrase 1: 11 beats
	phrase 4: 4 beats, *kempur*

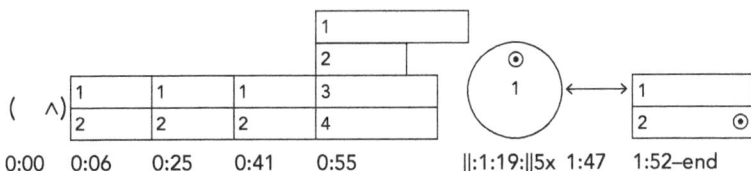

Timings: 0:00   0:06   0:25   0:41   0:55   ‖:1:19:‖5x 1:47   1:52–end

Pengiba Flow-Paths

Pengiba (feet) have the character of running and busyness (i.e., *ramé*). The seven *pengiba* in this repertoire are generally short, fastmoving cycles like many found in more modern pieces. In most, the *pokok* moves steadily at a standard two-beat pace and is elaborated by *kotekan ubit empat*, as well as unison passages. Below is a recording and Listening Guide for the *pengiba* from "Lutung Loncat" (no flow-path). This *pengiba*, along with the *pengiba* from "Sekar Jepun," are the only ones in the repertoire that are clearly constructed with one phrase-group consisting of four similar eight-beat phrases. In the recording, the whole section is played three times and fades out at the start of the fourth repetition. ((◀)) Recording 8.7, *Pengiba* from "Lutung Loncat")

RECORDING AND LISTENING GUIDE 8.7 *Pengiba* from "Lutung Loncat"

0:00–0:12	**Cue**
0:12–0:31	**Phrase-group:** four 8-beat phrases, standard/filled-in, *kotekan empat*, with unison near the end; *kempur*
0:32–1:22	Repeat three times
1:22–fade-out	Beginning fourth repeat

Three of the seven *pengiba* contain a *pokok* that is tuneful, taking the melodic shape of an ostinato; here, the *jegogan* notes move at the rate of one note per beat, creating a layer of rhythmic density and animation. The *pengiba* from "Tungtung Tangis," as discussed in chapter 7, illustrates this form. It consists of two ostinato *pokok* that end on different pitches: the first on pitch 3 and the second on pitch 1. The two cycles alternate their repeats, with the first cycle repeating far more times than the second, creating a kind of asymmetry within a symmetry. The pattern of repeats heard in the recording could, of course, be quite different in a different performance. A final phrase-group is constructed from four similar eight-beat phrases using a standard *pokok* and a simple elaboration. ((◀)) Recording 8.8, *Pengiba* from "Tungtung Tangis")

RECORDING, LISTENING GUIDE, AND FLOW-PATH 8.8 *Pengiba* from "Tungtung Tangis"

0:00–0:06	**Cue:** *ugal*
0:06–0:37	**Cycle 1:** one 8-beat phrase (ends on pitch 3); standard/filled-in, *kotekan empat*; played eight times; listen for *rincik* that cues the second cycle
0:37–0:48	**Cycle 2:** one 8-beat phrase (ends on pitch 1), played three times; accompanied by *kebyar*-like rhythmic accents with *rincik* prominent
0:48–1:45	**Cycle 1:** played sixteen times
1:45–1:53	**Cycle 2:** played three times
1:53–2:08	**Cycle 1:** played five times; at 2:02 there is a sudden slowing
2:08–end	**Phrase-group:** four 8-beat phrases; standard/simple, *kempur* (3)

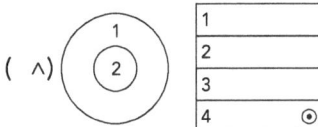

Timings: 0:00   c.1 0:06 :‖8x   2:08–end
             c.2 0:37 :‖3x
             c.1 0:48 :‖16x
             c.2 1:45 :‖3x
             c.1 1:53 :‖5x

Hybrid Flow-Paths

Although most sections in the cremation repertoire contain mixtures of different section-type characteristics, five rise to the level of hybrids. These are sections that begin in one style but quickly slide into another, and perhaps back again, to the point that it is difficult (at least for me) to assign them to a specific section-type. The third section of "Alis-Alis Ijo," for example, is nine phrases long. It begins as a *pemungkah*, complete with a standard *pokok*, filled-in elaboration, and a holding pattern, but switches to a *pengawak* in phrases two through four. Together, these four phrases form a phrase-group of one *pemungkah* plus three *pengawak* phrases. Phrases five through seven shorten this pattern, forming a three-phrase unit with one *pemungkah* phrase followed by two *pengawak* phrases; phrase eight begins with a hint of a *pengawak* opening but slides into *pemungkah* style, which continues to the end. Looking at the section as a whole unit, it appears to slowly contract, reducing itself to its true hybrid essence. (🔊 Recording 8.9, *Pemungkah/pengawak* hybrid from "Alis-Alis Ijo")

RECORDING, LISTENING GUIDE, AND FLOW-PATH 8.9 *Pemungkah/ pengawak* hybrid from "Alis-Alis Ijo"

0:00–0:08	**Cue**
0:08–0:44	**First phrase-group**
	phrase 1: 8 1/2 beats, standard/filled-in
	phrase 2: 8 1/2 beats, support
	phrase 3: 10 1/2 beats, standard
	phrase 4: 10 beats, support
0:44–1:09	**Second phrase-group**
	phrase 1: 10 1/2 beats, standard
	phrase 2: 8 1/2 beats, support
	phrase 3: 8 beats
1:09–end	**Third phrase-group**
	phrase 1: 8 beats, standard, variation of phrase 1 of first phrase-group
	phrase 2: 4 beats, *kempur*

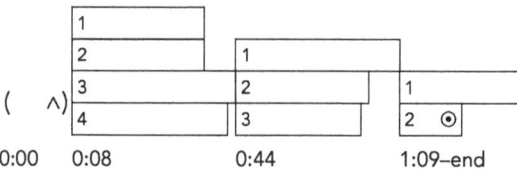

Timings: 0:00   0:08   0:44   1:09–end

Like "Alis-Alis Ijo," the third section of "Capung Manjus" is a hybrid that merges two section-types: a *pengawak* and *pengiba*. It is thirteen phrases long; the first two clearly conform to a *pengawak* style; but the remainder of the section is a *pengiba*, containing two separate internal cycles, both elaborated with a *kotekan empat*, and underlain by two different and tuneful ostinatos. The ending of the transition and the ending phrase of the cycle contain an unusual elaborative ornament: three full beats of pitch 4 leading into the *kempur*. (🔊 Recording 8.10, *Pengawak/Pengiba* hybrid from "Capung Manjus")

RECORDING, LISTENING GUIDE, AND FLOW-PATH 8.10 *Pengawak/Pengiba* hybrid from "Capung Manjus"

0:00–0:06	**Cue**
0:06–0:39	**Phrase group:** Four phrases
	phrase 1: 6 beats; support/filled-in
	phrase 2: 6 beats: standard
	phrase 3: 8 beats
	phrase 4: 4 beats, internal ending cell
0:39–1:12	**Cycle 1:** four 8-beat phrases, *kotekan ubit empat*; internal ending cell
1:12–4:00	Cycle repeated seven times, gradually accelerating, then slowing on last repeat
4:00–4:06	**Link:** one 10-beat phrase ending with 3 beats on pitch 4
4:06–4:32	**Cycle 2:** six phrases in two groups [8 + 8 + 8] [8 + 8 + 4] *kempur*
4:32–end	Cycle repeated four times, accelerating and slowing, as above

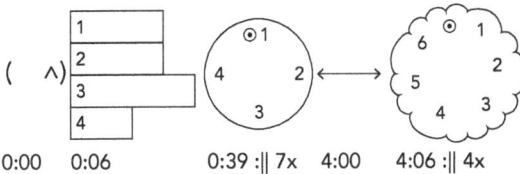

Timings: 0:00   0:06   0:39 :‖ 7x   4:00   4:06 :‖ 4x

Flow-Paths Compared

Looking at the flow-path diagrams above, it is easy to see that the three section-types unfold differently. Although using many of the same basic musical structures, such as phrase-groups or internal cycles, they create different paths of movement and stasis. *Pemungkah* are relatively uneventful, that is, they have a moderate number of changeable features. Most end with the same textural pacing and phrase lengths with which they began; textures, once set, remain the same throughout the section (with some exceptions). When textures and phrase lengths change, they do so in the middle or near the ends of sections, creating episodes of contraction and expansion; and short, syncopated passages are often used to end a phrase-group or a section.

Pengawak, on the other hand, show a remarkable flexibility and elasticity. Changes in texture and phrase-length occur throughout. There is far more use of fractional beats and breaths, indicated in the diagrams with uneven edges. Their slow tempos, combined with repeating single pitches of different duration at the beginnings of phrases, create a lulling or calming effect, while alternations between phrases with *pengawak* and *pemungkah*-like movement in the lower layer provide a bit of contrast. Further, *pengawak* are longer and consist of more contrasting textures, ragged, cloudlike internal cycles, and phrases that alternate between simple and filled-in elaborations or integrate these changes slowly. Indeed, textural and metric fluidity are hallmarks of this section-type and their flow-paths show this. These constant changes create a formal and tonal ambiguity that only heightens the wandering and emotionally deepening character of *pengawak*.

Pengiba* create the most concise and stable flow-paths, with their (usually) quick tempos, unchanging *pokok*, and elaboration pacing. Animation is created here by the prominence of cross-rhythmic accents that burst out of both *kotekan* and *ngempat* elaborations. Hybrids are the least integrated of all the sections. Changes in their textures and other contrasting elements occur more abruptly, highlighting their differences. It is possible that hybrids were constructed by fusing two different section-types or smaller segments together.

Section-types are also somewhat differentiated by their use of *saih angklung*. As stated above, pitches 3 and 1 dominate the repertoire overall. Pitch 3 is dominant in *pemungkah*, and *pengiba*, while pitch 1 dominates *pengawak*. What differentiates the use of *saih angklung* in *pengawak* from that in *pemungkah* and *pengiba*, though, is the length to which certain pitches remain prominent. For example, in many *pengawak*, each of the four pitches takes its turn at articulating the beginning rhythmic cell and dominating a region, with pitch 4 often occurring near the end.[9] This creates an ambiguous tonal field, with no pitch dominating. In *pemungkah* and *pengiba*, a firm tonal area is established at the beginning and it returns, with a few exceptions, at the end, which of course is also the beginning of a repetitive cycle. Whether *saih angklung* can be seen as modal, though, is a question still awaiting an answer.

Finally, I would like to suggest that, based on these analyses, each of the section-types entered the repertoire at a different historical time, although this is still a matter of conjecture. The continually changing musical characteristics of *pengawak*, for example, with their flexible phrasing, changing textures, and meters (or a lack of meter), mark them as the oldest. Clearly, they match the defining characteristics of other *tua* genres most closely. Pengiba* seem to be the youngest section-type, corresponding most closely

to newer forms developed during the *madya* period, with their more symmetric and formulaic structures, and their fast-playing tempos.

I divide *pengawak* between those with a simple elaboration and those
with a filled-in one. The use of a simpler elaboration suggests their more
tuneful nature and their possible origins in traditional *génggong, wayang,*
and *suling* tunes that were adapted to the *gamelan angklung.* I suggest that
these are older and might have developed alongside *pengawak* sometime
in the distant past. *Pemungkah* with filled-in elaborations more closely
resemble music composed during the *madya* period of Balinese music
history. They are longer, more integrated musically, and have more of the
formality of "classical" forms. Like the question posed above concerning
modes in *saih angklung,* however, these also await further study.

CHAPTER 9

In the Context of Performance

It is in the real-time context of a cremation that many important aspects of Balinese life and identity come together. Looking more closely at the ritual process of a cremation, as well as the role of music in this process, one can see a set of embedded performances that unfolds and extends way beyond the music, its *rasa*, or the even the ritual itself. Certainly, there are performances of music, each piece imbued with its own characteristic feelings/flavors, but there are also performances of place, family, and community; of ritual obligation; and of the past in the present that all come together in the context of cremation. This chapter examines how these multiple performances merge to create a deeply meaningful and effective experience for both the living and the dead.

The Order of Things

While I was recording and learning the music at my weekly sessions, using internal flow-paths such as the ones diagrammed in the previous chapter, I was also playing with the group at cremations. I immediately saw some major differences, the most important of which were playing order and the timing of individual sections. When performing for a cremation we never played a whole *gending* in section order (*pemungkah, pengawak, pengiba*); rather, we played strings of the same section-type taken from multiple *gending*. Further, once the *ugal* player had chosen a section to play, we might zip through it once with no repeats, or repeat it six or seven times; and one short internal cycle in a section might be repeated again and again, extending the playing time of the section considerably.

Thus, the idealized three-part order, as partially represented in Diagram 7.1 in chapter 7, essentially dissolves in performances at cremations, where, as opposed to concerts, all sections become independent pieces and all performances are unique. Sections still retain their individual characters, but are not linked together in any metaphorical, structural, or musical sense. Nor are they fixed in performance time; that is, their playing time can be extended or contracted at the will of the *ugal* or *rincik* players who cue repeats and endings. This made me wonder about the importance of ordering and what it could reveal about how the men conceptualized their repertoire in different ways.

Three separate but intersecting orderings of the thirty-two different sections in the repertoire were used by the men in differing contexts and for different purposes. When the men were teaching me the pieces, they made sure I recorded them in the order shown in Diagram 7.1, including those section repeats that appeared in different *gending*. This was the order in which they said they had learned them from their original teacher from Denpasar. To ensure accuracy, the head of the ensemble, Pak Rideng, brought a written list to the sessions to which he frequently referred. The men in the *sekehe* indicated the individual *gending* by their names and the individual sections by their number within the *gending* (not their more metaphoric names), as in "Tambun," *seksi satu* ("Tambun," section 1), not "Tambun, *pemungkah*." There were often disagreements among the men as to which section followed which, and an accidental switching of two sections in my first recordings, but eventually I recorded (and learned) the pieces in this order, which I call here the *official order*.

Later in my fieldwork, however, Pak Rideng gave me the more metaphorical names for these three, contrasting section-types: *pemungkah, pengawak,* and *pengiba.*[1] To illustrate the embodiment and general feeling of these terms, he pointed to the parts of his own body corresponding to each section, nodding his head leisurely for *pemungkah,* standing up straight and pointing to his midsection for *pengawak,* and moving his feet, as though running, for *pengiba* (Interview, Pak Rideng, December 16, 2008). His performance of these different feelings/flavors indicated that an ideal *gending* should include different, contrasting *rasa.* I call this the *rasa order.*

Neither the official nor *rasa* order were used at cremations. We always played the *pemungkah* from "Santun" (number 1 in Diagram 7.1) first and the *pengiba* "Jaran Nginjek" (number 15) last, but in between, we moved back and forth playing sections from all different *gending,* in what at first seemed to me to be random order. And, as I wrote above, the *ugal* player would sometimes sneak in a new, previously unknown section, usually a *pemungkah*, to teach us.

Although the specific order was different for each cremation, a common pattern emerged: we would most often begin with two or three *pemungkah*, followed by one *pengawak* (or one *pengiba*), followed by another set of *pemungkah*, etc., creating strings of different and contrasting section-types that mirrored the affect of the ritual. This ordering seemed to be consistent with the emotional contrasts of *rasa* order and, at the same time, also in keeping with the elasticity of the ritual itself, where one or another segment might be cut short or elongated. I call this the *performance order*.

These three orderings reveal differences in the way the men conceptualize and perform this repertoire. *Official order* is fixed (written down in Pak Rideng's notebook); it is not performed. It theoretically posits that the different sections, linked together to form the fifteen *gending*, were in place from the beginning and have remained so to the present day. It is a direct (perhaps imagined) link to the past, a reminder of the origins of the group, and a permanent and public record of *sekehe* ownership. *Rasa order* highlights the importance of emotional contrast, as signified in the metaphorical names given to the section-types. *Performance order* is an in-time, live musical expression of changing feelings, extended over many hours, and linked in time and place to an ongoing ritual.

At most cremations, *pemungkah* are the sections most played and repeated. As indicated above, they are often played at the beginning of a set, and for long stretches in between *pengawak* and *pengiba*. This imbues them with a kind of neutral or midground feeling, one that may regulate the more heightened feelings elicited by *pengawak* (sadness, quiet introspection, *sepi*) or *pengiba* (excitement, busyness, *ramé*). Further, each time we played a *pemungkah*, the playing time was greatly extended through multiple repeats. A *pemungkah* that might have taken around one minute for me to record would extend to over six or eight minutes when played at a cremation. *Pemungkah* could thus help to calm more heightened feelings, and its *rasa*, especially if prolonged, could act as a transition from one emotional state to another.

Pengawak were played less frequently than *pemungkah*. However, when a *pengawak* contained an internal cycle, the entire section might be played only once, but the internal cycle repeated many times. This technique, along with a far slower tempo, resulted in a total playing time that was similar to that of *pemungkah*. For example, at a performance on April 13, 2008, we played the same *pemungkah* three times, which lasted around four and a half minutes, followed by one *pengawak*, with an internal cycle that was repeated seven times, lasting about five minutes, so that the almost ten minutes of playing time was divided into two roughly equal parts, each with a different overall *rasa*.

Pengiba were the least played section-types. However, as the shortest and fastest sections, only a few of which contained inner cycles, they were often repeated ten or more times in performance, extending their individual playing time considerably as they reached almost unplayable speed. Their total playing time, though, was about the same as that of the other section-types. Thus, although the section-types alternated, no one section-type or *rasa* dominated and any could be shortened or lengthened, if needed.

Repeating an entire section or internal cycle often involved a specific tempo-dynamic plan. For example, in Recording 9.1 we hear a common repeat structure used during one performance of the *pemungkah* from "Capung Gantung," which we often played at cremations. Here, the entire section is played once and then repeated eight times, with the *rincik*, using a short damp, cueing us to slow down or speed up. (See ˆ in the diagram for *rincik* cues.) Diagram 9.1 illustrates a tempo-dynamic plan that creates a contracted route through a path of different short-term contrasts, with none dominating. The last repeat, with its abrupt slowing and moderate dynamic, signals an end to the *pemungkah*, as well as a return to its leisurely walking character. (◀ᴐ) Recording 9.1, *Pemungkah* from "Capung Gantung")

DIAGRAM 9.1 Tempo-dynamic plan of repeats: "Capung Gantung" B, *pemungkah*.

Playings	1 2 3 4^	5 6^	7 8^	9
Tempos	c. 120	100	140	80
Dynamics	medium loud	a bit softer	louder	medium loud

Cremation Flow-Paths

In chapter 8, I charted my own perceptions of the different affective flow-paths found in each section-type, illustrating my processes of learning and remembering the music. In the context of a cremation performance, however, the affective path is created over many hours by both the music and the ritual it accompanies. Here, certain musical performance practices, such as relative tempos, dynamics, and extended or contracted playing times, are combined with the flow of ritual activities to become the primary sources for an emotional and spiritual narrative.

This is not to suggest that there is much conscious attention paid to such practices, although I suspect that the *ugal* player, the person choosing what comes next, is aware, perhaps implicitly, of the ongoing ritual process and tries to mirror the flow of the music so that the right atmosphere of the cremation is maintained throughout.[2] I often asked the *ugal* player, Pak Madia, why he chose specific section-types or pieces to play at any one time, and why he took so many repeats in some places and so few in others; he never answered my questions directly, simply stating that he did so when the *rasa* needed to change (informal conversations with Pak Madia, 2007–8).

In chapter 5, a general timeline for a cremation was presented in Diagram 5.1 that showed its various stages. Our musical performance practices were briefly discussed in chapter 6. Here, we examine more closely one segment of the timeline in Diagram 5.1: sections D and E (items numbered 20 through 31, page 84), covering the day of the cremation itself, from its early morning beginnings at the home compound to its early to midafternoon ending at the *kuburan.*

I divide this space of about five hours into smaller segments, each a necessary part of the ceremony, during which certain activities, such as washing and wrapping the deceased's body, processing through the village, giving offerings, and burning the corpse are a part. What is crucial to the effectiveness of the day, however, is the constant maintenance of the right atmosphere, or right feeling (*rasa*), at times busy and excited (*ramé*), at other times, more thoughtful and poignant (*sepi*), but for the most part balanced between these two extremes. Thus, the music that is performed helps to create an affective supporting narrative that parallels the narrative of the ritual, mirroring its ebbs and flows.[3]

I have divided the five-hour period into three ninety-minute segments and one thirty-minute segment, each with its own function and overall feeling. This timeline and the written and graphic descriptions that follow are composites drawn from many cremations I participated in while in Bali. They are not meant to be exact recreations of a specific ceremony or of Balinese cremations in general but are representative of what I experienced. Times are approximate and, although section-types are identified, specific names of *gending* are not.

The timeline in Diagram 9.2 shows what happens during each period and where it happens. Beneath the timeline is a written description of each segment and a graphic illustration showing the basic atmosphere created by the musical and ritual activities performed during that period. Here, actual performance segments drawn from my own field recordings are used to illustrate these points, showing what section-types we played and in what order. To indicate the different section-types, a single letter found in each word is used: K, for *pemungKah*; W, for *pengaWak*; and B, for *pengiBa*, as well as simple lines to indicate their general affect: *pemungkah* (steadiness/neutrality: a straight line), *pengawak* (deepening/slowing: a downward line), and *pengiba* (heightening/animating: an upward line). When connected, they create a cremation flow-path not unlike those illustrated in chapter 8, but here it is a path covering a five-hour-long cremation ceremony, with its accompanying musical choices, and the major points of most heightened and deepened feeling.

DIAGRAM 9.2 Timeline of a typical cremation.

home compound	walking through the village	at the *kuburan*	back to the *balé*	
c. 7:00 a.m.	c. 8:30 a.m.	c. 10:00 a.m.	c. 11:30 a.m.	noon
1. arrival	2. separating/ processing/ rejoining	3. remembering/ grieving/ celebrating	4. burning/ departure	

Description of Events

1. Arrival c. 7:00 a.m.–c. 8:30 a.m.: We arrive at the home compound in Pak Budiarta's truck, unload the instruments, and Pak Winaja (the priest) blesses them. The family is finishing the construction of the *wadah* (cremation tower) and bier (platform that carries the *wadah*) that will carry the corpse to the *kuburan*. Food and coffee are served while the corpse, still inside the compound, is being washed and wrapped for the final time in preparation for the journey to the *kuburan* and beyond. We play on and off, taking coffee breaks every half-hour or so.

There is a general feeling of awakening, of newly invigorating the living and the dead for what is to come, and a growing sense of focus. As more and more people arrive, a feeling of excitement builds slowly until the body is finally carried out from inside and placed in the *wadah*, now resting on its platform, which is attached to many long bamboo poles. This beginning time segment has an upward or quickening trajectory overall, from a gentle awakening to a growing sense of purpose.

Diagram 9.3 shows the different section-types we played and the order in which we played them for a cremation ceremony at Desa Sambung, Badung, on September 14, 2007. As always, we begin with the *pemungkah* from "Santun" and follow with an eight-section string of interlaced *pemungkah* and *pengawak*. Moving on, we play two *pengiba*, followed by another string of *pengawak* and *pemungkah*, ending with two *pengiba*, the last of which is "Jaran Nginjek." We have played twenty sections over a ninety-minute period, which also included two breaks (not shown). Diagram 9.3, below, shows the musical flow-path in relation to the general *rasa* (atmosphere or feeling) for that segment. It is significant that of the twenty sections played, half are *pemungkah*, with a heightening excitement mirrored by the two *pengiba* in the middle and at the end of the segment.

DIAGRAM 9.3 Ritual and musical flow-path of arrival segment, from cremation at Desa Sambung, Badung, September 14, 2007.

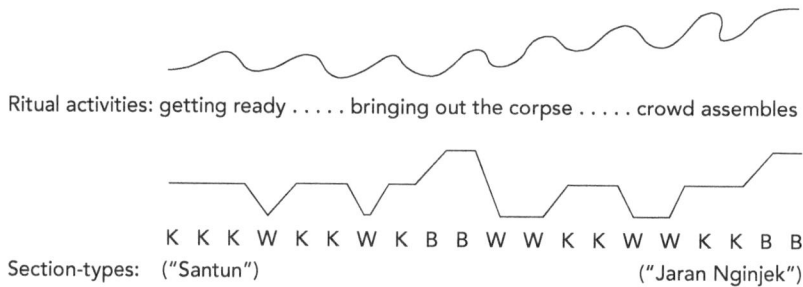

Ritual activities: getting ready . . . . . bringing out the corpse . . . . . crowd assembles

K K K W K K W K B B W W K K W W K K B B

Section-types: ("Santun")   ("Jaran Nginjek")

2. Processing/Separating/Rejoining c. 8:30 a.m.–10:00 a.m.: When all family members, friends, and others in the community have arrived, and the body of the deceased is now inside the *wadah*, we stop playing. The assembled crowd forms a line, headed by six or eight women carrying tall pyramids of fruit on their heads. Each person in the line grasps part of a long white cloth that will be held during the procession through the village and into the *kuburan*. The cloth, pure white—the color of death— effectively holds the group together, both symbolically and literally, and ensures that no one gets lost on the journey, which can in some cases be a few miles long. The platform, supported by bamboo poles, is lifted onto the shoulders of four to eight strong men and boys, usually family members, and moves into the line of participants. As you can see in the picture below, the *wadah* is constructed in three parts, symbolizing the lower, middle, and upper worlds of the Balinese universe (Bakan 1999:67–77).

At this point, about half of the men from our *gamelan angklung* leave the group to form a *beleganjur* ensemble, consisting of our eight *réong* pots and our midsized gong (*kempur*). The *beleganjur* ensemble walks through the village ahead of the *wadah* and plays a short eight-beat *kotekan empat*, one

FIGURE 9.1 Lifting the *wadah*.

FIGURE 9.2 Members of
Taman Sari walking ahead
of the *wadah*, playing
beleganjur music.

pot per person. On the way, the men holding the platform twist, turn, and twirl it vigorously when passing over various street intersections and other spaces where evil and mischievous spirits linger; this is done to confuse these troublemakers and prevent them from causing harm. Excitement builds as the procession moves along.

Meanwhile, I go to the *kuburan*, along with the remaining men and instruments, in the truck. There we set up the instruments again where they wait in the shade under a large, imposing banyan tree for the procession to arrive; then we take a break. When it arrives, the *wadah* is placed in the center of the field and is again twirled to the accompaniment of the *beleganjur* ensemble and loud, raucous laughter, shouting, and sometimes, mock fighting, where the forces of evil and good vie for possession of the deceased's spirit (Bakan 2016).

There is a feeling of growing excitement, even potential chaos in the music performed by the *beleganjur* ensemble and in the many, almost out-of-control actions of the men carrying the *wadah*. When this is completed, the men who have been playing in the *beleganjur* ensemble return to us and our *gamelan angklung* group is reunited.

DIAGRAM 9.4 Ritual and musical flow-path of separation/procession segment.

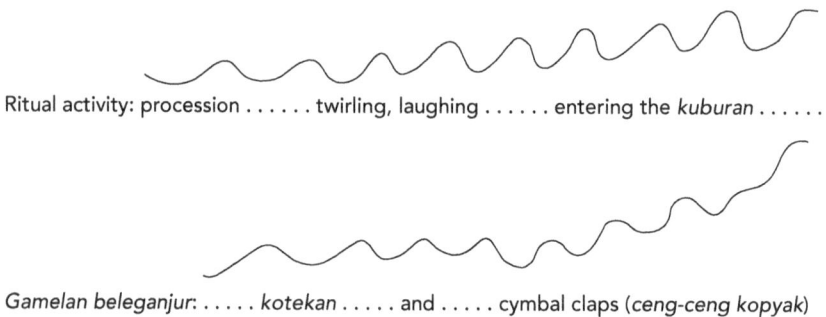

Ritual activity: procession . . . . . . twirling, laughing . . . . . . entering the *kuburan* . . . . . .

Gamelan *beleganjur*: . . . . . *kotekan* . . . . . and . . . . . cymbal claps (*ceng-ceng kopyak*)

3. Remembering/Grieving/Celebrating 10:00 a.m.–11:30 a.m.: During the next period, the overall heightened feeling created by the entrance of the *wadah* and the *beleganjur* ensemble recedes, becoming quieter, more relaxed, and contemplative. This is a time of remembrance, mourning, and celebration. Prayers are chanted and offerings of holy water, flowers, and objects belonging to the deceased are placed on the platform as family and community members take time to sit for the last time with the deceased and to pray for the spirit's safe journey to eventual reincarnation.

If the deceased has lived long enough to have grandchildren, they form a separate group near the *wadah* and share their memories (Interview, Hiranmayena, February 16, 2023).

We play throughout this period, with breaks here and there. Although the section-type played most often is still *pemungkah, pengawak* are played more here than in any other period. For example, on October 13, 2007, we played a ninety-minute set of nine *pemungkah*, nine *pengawak*, and five *pengiba* in the order seen in Diagram 9.5 below. This pattern, with its alternating *rasa*, suggests a path of basic steadiness mixed with a deepening sadness along the way, perhaps a sonic enactment of the spirit's journey. Thus, the balance between the different section-types and the general atmosphere accompanying the ritual activity changes here.[4]

DIAGRAM 9.5 Ritual and musical flow-path of remembering/grieving/celebrating segment, from cremation in Samsam, Kerambitan, Tabanan, October 13, 2007.

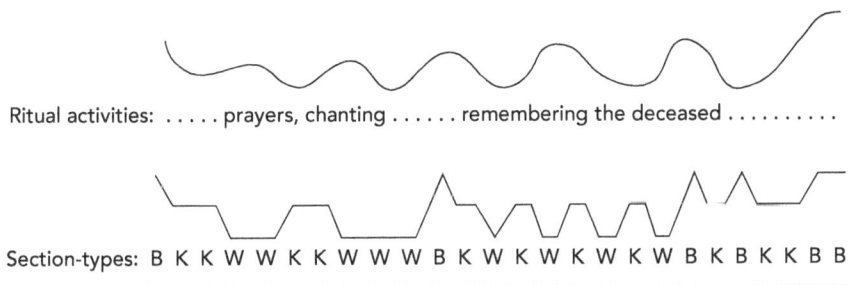

Ritual activities: . . . . . prayers, chanting . . . . . . remembering the deceased . . . .

Section-types: B K K W W K K W W W B K W K W K W K W B K B K K B B

4. Burning/Departure 11:30 a.m.–noon: Eventually, the corpse, or its effigy, is removed from the *wadah* and carried to the pyre in preparation for burning. The pyre is lit and the corpse burns quickly. We continue to play *pemungkah*, interlaced now with more *pengiba*. The atmosphere has shifted again, from a quieter feel to one of more animation and hopefulness. It is time for the final goodbye to the earthly embodiment of the deceased. The burning ends, and we hear the cue for "Jaran Nginjek." We end, quickly load the instruments onto the truck, and drive back to the *balé banjar*. This is the shortest segment and *pengiba* dominate here. As the ritual activities come to an end, the atmosphere moves away from quiet contemplation and sadness to celebration.

I had always wondered why our departure from the *kuburan* was so hurried. It seemed to me that this was disrespectful of the solemnity of

FIGURE 9.3 Corpse burning.

the event. I later learned that if the music of the *gamelan angklung* (or any other ensemble) continues to sound after the body is burned, it could inadvertently lure the deceased's spirit back to the earthly realm, causing a delay or possible termination of the spirit's journey (Interview, Hiranmayena, February 16, 2023). Below is the flow-path of this segment, taken from a cremation we played on September 17, 2007, in *banjar* Baturiti.

DIAGRAM 9.6 Ritual and musical flow-path of burning/departure segment, from a cremation in *banjar* Baturiti on September 17, 2007.

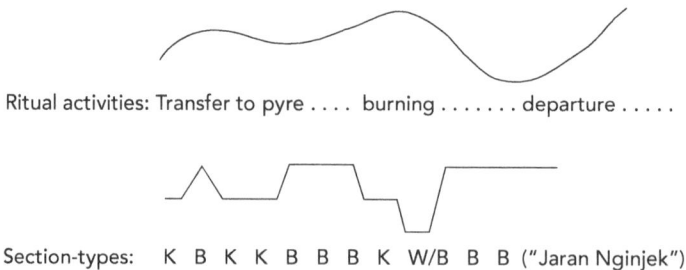

Ritual activities: Transfer to pyre . . . . burning . . . . departure . . . . .

Section-types: K B K K B B B K W/B B B ("Jaran Nginjek")

Connecting the sections of the timeline results in a five-hour flow-path showing the combined ups and downs of the ritual process and of the music that accompanies it.

DIAGRAM 9.7 Cremation flow-path.

Ritual flow-path:

KKKWKKWKBBWWKKWWKKBB; *beleganjur*; BKKWWKKWWWBKWKW KWKWB; KBKKBBBKW/BBB
Music flow-path:

Looking at Diagram 9.7 more closely, you can see that both the ritual process and the parallel musical choices together create an uncertain path: one of comfort and familiarity, but also one of ambiguity: Will the deceased's spirit accomplish its journey successfully with a minimum of difficulty? Will the living be able to express their feelings toward the deceased without being overcome by grief or anger? The possibilities of trouble along the spirit's path are endless; and for the living, a serious breach of public conduct is always a looming threat.

The people with whom I experienced cremations did not outwardly express these extreme feelings in the public context of the ritual. Indeed, most people were smiling, even laughing throughout, busily presenting offerings, chatting with their neighbors, or boisterously helping twirl the *wadah*. Nor did they equate, in any explicit way, the specific sounds of any section in the cremation repertoire with any emotion or ritual activity.

However, this analysis, although speculative, resonates with what I wrote earlier about Balinese responses to life's vicissitudes, based on two important sources: Unni Wikan's book *Managing Turbulent Hearts: A Balinese Formula for Living* (1990) and Fred Eiseman's two-volume set *Bali: Sekala and Niskala* (1990). In the context of a cremation, where an expression of grief might be expected (as in Western cultures), in Bali, where people feel so connected to and responsible for each other and their ancestral spirits, a public display of grief can have real and lasting harmful consequences for oneself, one's community, and most importantly, for the spirit of the deceased.

Although the living might feel great sadness or grief internally, showing these emotions outwardly by crying, brooding, or acting in anger is discouraged in public contexts because these actions might adversely affect those around you or the wider community, causing everyone to be overcome by emotion. An out-of-control emotional state (grief, anger, or elation) effectively separates individuals, in that it focuses too much attention on the individual's feelings and creates a gap for malicious entities to fill.

Performing the Individual, Social, and Spiritual Self

The act of performing *gamelan angklung* music at a cremation also creates an ideal space for other performances—those of self and social identity. Attending a cremation can be an overwhelming experience. Hundreds of people are packed into a relatively small outdoor space; everyone is talking, laughing, or shouting; children are running freely; the smell of incense saturates the air; and many *gamelan* (*angklung, gong kebyar, gambang, gender wayang,* etc.) are often playing simultaneously. Although this may seem like a random and chaotic mass of human activity, sound, and smell, the Balinese see this as a necessary and effective atmosphere (*ramé*) for a cremation. It is in this space that the men of Taman Sari are the most performative, that is, most able to call up, act out, and maintain their individual and social identities.

Each performer, for example, is carrying out his own *dharma*, that is, performing his ritual obligations to his community through his act of performing the necessary music for this event. The performers, all from the same *banjar* (or interconnected *banjar*), are performing together with their lifelong friends and relatives, each contributing something to the whole. The *kuburan*, usually within walking distance of home, is not only a cremation ground but also the neighborhood playground where the men played soccer and ran together as children. Their playing at a cremation is not about musical accuracy or technique but, rather, about this communal experience and memory. And the specific sounds of their own *gamelan angklung* define them as members of a unique ritual and musical group.

Playing music in their own village also reconnects the men to their families, including their deified ancestors who reside in the form of effigies in small family shrines within their home compounds. Attended to daily, these shrines permanently attach the family to a specific place, time, and context. Also found within the compound are the placenta, umbilical cord, and other remains of the birthing process of children born to this family, a practice that ensures that a newborn, regarded as a reincarnation of a revered ancestor, will be accompanied by a protective spirit in life.

These symbols of life, death, and reincarnation, readily at hand in the compound and a significant part of daily life, constitute a representation of the cosmic world, where past, present, and future, as well as seen and unseen realities (*sekala* and *niskala*) exist simultaneously. Even the music itself can be seen as a sonic interpretation of the journey to reincarnation. Its inconsistent meters, changing phrase lengths, wandering elaborations, and constantly varied textures mirror the uncertainties that await the spirit as it moves through its various stages toward rebirth.

Further, the unifying give-and-take of communal reciprocity (*patus*) unites the men even more during this ceremony. One of the most important responsibilities for members of one's *banjar* is to provide help at a cremation in the form of cooking, providing cloth, making offerings, and playing music, among many other activities. These acts are significant: one day they will be performed for you. This loving, reciprocal relationship forever binds the community together.

Finally, performing at a cremation also allows the past—as conceived by contemporary Balinese—to be reconstructed in the present. First, the sounds of musical oldness are encoded in the cremation music they play today; second, the cremation ceremony itself is conceptualized as part of an ancient village tradition, unconnected to a more hierarchic court life or a life moderated by the internet; and, third, the members themselves are old—many of them have been playing in the *gamelan angklung* for decades. It is their responsibility and honor to perform this traditional music and to pass it to the next generation.

The ultimate purpose of a cremation in Bali is to cleanse, lift, and guide the spirit of the deceased to its proper place. But it is also an important space for living participants to renew their commitments to themselves, their families, and their communities. The music of the *gamelan angklung* is an ideal companion, as its music's bittersweetness and structural flexibility combine to create the proper and most effective atmosphere for a cremation, providing both a familiar and comfortable sound presence, as well as the space to safely call up, negotiate, and fully experience the intermingled feelings of bittersweet sadness and celebration that accompany the death of a family member or friend.

• • •

The three *gamelan angklung* stories from the Introduction of this book—one based on existing scholarship, one told by the men of *sekehe* Taman Sari, and one focusing on my own musical interests—are, as I wrote, neither complete nor completely accurate; all are true in some sense, and all are valuable. Early scholarship largely ignored *gamelan angklung* or places it within newly formed historical categories defined by musical structures vis-à-vis other contemporaneous repertoires. The men's story focuses almost exclusively on ritual obligation and communal responsibility, without much mention of music. My story is about coming to some understanding of the music's everchanging structures through the use of flow-paths.

However, when merged into one narrative, these stories become more than the simple sum of their parts. Far from being mere ambient sound, *gamelan angklung* cremation music is a sounded performance of all three stories, told at once, yet from different perspectives. Pieces of thought-to-be-old music/sound/*dharma*, carrying appropriate cremation feelings/flavors/*rasa*, are learned orally/aurally/cognitively over a lifetime through countless repetition. Experiencing this music at a cremation thus effectively reinscribes an already well-marked path to spiritual, social, and personal worlds inhabited by contemporary Balinese. The presence of *gamelan angklung* and its cremation music thus enables those who hear it—both living and dead—to avoid the potential harm that can result from the distraction and disconnectedness of grief, while also allowing them to celebrate and move forward.

Notes

Introduction

1. I Wayan Dapet (d. 2018) was his formal, legal name; Nang Suadin was the name by which he was known in his village.

2. There was another earlier article by McPhee, "Angkloeng Gamelan in Bali," published in 1937, which I discovered later.

3. In her 2010 PhD dissertation "Representing Balinese Music: A Study of the Practice and Theorization of Balinese Music," Catherine Elizabeth Wakeling deconstructs much of this scholarship, with a lengthy historiography, highlighting the explicit motives as well as the implicit assumptions, or unconscious biases, of their authors. These assumptions, Wakeling writes, led to a literature dominated by contemporaneous Western academic music concerns, largely ignoring the knowledge and concerns of the musicians themselves.

4. I am grateful to Sidra Lawrence (2023:09) for this insight.

5. Many Balinese musicians now learn new pieces through recordings, especially since the invention and mass distribution of portable recording devices and batteries in the mid-twentieth century.

Chapter 1. Balinese Village Life

1. It is also the birthplace of the famous dancer I Ketut Maria (1897–1968), who ushered in the era of *gamelan gong kebyar*, and the site of a mass suicide (*puputan*), which occurred as a last resort against the Dutch in 1906.

2. See Eiseman 1990 and Herbst 1981 for fuller descriptions.

3. See, for example, Bateson and Mead 1942; Geertz 1966, 1980; Pringle 2004; Lansing 1987; and Howe 2005, among others, for fuller discussions.

4. The Balinese *subak* was designated a World Cultural Heritage Site by UNESCO in 2012.

5. As a woman and a foreigner, I was unable to be a member of *banjar* Wani or Baturiti, but I did pay $50 to Baturiti for "*banjar* protection."

6. Today, clans and castes are not always aligned. For example, the group known as *pandé* is a clan and, sometimes, a caste. It is a clan because it is a group defined by its genetic makeup as descended from a common ancestor; it is also a caste in that many of the men of the *pandé* clan have professions dealing with fire, such as smithies, or metal workers who construct the bronze and iron keys of *gamelan* ensembles. But a person born into the *pandé* clan can also become part of another subcaste not associated with fire (Eiseman vol. 2, 1990:24).

7. For a fuller discussion of Rembang and a chart of historicized musical forms, see Tenzer 2000:149.

Chapter 2. *Gamelan Angklung* Today

1. The word *angklung* also refers to a xylophone of twelve to fourteen bamboo tubes set in a frame found only in Banyuwangi, East Java. It belongs to an ensemble called *gamelan angklung* (Kartomi 2001, Oxford Online).

2. The sole exception here is the Canadian composer Colin McPhee (1900–1964), who in his discussions of *gamelan angklung* distinguished three different ensembles: old (i.e., those he found in Karangasam, still using *angklung kocok*); classic (those found in Gianyar, without *angklung kocok*); and new (the northern five-tone ensemble, with larger drums and gong). It is McPhee's classic category that is the focus here.

3. Recordings of the fifteen cremation *gending* that make up the Taman Sari cremation repertoire are found on the companion website to this book.

4. Occasionally, I was told that *kambang kiring* meant "lacking a flower."

5. This term is used in the *gender wayang* tradition to denote the beginning piece.

6. I am using the Balinese counting system here: beat 1 comes after the *kempur*; the cycle ends with the *kempur*, sounding on beat 16.

7. See Ornstein 1971.

Chapter 3. *Gamelan Angklung* Scholarship and Its Legacies

1. See *Bali South*, notes, 2003 and Picard 2012.

2. See Tenzer 2000:144–82 for a complete history.

3. *Gamelan joged bumbung* is also a *slendro*-tuned ensemble, but it's uncertain if McPhee ever heard one.

4. McPhee 1966:39–40; see also Wakeling 2010:93.

5. McPhee uses *sangsih* for pitches 1–2 and *molos* for pitches 3–4.

6. *Gamelan gong bheri* only exists in one place and will not be discussed here. Tenzer adds four vocal genres to the *tua* category (2000:149): *raré, sanghyang, sloka,* and *kakawin,* all of which were accompanied by one or more of the first four on Rembang's list, but will not concern us here.

7. See Wakeling 2010; McGraw 1999.

8. For a complete history of the scholarship on *tua*, *madya*, and *baru* ensembles, see Tenzer 2000:145–68.

9. For a full discussion of this history and its deconstruction, see especially Perlman 2004 and Wakeling 2010.

10. See Rai (2004), Rahn (1996), and Wakeling (2010).

11. For example, the tuning of *gamelan gambang* relies on a forked *panggul*.

12. See Perlman 2004 for a fuller discussion.

13. The Balinese sometimes use the metaphors of "small" and "large" to describe what we in the West call "high" and "low," as in pitch quality. Sometimes *saih angklung* is called *slendro alit* (small slendro) when referring to its high pitch ambitus.

Chapter 4. Three Possible *Gamelan Angklung* Ancestors

1. The instrument is called Jew's harp in English and German. The first document using the term "Jew's harp" is a 1481 French petty customs account, where these instruments were listed as *jue harpes* (harp players) or *jue trumpes* (trumpet players) (Wright 2004).

2. For a definitive history and description of this instrument, see Deirdre Morgan's "Organs and Bodies: The Jew's Harp and the Anthropology of Musical Instruments."

3. In 1994, while visiting Disneyland with my family, I was surprised to see a barbershop quartet using four diatonically tuned *angklung kocok* to create tonic and dominant chords to accompany their singing. *Angklung kocok* was also named by UNESCO as an Intangible Cultural Heritage in 2010.

Chapter 5. Work for the Dead

1. See *Jero Tapakan: Balinese Healer* 1986, *Jero on Jero: A Balinese Trance Séance* 1986, and *Releasing the Spirits: A Village Cremation in Bali* 1991, illustrating this practice.

2. See especially Geertz 2000 [1966] and 1980; and Bateson and Mead 1942.

3. Every week I would travel to Ubud and check my email at an internet café. At different times during the day the proprietor would place offerings on the tops of the computer monitors.

Chapter 6. Work for the Community

1. *Jero* (also *jro*) is a word that signifies "insider." It is also a polite title for a lay priest (*pemangku*) and refers to the homes where members of the *satria* caste live. https://www.baliadvertiser.biz/what-does-jro-mean/.

2. In honor of the movie musical *The King and I*, released in 1956 by Twentieth Century Fox.

3. Euphemism for a sexual transgression.

Chapter 7. *Gamelan Angklung* Cremation Music Today

1. I borrow the term *gihing* (backbone) from McPhee (1966), who borrowed it from the *wayang kulit* tradition to describe the opening cues used by the *gamelan angklung* he saw in Karangasem in the 1930s.

2. Pak Rideng was the only member of the *sekehe* who used these terms; the rest of the men used numbers.

3. Pak Rideng had written down the names of the *gending* and their section designations in a notebook, which he brought with him and often consulted during recording sessions.

4. In a conversation with Michael Tenzer, I Madé Bandem stated that these terms were first applied to instrumental music by Gusti Putu Madé Griya, who adapted them from poetry and song. Griya was one of the first conservatory teachers during the 1950s and 60s, where he institutionalized them (Tenzer, personal communication, December 8, 2023).

5. In Karangasem, McPhee notes, compositions were sometimes paired (i.e., *pengawak-pangecet*) but also often played singly (1966:240).

6. Bakan (1999:118f) also makes the case for a similar flexibility in ritual *beleganjur* cremation music, as opposed to *kreasi beleganjur* (new music for *beleganjur* competitions), which adheres more closely to the three-part form.

7. See Walton (2007) and Herbst (1981).

8. Tenzer writes, "[M]usicians prefer considering the music in its larger context, responding to questions by deferring to the concept of *rasa* (feeling)" (2000:233 n.32).

9. I have labeled this "standard" because it is the metric unit most often used in Western scholarship to illustrate the pacing of the *pokok*, carried by the *jublag* or *calung* in *gamelan gong kebyar*, the most heavily researched and familiar ensemble to Western audiences.

10. The terms "simple" and "filled-in" are taken from I Nyoman Suadin, who uses them consistently to distinguish these styles.

11. The opposite, however, is not true. If the elaboration moves to pitch 4, it is played in unison by *polos* and *sangsih*.

12. The twoness of these is reminiscent of older *réong*, where the pots were attached to the two ends of a pole for easy playing and carrying.

13. See Tenzer 2000:183–248 for a discussion of all *kotekan* types.

14. *Kotekan ubit telu* (interlocking over a span of three notes also exists, where *polos* and *sangsih* coincide on pitch 3). This occurs most often in the opening cue.

15. There is a small break in the second half of this *pengiba*, highlighted by the *rincik*. It is similar to an *angsel*, a rhythmic cue shared by the *rincik* and drummer in a dance form.

16. Again, it is unclear here what McPhee meant by "short melodic sections." The confusion lies, as in the previous discussion, in what he is defining

as a melody, the *pokok* (what most scholars call the melody) or the elaboration, which in some cases is melodylike. And many kinds of musical gestures are used for "contrast," not only "ostinatos with figuration."

Chapter 8. Flow-Paths

1. Chunking is a short-term memory aid that divides longer units of music, text, etc., into shorter, manageable segments.

2. I am not suggesting that my specific way of chunking is the best or the only way to parse this music. Indeed, not everyone (or maybe anyone) hears and processes musical information in the same way.

3. Concepts of time in relation to *gamelan* music in Bali have been discussed frequently in the literature. See, for example, Geertz 1966; McGraw 2008; and Tenzer 2000, among others. Here, I am referring to my own, commonsense perceptions of flow and pacing, not to concepts of time, especially cyclical time, as used by Balinese musicians, or of time more generally.

4. See Tenzer (2000:224–27) for a discussion of movement and stasis in Balinese music, and note 6, below.

5. In performance, there is a tendency to speed up all sections as they are repeated, so that beginning and ending tempos are often quite far apart.

6. Tenzer, drawing on his discussions with Pak Rai (2000:178–82), has called these patterns *ngubeng*, meaning little movement, or "stuck in place," as opposed to *majalan*, or "moving purposefully," but also adds that these terms are most often reserved for court genres (2000:178).

7. Not unlike a *tihai* in Indian classical music.

8. See Bakan 1999:70–75 for a similar description of cremation time elasticity.

9. Pitch 4 appearing near the end is also a characteristic of many *pemungkah*.

Chapter 9. In the Context of Performance

1. Only Pak Rideng knew these terms; the others did not use them.

2. Both Michael Bakan (1999, 2016) and Lisa Gold (1998) have also written about maintaining the correct atmosphere at cremations.

3. Emphasizing the importance of maintaining a "right atmosphere" at cremations was echoed in discussions I had with the Balinese American composer I Putu Tangkas Adi Hiranmayena, now a professor at Grinnell College in Iowa. After Putu and I met (over Zoom) in early 2022, when we talked at length about *gamelan angklung*, he returned to Bali for the summer and talked with three master musicians there—I Madé Lasmawan (his father), composer and scholar I Ketut Gedé Asnawa, and I Bagus Aji, cofounder of the group Çudamani—about the music and why certain musical choices were made during a cremation. Putu shared the comments he had collected with

me on February 16, 2023. His wife, Ni Dewa Ayu Eka Putri, joined us near the end. These comments inform my discussion of changing atmospheres in this section.

4. A notable exception occurred on September 17, 2007, where we played a string of four *pemungkah*, followed by a string of six *pengiba*, over a thirty-minute period. Together, the six *pengiba* constituted a set of one performance, plus five repeats of a new piece the *ugal* player was trying to teach us.

Glossary

adharma: Lack of adherence to one's duty (see *dharma*); immorality; chaos.

agama: Religion. Expressed various ways: Agama Bali (religion of Bali); Agama Hindu Bali (Hindu religion of Bali, as opposed to India); Agama Tirtha (Religion of Water).

ageng: Large; in music, deep, low-pitched.

alit: Small; in music, high-pitched.

angklung: (also *angklung kocok*) A tuned, shaken, bamboo rattle, traditionally used in Sunda (West Java) to accompany rice harvests.

angklung-kebyar: A bright, new style of music for *gamelan angklung*, with added instruments and drums, using *gong kebyar* musical gestures and textures.

angklung kléntangan: An old name for the bronze-keyed *gamelan angklung* cremation ensemble; from *kléntangan* (bells), referring to the bell-like sounds of the *réong*.

ASTI: Acronym for the Academi Seni Tari Indonesia (renamed Sekolah Tinggi Seni Indonesia [STSI]), Academy of Indonesian Arts, a university-level conservatory system for the arts found throughout Indonesia.

balé: Meeting place; pavilion.

balé banjar: Community meeting place, often used for rehearsals, where musical instruments, costumes, and other important ritual items are kept.

Bali Aga: Name given to people believed to be Indigenous to Bali.

bali-balihan (see also *bebali* and *wali*): A category of public performances, mainly for tourists.

balian: Traditional healer; spirit guide.

banjar: Neighborhood association made up of fifty to a hundred interrelated families that share various ritual and civic responsibilities.

baru: New, as in *kriasi baru* (new creations).

bebali: (see also *bali-balihan* and *wali*): A category of ceremonial performances for Balinese and non-Balinese.

beleganjur: Music played by the *gamelan beleganjur*, often at cremations, consisting of interlocking patterns executed by large crash cymbals and drums.

bhuta (and kala): General names for evil spirits or destructive forces.

bossed gong: A gong with a protruding knob in its center, found in various sizes in a *gamelan*.

bumbung: A length of bamboo, measured from one node to the next; a musical instrument made from bamboo, often used in contexts of light entertainment.

byar: To flare up; refers to the bright sound and sudden accents of *gamelan gong kebyar* music.

candétan: polyrhythmic passages created during rice-pounding; an older term for interlocking parts.

ceng-ceng kecek: A set of small hand cymbals attached to a carved wooden base; in *gamelan angklung*, used to accent certain rhythms and as a cueing instrument.

ceng-ceng kopyak: A set of large crash cymbals used in processions, especially in *beleganjur* ensembles.

desa adat: Traditional village governing system.

desa dinas: Official, national governing system.

Dewi Sri: Hindu goddess of rice.

dharma: Religious duty according to one's place (i.e., one's caste, gender, age, historical time).

ending cell: A one- or two-beat rhythmic pattern that cues the ending of a phrase-group or section.

flow-path: A diagram of a section's pacing, based on changes in texture, meter, and phrase length.

gamelan: An ensemble, chiefly made up of bronze-keyed percussion instruments, gongs, and drums used in Bali and Java; thought to be an inseparable family.

gamelan angklung: A four- or five-tone ensemble of bronze metallophones, pot-gongs, drums, hand cymbals, and a medium-sized gong used for cremations, and, with added instruments, for other ceremonial events.

gamelan angklung kocok: An ensemble composed of tuned, shaken, bamboo rattles.

gamelan gambang: A sacred seven-tone ensemble of wooden-keyed instruments often played at cremations.

gamelan gambuh: An old ensemble using large, end-blown *suling* (bamboo flutes) and *rebab* (two-stringed, spike fiddle), for accompanying court-dramas.

gamelan gender wayang (sometimes, *gamelan gender*): An ensemble of four ten-keyed, *slendro*-tuned, bronze-keyed instruments that accompanies *wayang kulit* (leather shadow-puppet) stories.

gamelan génggong: An ensemble of *génggong* (Jew's/jeu harp) used to accompany local stories, usually about frogs and other natural creatures.

gamelan gong ageng: A large *pélog*-tuned *gamelan*, popular during the end of the *madya* period of Balinese music history that inherited many of the performance conventions and repertoires of *gong gdé*.

gamelan gong gdé: *Gamelan* of the great gong. A colossal and stately *pélog*-tuned ensemble used during the height of the *madya* period of Balinese music history for court ceremonies and rituals; played long, slow compositions called *lelambatan*.

gamelan gong kebyar: A *pélog*-tuned ensemble of bronze-keyed instruments, gongs, and drums that developed in the early twentieth century, whose rhythmic accents and interlockings produce a bright, energetic sound.

gamelan jegog: A four-tone, *pélog*-tuned ensemble of instruments constructed from unusually large bamboo tubes held together in a wooden case. Players often mount the instruments to play.

gamelan luang: A rare and sacred ensemble of bronze-keyed instruments using a seven-tone scale.

gangsa: A family of multi-keyed, multi-octave bronze instruments found in most Balinese *gamelan*.

gangsa kantilan: Higher-pitched *gangsa*.

gangsa pemadé: Lower-pitched *gangsa*, tuned one octave below *gangsa kantilan*.

gending: A musical composition.

génggong: A Jew's harp.

gihing: Backbone; used in *gender wayang* terminology to signify a beginning melodic cue.

ginneman: A nonmetered, semi-improvisatory introduction to a larger composition.

gongan: One gong cycle.

Ibu: Mother; an honorific given to older women as a sign of respect.

internal cycle: A cycle embedded within a longer cyclical section.

ISI: Institut Seni Indonesia (Institute of Indonesian Arts). The highest-level arts conservatory system in Indonesia.

jegogan: The largest and lowest member of the *gangsa* family in a *gamelan angklung*.

kain: A large piece of cloth wrapped around the lower half of the body; worn in all temple festivals and ceremonies.

kajar: A medium-sized bossed gong used as a timekeeper in a *gamelan gong kebyar*.

kantilan: The higher-pitched *gangsa* in a *gamelan angklung*.

Kawi: A literary language evolved from Sanskrit.

kebaya: A special blouse worn by women for ceremonial and ritual events.

kebyar: To flare up; a musical style associated with *gamelan gong kebyar*.

kempli: A small, bossed gong attached to a wooden base, used to punctuate a gong cycle.

kempur (kempul, pur): The medium-sized hanging bossed gong used in *gamelan angklung* to mark the endings/beginnings of sections.

kendang: The general word for drum. When two drums are used, as in *gamelan gong kebyar*, they are divided into male (*lanang*) and female (*wadon*), with the *wadon* being slightly larger and lower in pitch.

kilitan: Locking in, or binding together; in *gamelan angklung*, used in reference to performing *kotekan empat*, where a player plays pitches 2 and 3 of *saih angklung* to bind the *kotekan* together.

KOKAR: (see Sekolah Menengah Karawitan Indonesia).

kotekan: General term for interlocking. In *gamelan angklung*, a style of elaboration (also called *kotekan ubit empat*), where the four tones of *saih angklung* are divided between two groups of players (*polos* and *sangsih*). Each group plays syncopated patterns that combine to form a continuous elaborative stream. Pitches 1 and 4 sound simultaneously, creating cross-accents. Also, an older term for the polyrhythmic patterns created by rice-pounding.

kotekan empat: Interlocking over four notes.

kotekan katak ngongkek: Croaking-frog interlocking, a name given to rice-pounding patterns that result in cross-accents (3 + 3 + 2) over eight pulses.

kreasi baru: New creations, mostly referring to musical compositions from the mid-twentieth century onward.

kuburan: Cremation ground; also, the place bodies are buried when they are not immediately cremated.

kulkul: A set of large bamboo tubes (slit drums) that hang in the tower of a *balé* and are struck in various patterns to summon villagers.

lagu: A melody or piece of music.

lanang (with wadon): (See *kendang*.)

lelambatan: Slow music; a stately genre of *gamelan* music performed during the *madya* period of Balinese music history for court-related ceremonies.

leyak: A person who practices evil magic, or the magic itself; an evil spirit.

lontar: A palm-leaf manuscript that contains verses or inscriptions in Kawi; sometimes used to notate the *pokok* of a musical composition.

madya: Middle, referring to the middle period of Balinese music history.

Majapahit: A Hindu-Buddhist kingdom of East Java that migrated to Bali in the fourteenth and fifteenth centuries; for many, its arrival marks the beginnings of modern Balinese history.

manis: Sweet, referring to an important quality of *saih angklung* as heard in *gamelan angklung* music.

neng, nung, nang, ning, nong: Syllables used by trained musicians when learning, teaching, or remembering pieces that use the pentatonic *pélog* or *slendro* systems.

ngabén: Cremation ceremony.

ngempat: A vertical interval created in the elaborative layer where pitches 1 and 4 sound together.

niskala: Intangible; invisible.

ócètan: A technique of alternating tones used in *génggong* playing.

odalan: A temple ceremony or festival usually celebrating an anniversary or an important day in the Balinese calendar.

ombak: Wave, referring to the shimmering sound of instruments tuned slightly off one another.

oncangan: Syncopated patterns created by strikes on the rims of rice troughs.

ostinato: A short melodic or rhythmic pattern repeated, usually in the lower layer, throughout a musical composition.

padi: A rice plant.

Pak: Father; an honorific showing respect for an older man.

palet: A metric unit within a gong cycle, sounded by gongs.

pancoran: An area where pure, natural water flows.

pandé: Metalsmith; a person responsible for building and tuning a *gamelan*, and for forging gongs and other metallophones.

panggul: The general word for a stick, hammer, or mallet used to strike an instrument in a *gamelan*.

pasar: Market.

patus: A strong, reciprocal social bond that ensures the cohesion and stability of a community.

pedanda: A Hindu priest, either male or female, of the Brahmin caste.

pélog: One of two modal systems used in Javanese and Balinese music; a set of seven pitches to the octave from which five are chosen to create different modes used in *gamelan* composition (see also *slendro*). Internal intervals are both wide (200–300 cents) and narrow (100–200 cents).

pélog selisir: One of the most common sets of five pitches derived from the seven-tone *pélog*, used in *gamelan gong kebyar* and other ensembles.

pemadé: The lower octave *gangsa* in *gamelan angklung*; used singly, as *ugal* (a cue instrument) and, as a group, in elaborating.

pemangku (manku): A lay priest who is the guardian and keeper of a temple, often of the *sudra* caste.

pemungkah: An opening piece; term taken from *gender wayang* to signify music that plays while the *dalang* (puppeteer) sets up the puppets.

pengawak: A standard term for the second, slow piece in a multisectional composition. The main body of a composition.

pengiba: A fast, concluding section of a *gending*, often using the elaborating technique of *kotekan ubit empat*.

phrase-group: Two or more consecutive phrases that are repeated, varied, or related and come to an end.

PKB: An acronym for Pesta Kesenian (Bali Arts Festival), held annually.

pokok: A slow-moving musical contour that is elaborated by higher, faster-moving instruments; often called a "core melody" in Western scholarship.

polos: Basic, simple; in *gamelan angklung*, the lower pitches of *saih angklung* (pitches 1 and 2) played in *kotekan* elaboration, which interlock with the *sangsih* pitches (3 and 4). *Polos* pitches often coincide with the *pokok*.

pura: A Balinese temple.

puri: The home of a Balinese raja; a palace.

ramé: An atmosphere of busyness or crowdedness.

rasa: Taste, flavor, mood, or atmosphere.

réong: A set of small, bossed, pot-gongs (gong chimes) used in *gamelan angklung* and other Balinese ensembles.

rincik: A set of small hand cymbals attached to a wooden frame, used in *gamelan gong kebyar*.

saih: Set, or row, referring to the set of pitches used in different Balinese *gamelan*.

saih angklung: A set of four pitches, with relatively equal space between them, used in *gamelan angklung* music.

saih gender: The set of *slendro*-tuned pitches used in *gender wayang* (shadow puppet) performances.

saih génggong: The set of four pitches, related to *saih angklung*, used in *génggong* music.

saih lima: Any of the five-tone sets of pitches derived from *saih pitu* (a seven-tone row).

saih pitu: A seven-tone set of pitches used in older *gamelan*, such as *gambuh*, *luang*, etc. (See also *pélog*.)

samsara: Rebirth, reincarnation; a basic Hindu-Buddhist belief that after death, one is reborn into a new status, dependent upon one's actions (*karma*) in the previous life.

sanggah: A family temple, or shrine to the family's ancestors.

sangsih: Different, filled-in; in *gamelan angklung*, the higher pitches of *saih angklung* (pitches 3 and 4) played in *kotekan* elaboration, which interlock with *polos* pitches (1 and 2).

saput: A piece of cloth worn by men covering their waist and thighs; used when in a temple or when participating in a ceremony.

sekala: Tangible; seen or experienced by the senses, as opposed to *niskala*.

sekehe (also sekaha): A voluntary club or group within a *banjar*.

sekehe gamelan angklung: A group that plays *gamelan angklung* music.

seksi: Term used by the men of *gamelan* Taman Sari to indicate a specific section within a *gending*.

seni: Arts.

seni profan: Literally, profane arts; referring to secular music not related to sacred rituals or ceremonies. Performances for non-Balinese audiences.

seni sacral: Sacred arts; arts performances for sacred rituals and ceremonies; for Balinese audiences.

sepi: An atmosphere of emptiness.

siem: The term used by the men of *gamelan* Taman Sari for a specific *gangsa pemadé* that protects the rest of the instruments.

slendro: One of two modal systems (along with *pélog*) used in Balinese *gamelan* music, consisting of five notes to the octave, with wide internal intervals (200–300 cents) of relatively equal size.

slendro alit: Small, or high *slendro*; another name given to *saih angklung* by those who believe that *saih angklung* is derived from *slendro* to distinguish it from *saih gender*.

slendro gedé: Large, or low *slendro*; another name for *saih gender*.

slendro kirang: Literally, *slendro* without its first note, or *slendro* without a flower; a nickname for *saih angklung*.

SMKI: An acronym for Sekolah Menengah Karawitan Indonesia (High School for Indonesian Music), also known as KOKAR.

sudra: Lowest of the four Hindu castes, comprising over 90 percent of the Balinese population.

suling: Bamboo, end-blown flute.

tabuh: A musical form using a fixed gong punctuation; today, refers to a musical composition.

tabuh telu: Literally, form of three; refers to a threefold pattern in the punctuating gongs of older genres.

Taman Sari: Sweet Nectar; the name of *banjar* Baturiti's *gamelan sekehe* (group).

tawa-tawa: A medium-sized, bossed gong used as a beat-keeper in *gamelan angklung*; held in the lap and struck with a padded *panggul*.

tekep: To cover or close; refers to covering one or more of the holes carved into a *suling*, used in *gambuh* to determine different five-pitch sets.

tingkadan: Alternating strikes of large bamboo tubes used in rice-pounding.

Tri Hita Karana: The Three Causes of Wellbeing, or Prosperity.

triwangsa: The three upper castes of Hinduism.

trompong: A set of ten bossed pot-gongs set in a line; used in older compositions of the *gamelan gong gdé*; played by one player.

tua: Old; here, refers to a classification of *gamelan* genres without drums and gongs, thought to have originated in Bali before the entrance of Hinduism.

ubit-ubitan: A kind of interlocking over four notes where pitches 1 and 4 strike simultaneously.

ugal: The leader of the *gangsa* who cues the beginnings of pieces; refers to both the instrument (*gangsa pemadé*) and the person who plays it.

Vedas: From Sanskrit; collectively, the four books of sacred texts in Hinduism.

wadah: Container; refers to the cremation tower that carries a body or effigy to the cremation grounds.

wadon (with *lanang*): Female. The slightly lower and larger of a set of two instruments, such as a pair of drums or gongs.

wali (see also *bali-balihan* and *bebali*): A sacred performance for Balinese only.

wantilan: A large performance space used for musical events and cock fights.

warung: A small eatery or café along a path where people go to snack, smoke, and chat.

wayang kulit: Shadow puppetry using tooled leather stick puppets; reenacts stories from the Hindu epics, *Ramayana* and *Mahabharata*, as well as local stories and current events.

References

Adams, Jonathan Stuart. 2012. *"Pupuh Gambang*: Manuscript, Melody, and Music." PhD Dissertation, University of British Columbia.

Agung, Anak Agung Ngurah Madé. 1990. "Tata Nada Gambelan Angklung." *Laporan Penelitian*. Denpasar: Program Studi Fisiki, Universitas Udayana.

Asnawa, I Ketut Gedé. 1991. "The Kendang Gambuh in Balinese Music." MA Thesis, University of Maryland.

Baier, Randal. 1986. "The Angklung Ensemble of West Java: Continuity of an Agricultural Tradition." *Balungan: Journal of the American Gamelan Institute*, Vol. 2:1–2, Fall/Winter 1, pp. 8–16.

Bakan, Michael B. 1999. *Music of Death and New Creation: Experiences in the World of Balinese Beleganjur*. Chicago: University of Chicago Press, 1999.

———. 2016. "War of the Worlds: Music and Cosmological Battles in the Balinese Cremation Procession." *Yale Journal of Music & Religion*: Vol. 2: No. 2, Article 8.

Balinese Requiem (DVD). 1992. Yasuhiro Omori, dir. Documentary Educational Resources.

Bali South: Gamelan Gong Kebyar and Gamelan Angklung. 2003. (CD) I Nyoman Wenten and Gertrude Rivers Robinson, notes. UCLA Ethnomusicology Productions.

Bandem, I Madé. 1983. *Ensiklopedi Gambelan Bali*. Dibiayai dan dicetak oleh Proyek Penggalian, Pembinaan, Pengembangan Seni Klasik/Tradisional dan Kesenian Baru, Pemerintah Daerah Tingkat I Bali.

Bandem, I Madé and Fredrik deBoer. 1978. "Gambuh: A Classical Balinese Dance-Drama." *Asian Music* 10(1):115–27.

Barth, Frederick. 1993. *Balinese Worlds*. Chicago: University of Chicago Press.

Bateson, Gregory and Margaret Mead. 1942. *Balinese Character: A Photographic Analysis*. Vol. 2, Special Publications of the New York Academy of Sciences.

Belo, Jane. 1953. *Bali: Temple Festival*. Locust Valley, NY: J. J. Augustin.

———. 1970. *Traditional Balinese Culture*. NY: Columbia University Press.

Benamou, Marc. 2010. *Rasa: Affect and Intuition in Javanese Musical Aesthetics*. Oxford: Oxford University Press.

Bohlman, Philip V. 1988. *The Study of Folk Music in the Modern World*. Bloomington: Indiana University Press.

Boomkamp, Jacoba Hooykaas-Van Leeuwen. 1961. *Ritual Purification of a Balinese Temple*. Amsterdam: Noord-Hollandsche Uitgevern Maatschappij.

Boon, James A. 1977. *The Anthropological Romance of Bali 1597–1972*. Cambridge: Cambridge University Press.

———. 1986. *Other Tribes, Other Scribes: Symbolic Anthropology in the Comparative Study of Cultures, Histories, Religions, and Texts*. Cambridge: Cambridge University Press.

Brandts Buys, J. S. and A. Brandts Buys-Van Zijp. 1926. "Over Muziek in het Banjoewangische." *Djawa* 6:205–28.

Brockington, John. 2004. "The Concept of 'Dharma' in the Rāmāyana." *Journal of Indian Philosophy*, 5/6:655–70.

Bundi Dinda Satya Upiah. 2014. "Perkembangan (Instrument) Angklung." *Jurnal Ilmiah Awilaras* Vol. 1:1, Juli, pp. 21–37.

Connor, Linda. 1995. "The Action of the Body on Society: Washing a Corpse in Bali." *The Journal of the Royal Anthropological Institute* 1(3):537–59.

Covarrubias, Miguel. 1937. "Festival of Death." *Asia* 37(7):518–21.

Creel, Austin B. 1972. "Dharma as an Ethical Category Relating to Freedom and Responsibility." *Philosophy East and West*, Vol. 22(2):155–68. Honolulu: University of Hawai'i Press.

Davidson, Lyle and Bruce Torff. 1992. "Situated Cognition in Music." *The World of Music* 34(3):120–39. Verlag für Wissenschaft und Bildung.

Davies, Stephan. 2007. "Balinese Aesthetics." *Journal of Aesthetics and Art Criticism*, 65(1):21–29.

Dibia, I Wayan. 1985. "Odalan of Hindu Bali: A Religious Festival, a Social Occasion, and a Theatrical Event." *Asian Theatre Journal*, Vol. 2:161–65. University of Hawai'i Press.

Eiseman, Jr., Fred B. 1990. *Bali: Sekala and Niskala*: Vol. 1: Essays on Religion, Ritual, and Art. Vol. 2: Essays on Society, Tradition, and Craft. Jakarta: Periplus.

Fox, Richard. 2010. "Why Media Matter: Critical Reflections on Religion and the Recent History of 'the Balinese.'" *History of Religions*, Vol. 49(4):354–92. University of Chicago Press.

———. 2015. "Why Do Balinese Make Offerings? On Religion, Teleology and Complexity." *Bijdragen tot de Taal-, Land- en Volkenkunde*, Vol. 171(1):29–55, Brill.

From Kuno to Kebyar: Balinese Gamelan Angklung. 2010. Recorded and annotated by Ruby Ornstein. Smithsonian Recordings. Washington, DC.

Geertz, Clifford. 1966. "Person, Time, and Conduct in Bali: An Essay in Cultural Analysis." *Cultural Reports Series*, 14, Southeast Asia Studies. New Haven: Yale University Press, pp. 360–411.

——. 1980. *Negara: The Theatre State in Nineteenth-Century Bali*. Princeton: Princeton University Press.

Geertz, Hildred, and Clifford Geertz. 1975. *Kinship in Bali*. Chicago: University of Chicago Press.

Génggong: Balinese Jews' Harp Orchestra. 1990. CD. Sekehe Genggong Batuan. King Record Company. Tokyo, Japan.

Gold, Lisa. 1998. "The Gender Wayang Repertoire in Theater and Ritual: A Study of Balinese Musical Meaning." PhD Dissertation, University of California: Berkeley.

——. 2005. *Bali: Experiencing Music, Expressing Culture*. Oxford: Oxford University Press.

Goris, Rolf. 1960. "The Religious Character of the Village Community." In *Bali: Studies in Life, Thought, and Ritual*, Vol. 5. *Selected Studies on Indonesia by Dutch Scholars*. The Hague: W. Van Hoeve, 77–100.

——. 1960. "Holidays and Holi Days." In *Bali: Studies in Life, Thought, and Ritual*, Vol. 5. *Selected Studies on Indonesia by Dutch Scholars*. The Hague: W. Van Hoeve, 113–30.

——. 1960. "The Temple System." In *Bali: Studies in Life, Thought, and Ritual*, Vol. 5. *Selected Studies on Indonesia by Dutch Scholars*. The Hague: W. Van Hoeve, 101–11.

Habenstein, Robert Wesley. 1960. *Funeral Customs the World Over*. Milwaukee: Bulfin.

Hägerdal, Hans. 1995. "Bali in the Sixteenth and Seventeenth Centuries; Suggestions for a Chronology of the Gelgel Period." *Bijdragen tot de Taal-, Land- en Volkenkunde* 151 (1995), No. 1, Leiden, 101–24. Downloaded from http://www.kitlv-journals.nl.

Harnish, David. 1988. "Music at Balinese Temple Festivals: Five Criteria for Investigating the Meaning of Music in Ritual Contexts." Paper delivered at Society for Ethnomusicology national conference, Boston.

——. 1998. "Bali." In *Garland Encyclopedia of World Music*, Vol. 4, "Southeast Asia," pp. 729–61.

Hatch, Vaughan. 2016. "What Is Angklung?" Mekar Bhuana, balimusicanddance.com.

Hauser-Schäublin, Brigitta. 2004. "'Bali Aga' and Islam: Ethnicity, Ritual Practice, and 'Old-Balinese' as an Anthropological Construct." *Indonesia* 77:27–55, Cornell University. Southeast Asia Program.

——. 2005. "Temple and King: Resource Management, Rituals and Redistribution in Early Bali." *The Journal of the Royal Anthropological Institute* 11(4):747–71. Royal Anthropological Institute of Great Britain and Ireland.

Hayes, Jordan. 2011. "Balinese Angklung Kebyar: I Nyoman Suadin's Process of Transferring 'Puspanjali.'" MA Thesis, University of Rochester.

Heimarck, Brita Renée. 2003. *Balinese Discourses on Music and Modernization: Village Voices and Urban Views*. NY: Routledge.

Herbst, Edward. 1981. "Intrinsic Aesthetics in Balinese Artistic and Spiritual Practice." *Asian Music* 13(1):43–53.

——. 1997. *Voices in Bali: Energies and Perceptions in the Vocal Music and Dance Theater*. Hanover: University Press of New England.

——. 2001. "Notes." *Roots of Gamelan, The First Recordings Bali, 1928, New York, 1941*. CD. NY: Arbiter of Cultural Traditions, pp. 1–26.

——. 2016. "Notes." *Roots of Gamelan, The First Recordings Bali, 1928, New York, 1941: Gamelan Gong Kebyar*. CD. NY: Arbiter of Cultural Traditions, pp. 1–15.

Hinduism. *International Journal of Dharma Studies* 5:20, DOI 10.1186/s40613 -017 0056, pp. 1–14.

Hobart, Mark. 1997. "The Missing Subject: Balinese Time and the Elimination of History." *Review of Indonesian and Malaysian Studies* 31, 1:123–72.

Hobart, Mark and Ni Madé Pujawati. 2020. *The Transformable Balinese Body*, a Lecture-Performance, accessed June 2020.

Hood, Mantle. 1966. "Slendro and Pelog Redefined." *Selected Reports in Ethnomusicology* 1:1–28.

Hooykaas, C. 1974. *Cosmology and Creation in Balinese Tradition*. The Hague: Martinus Nijhoff.

——. 1976a. "Balinese Death Ritual: As Described and Explained from the Inside." *Review of Indonesian and Malaysian Affairs* 10(2):35–49.

——. 1976b. "Counsel and Advice to the Soul of the Dead." *Review of Indonesian and Malaysian Affairs* 10(1):39–50.

Hornbacher, Nanette. 2014. "Contested Moksa in Balinese Agama Hindu. Balinese Death Rituals between Ancestor Worship and Modern Hinduism: Magic and Modernity." *Dynamics of Religion in Southeast Asia*, 237–60.

Howe, Leopold. 1981. "The Social Determination of Knowledge: Maurice Bloch and Balinese Time." *Man, New Series* 16(2):220–34. Royal Anthropological Institute of Great Britain and Ireland.

——. 1984. "Gods, People, Spirits and Witches: The Balinese System of Person Definition." *Bijdragen tot de Taal-, Land- en Volkenkunde*, Deel 140, 2/3de Afl., 193–222. Brill.

——. 2005. *The Changing World of Bali: Religion, Society, and Tourism*. NY: Routledge.

Hutterer, Karl L. 1998. "Southeast Asia in History." In *Garland Encyclopedia of World Music*, Vol. 4, "Southeast Asia." New York: Garland Publishing, Inc., pp. 32–47.

Jero on Jero: A Balinese Trance Séance. 1986. Linda Connor, Patsy Asch, and Timothy Asch, dirs. UCLA Media Studies.

Jero Tapakan: Balinese Healer. 1986. Linda Connor, Patsy Asch, and Timothy Asch, dirs. UCLA Media Studies.

Kahyangan: The Balinese Journey of the Soul. 2010. Linda Burman-Hall and Eli Hollander, dirs. Berkeley Media, LLC. Berkeley, CA.

Kam, Garrett. 2018. "Farewell by Fire: Cremations in Bali and Thailand." Conference presentation, East-West Center, University of Hawai'i, Honolulu, April 6.

Kartomi, Margaret J. 2001. "Angklung Kocok." Oxford Online, oxfordmusic online.com. Accessed June 14, 2020.

Kawitan: Creating Childhood in Bali. 2002 (DVD). Linda Burman-Hall, notes and Eli Hollander, dir. Berkeley Media, University of California: Berkeley.

Koskoff, Ellen. 2011. "Musical Bodies in Bali." *Embodiments of Cultural Encounters, Cultural Encounters and the Discourses of Scholarship*, Sebastian Jobs and Gesa Mackenthun, eds. Wuster: Maxmann, pp. 217–34.

———. 2021. "Rethinking Musical Mode." Notes taken from Conference in Graz, November 11–12, 2021.

Kunst, Jaap and C. J. A. Kunst-van Wely. 1925. "On Balinese Music." In *De Toonkunst van Bali*. Batavia, pp. 194–96.

Kunst, Jaap. 1934. *De Toonkunst van Bali*. The Hague.

———. 1968. *Hindu-Javanese Musical Instruments*, 2nd ed., Martinus Nijhoff.

Lansing, J. Stephen. 1983. "The 'Indianization' of Bali." *Journal of Southeast Asian Studies,* Vol. 14, No. 2:409–21. Cambridge: Cambridge University Press on behalf of Department of History, National University of Singapore.

———. 1987. "Balinese Water Temples and the Management of Irrigation." *American Anthropologist*, New Series, Vol. 89:2, pp. 326–41. American Anthropological Association.

———. 1991. *Priests and Programmers: Technologies of Power in the Engineered Landscape of Bali*. Princeton: Princeton University Press.

Lansing, J. Stephen and Karyn M. Fox. 2011. "Niche Construction on Bali: The Gods of the Countryside." *Philosophical Transactions: Biological Sciences*, Vol. 366:1566, pp. 927–34.

Lawrence, Sidra. 2023. "Introduction: On Intimate Entanglements." In *Intimate Entanglements in the Ethnography of Performance: Race, Gender, Vulnerability*. Sidra Lawrence and Michelle Kisliuk, eds. Rochester, NY: University of Rochester Press, pp. 1–22.

Living Art, Sounding Spirit: The Bali Sessions. 1999. Mickey Hart, producer. 360 Degrees Productions. Sebastopol: CA.

McDaniel, June. 2017. "Religious Change and Experimentation in Indonesian Hinduism." *International Journal of Dharma Studies* 5:20, DOI 10.1186 /s40613-017-0056, pp. 1–14.

McGraw, Andrew C. 1999. "The Development of the *Gamelan Semara Dana* and the Expansion of the Modal System in Bali, Indonesia." *Asian Music* 31(1):63–93.

——. 2008. "The Perception and Cognition of Time in Balinese Music." *Empirical Musicology Review*, Vol. 3(2):38–54.

McPhee, Colin. 1937. "Angkloeng Gamelans in Bali." *Djawa, jrg.* 17:5–6, 322–66.

——. 1947. *A House in Bali*. London: Victor Gollancz Ltd.

——. 1948. *A Club of Small Men*. NY: J. Day Co.

——. 1949. "Five-Tone Gamelan Music of Bali." *The Musical Quarterly*, April, 250–81.

——. 1955. "Children and Music in Bali." *Childhood in Contemporary Culture*, Margaret Mead and Martha Wolfenstein, eds. Chicago: University of Chicago Press, pp. 70–98.

——. 1966. *Music in Bali: A Study in Form and Instrumental Organization in Balinese Orchestral Music*. New Haven: Yale University Press.

Metcalf, Peter and Richard Huntington, eds. 1991. *Celebrations of Death: The Anthropology of Mortuary Ritual*. NY: Cambridge University Press.

Morgan, Deirdre Anne Elizabeth. 2008. "Organs and Bodies: The Jew's Harp and the Anthropology of Musical Instruments." MA Thesis, University of British Columbia, Vancouver.

Nagafuchi, Yasuyuki. 1988. "Transformation of Burial Rites in Bali." *Minzokugaku Kenkyu (Japanese Journal of Ethnology)* 53(3): 253–79. *Oceania* 64.1 (Sept. 1993):36–62.

Oja, Carol. 1980. *Distant Tones: Excerpts from the Field Notes of Colin McPhee*. Berkeley: The Aliquando Press.

——. 2004. *Colin McPhee: Composer in Two Worlds*. University of Illinois Press.

Ornstein, Ruby. 1971. "The Five-Tone *Gamelan Angklung* of North Bali." *Ethnomusicology* 15(1):71–80.

Perlman, Mark. 2004. *Unplayed Melodies: Javanese Gamelan and the Genesis of Music Theory*. University of California Press.

Perris, Arnold B. 1971. "The Resurgence of the Javanese *Angklung*." *Ethnomusicology* 15:1:403–7.

Picard, Michel. 2012. "What's in a Name? An Enquiry About the Interpretation of *Agama Hindu* as 'Hinduism.'" *Journal Kajian Bali*, 2:2:113–40.

Picard, Michel and Rémy Madinier. 2011. *The Politics of Religion in Indonesia: Syncretism, Orthodoxy, and Religious Contention in Java and Bali*. NY: Routledge Taylor and Francis Group.

——. 2011. "Balinese Religion in Search of Recognition: From 'Agama Hindu Bali' to 'Agama Hindu' (1945–1965)." *Bijdragen tot de Taal-, Land- en Volkenkunde*, Vol. 167:4:482–510, Brill.

Picken, Laurence. 1957. "The Music of Far Eastern Asia." *New Oxford History of Music, Volume 1: Ancient and Oriental Music*, Egon Wellesz, ed. NY: Oxford University Press, pp. 135–89.

Pringle, Robert. 2004. *A Short History of Bali: Indonesia's Hindu Realm*. Australia: Allen and Unwin.

Putra, I Nyoman Darma. 2011. "Balinese and Westerners." In *A Literary Mirror: Balinese Reflections on Modernity and Identity in the Twentieth Century*. Brill.

Raffles, Sir Thomas Stamford. 1817. *The History of Java*, Vol. 1. London: Gilbert and Rivington Printers.

Rahn, Jay. 1996. "Perceptual Aspects of Tuning in a Balinese *Gamelan Angklung* for North American Students." *Canadian University Music Review* 62:1–42.

Rai, I Wayan. 2004. "Scale of *Génggong* and Its Relations to the Four Tone *Slendro* Tuning System in Bali." *Mudra: Jurnal Seni Budaya*, Special Edition, 30–40.

Ramseyer, Urs. *Bali, Distrikt Karangasem—Figurationsrhythmik in der Balinesischen Musik*. 1973/1978. (DVD), E2163, Geistesse Wissenshaften Humanities.

Ramstedt, Martin. (n.d.) "Negotiating Identities: 'Hinduism' in Modern Indonesia." *International Institute for Asian Studies (IIAS) Newsletter Online* No. 17 Omori Yasuhiro, dir.

——, ed. 2004. *Hinduism in Modern Indonesia: A Minority Religion Between Local, National, and Global Interests*. London: Routledge Curzon.

Releasing the Spirits: A Village Cremation in Bali. 1991. Linda Connor and Patsy Asch, dirs. UCLA Media Studies.

Richter, Karl. 1992. "Slendro-Pelog and the Conceptualization of Balinese Music: Remarks on the *Gambuh* Tone System." In Danker Schaareman, ed., *Balinese Music in Context*. Frankfurt: Amadeus.

Ricklefs, M. C. 2001, 3rd ed. *A History of Modern Indonesia Since 1300*. Stanford: Stanford University Press.

Robinson, Gertrude Rivers. 1976. *The Ceremonial Repertoire of the Balinese Gamelan Angklung: A Study in Regional Variation and Compositional Transference*. PhD Dissertation, University of California: Los Angeles. Archives at Indiana University (SC 20).

Rosaldo, Renato. 1989. "Grief and a Headhunter's Rage." In *Culture and Truth: The Remaking of Social Analysis*. Boston: Beacon Press.

Rubenstein, Raechelle and Linda Connor, eds. 1999. *Staying Local in the Global Village: Bali in the Twentieth Century*. Honolulu: University of Hawai'i Press.

Saung Angklung Udjo. Web: http://www.angklung-udjo.co.id Bandung, West Java (Sunda). *Saung Angklung* (Udjo's House of *Angklung*).

Schaareman, Danker. 1980. *Ethnomusicology* 24(3):465–82, *Journal of the Society for Ethnomusicology*.

——, ed. 1992. *Balinese Music in Context*. Frankfurt: Amadeus.

Schlager Ernst. 1965. "Von Arbeitsrhythmus zur Bali." In *Festschrift Alfred Buhler/hrsg. von Carl A. Schmitz, Robert Wildhaber*. Basel: Pharos, Verlag Hansrudolf Schwabe.

——. 1976. *Rituelle Siebenton-Musik auf Bali*. Winterthur: Amadeus Verlag, Forum Ethnomusicologicum 1.

Seebass, Tillman. 1982. "Notes and Paradigms." (Sasak, Lombok). Meeting of the International Musicological Society.

——. 1990. "Theory (English) and Lehre (German) versus Téori (Indonesian)." XIV Congresso Della Societa Internazionale di Musicologia. E. D. T. Edizioni di Torino. Torino, Italy, 202–9.

Shulte, Nordholt. 1989. "The Spell of Powers." *Bijdragen tot de Taal-, Land- en Volkenkunde*, Deel 145, 1ste Afl., pp. 47–71, Brill.

Spiller, Henry. 2018. "From the Rice Harvest to 'Bohemian Rhapsody': Diachronic Modernity in *Angklung* Performance." In *Making Waves: Traveling Musics in Hawai'i, Asia, and the Pacific*, Frederick Lau and Christine R. Yano, eds. Honolulu: University of Hawai'i. 19–38.

Stuart-Fox, David J. 1992. *Bibliography of Bali: Publications from 1920 to 1990*. Leiden: KITLV Press.

Suanda, Endo. 1995. "The History of Bamboo Musical Instruments in Indonesia." *The Jakarta Post*. PT Bina Media Tenggara, Indonesia.

Suartari, Kadek. 1985. "Génggong de Desa Batuan." *Academi Seni Tari Indonesia*.

Sudirana, I Wayan. 2013. "Gamelan Gong Luang: Ritual, Time, Place, Music, and Change in a Balinese Sacred Ensemble." PhD Dissertation, University of British Columbia, Vancouver.

Suryani, Luh Ketut and Gordon D. Jensen. 1995. *Trance and Possession in Bali: A Window on Western Multiple Personality, Possession Disorder, and Suicide*. Kuala Lumpur: Oxford University Press.

Susilo, Emiko. 1997. "Continuity and Change in the Spiritual and Political Power of Balinese Performing Arts." *Explorations in Southeast Asian Studies: A Journal of the Southeast Asian Studies Student Association* 1(2).

Swellengrebel, J. L., ed. 1960. *Bali: Studies in Life, Thought, and Ritual*. The Hague: W. van Hoeve, Ltd.

Tenzer, Michael. *Balinese Music*. 1991. Jakarta: Periplus Press.

——. 2000. *Gamelan Gong Kebyar: The Art of Twentieth-Century Balinese Music*. Chicago: University of Chicago Press.

——. 2011. "Generalized Representations of Musical Time and Periodic Structures." *Ethnomusicology*, Vol. 55, No. 3, pp. 369–86.

Toth, Andrew. 1975. "The Gamelan Luang of Tankas, Bali." *Selected Reports in Ethnomusicology*, 11/2:65–79.

Tucker, Annie. (n.d.) Film Guide for "*Ngaben*: Emotion and Restraint in a Balinese Heart." Robert Lemelson, Julia Zsolnay, and Adia White, eds. Elemental Productions, Los Angeles.

Vervoort, M. 1927. "The Flaming Road to Heaven." *Inter-Ocean* 8(7): 409–13.

Vickers, Adrian. 1985. "The Realm of the Senses: Images of the Court Music of Pre-Colonial Bali." *Imago Musicae* 2:43–77.

——. 1989. Bali: *A Paradise Created*. Jakarta: Periplus.

——, ed. 1996. *Being Modern in Bali: Image and Change*.

Vitale, Wayne. 1990. "Gamelan Angklung in Denver." *Balungan* 4(2):15–23.

———. 2014. *Gamelan Angklung: Bali's 4-Tone Bronze Gamelan Orchestra* (CD). Vital Records, Notes. Historical Recording Series, Recorded in 1992.

Wakeling, Katherine Elizabeth. 2010. "Representing Balinese Music: A Study of the Practice and Theorization of Balinese Gamelan." PhD Dissertation, University of London, School of Oriental and African Studies.

Wallis, Richard. 1979. "The Voice as a Mode of Cultural Expression in Bali." PhD Dissertation, University of Michigan, Ann Arbor.

Walton, Susan Pratt. 2007. "Aesthetic and Spiritual Correlations in Javanese Gamelan Music." *Journal of Aesthetics and Arts Criticism*, pp. 31–41.

Warren, Carol. 1996. "Disrupted Death Ceremonies: Popular Culture and the Ethnography of Bali." *Oceania* 64(1), 36–56.

Wessing, Robert. 1998. "Bamboo, Rice, Water." *Garland Encyclopedia of World Music*, Vol. 4: Southeast Asia Routledge Books, pp. 47–55.

Wiener, Margaret J. 1995. *Visible and Invisible Realms: Power, Magic, and Colonial Conquest in Bali*. Chicago: University of Chicago Press.

Wikan, Unni. 1990. *Managing Turbulent Hearts: A Balinese Formula for Living*. Chicago: University of Chicago Press.

Wolbers, Paul Arthur. 1986. "*Gandrung* and *Angklung* from Banyuwangi: Remnants of a Past Shared with Bali." *Asian Music* 18(1):71–90.

———. 1987. "Account of an *Angklung Caruk*." *Indonesia* 43:67–74.

Wright, Michael. 2004. "Jue Harpes, Jue Trumpes, 1481." *Journal of the International Jew's Harp Society*. n.p.

———. The Search for the Origins of the Jew's Harp. silkroadfoundation.org /Newsletter/ Vol. 2:1.

Yamashita, Shinji. 2003. *Bali and Beyond: Explorations in the Anthropology of Tourism*. NY: Berghahn Books.

Zanten, Wim van. "Aspects of Baduy Music in Its Sociocultural Context, with Special Reference to Singing and *Angklung*." *Bijdragen tot de Taal-, Land- en Volkenkunde*, Deel 151, 4deAfl., *Performing Arts in Southeast Asia* (1995), pp. 516–44.

Zobel, Myron. 1926. "Fires of the Dead." *Inter-Ocean* 7(12):705–10.

Index

ELLEN KOSKOFF is Professor Emerita of Ethnomusicology at the Eastman School of Music at the University of Rochester. Her many books include the award-winning *Music in Lubavitcher Life* and *A Feminist Ethnomusicology: Writings on Music and Gender*.

The University of Illinois Press
is a founding member of the
Association of University Presses.

———————————————————————

Composed in 10.5/13 Mercury Text G1
with Avenir LT Std display
by Kirsten Dennison
at the University of Illinois Press

University of Illinois Press
1325 South Oak Street
Champaign, IL 61820-6903
www.press.uillinois.edu